Purdah to *piccadilly*

Purdah to Piccadilly

A Muslim Woman's Struggle for Identity

ZARINA BHATTY

SAGE www.sagepublishing.com
Los Angeles | London | New Delhi | Singapore | Washington DC | Melbourne

First published in 2016 by

SAGE Publications India Pvt Ltd
B1/I-1 Mohan Cooperative Industrial Area
Mathura Road, New Delhi 110 044, India
www.sagepub.in

SAGE Publications Inc
2455 Teller Road
Thousand Oaks, California 91320, USA

SAGE Publications Ltd
1 Oliver's Yard, 55 City Road
London EC1Y 1SP, United Kingdom

SAGE Publications Asia-Pacific Pte Ltd
3 Church Street
#10-04 Samsung Hub
Singapore 049483

Published by Vivek Mehra for SAGE Publications India Pvt Ltd, typeset in 10.5/12.5 pt Minion by Zaza Eunice, Hosur, Tamil Nadu and printed at Chaman Enterprises, New Delhi.

Library of Congress Cataloging-in-Publication Data

Name: Bhatty, Zarina.
Title: Purdah to Piccadilly : a Muslim woman's struggle for identity / Zarina Bhatty.
Description: Thousand Oaks : SAGE Publications India Pvt. Ltd, 2015.
Identifiers: LCCN 2015039347| ISBN 9789351508243 (hardback : alk. paper) | ISBN 9789351508236 (ebook) | ISBN 9789351508250 (epub)
Subjects: LCSH: Bhatty, Zarina. | Muslim women–India–Biography. | Feminism–India–History.
Classification: LCC HQ1170 .B4445 2015 | DDC 305.48/6970954–dc23 LC record available at http://lccn.loc.gov/2015039347

ISBN: 978-93-515-0824-3 (HB)

The SAGE Team: Aditi Chopra, Saima Ghaffar, Megha Dabral and Vinitha Nair

I dedicate my memoir to my parents, Mohammadi Begum and Faridul Haq for their ability to accept change with grace.

Contents

Preface

Memoirs are usually written by distinguished persons such as scholars, philosophers, and artists, who have made important contributions to knowledge, art, and culture. I cannot claim any such distinction, and yet I have narrated my life and experiences from my long journey of 80 years. I have done so, suggested and motivated by my three daughters who believe that my life has been somewhat different from that of an average Muslim woman, as I struggled against the established social norms of my time and carved out my own identity. I also had a desire to record the massive socio-cultural changes that I have been witness to during the last century. India, after being established as a sovereign democratic state, launched a massive program of socio-economic development, questioning the caste system and traditional gender relationships. It gave itself a secular democratic constitution that guaranteed equality to all Indian citizens "irrespective of caste, creed, and sex."

In the following pages, I have described social and political upheaval of pre- and post-independence India and have reflected on the emergence of notions of socio-economic equality and social justice which attempted to demolish the caste, class, and gender boundaries. These notions, along with the environment of protest against the rigid and outdated social structure, affected not only the social fabric of the country but also individual aspirations and lifestyles.

I have also highlighted how the political changes in post-independence India and after the partition of the country affected the Indian Muslims who had been an integral part of Indian society and polity. They felt torn between their religious and cultural loyalties. Religious zeal pulled them toward Pakistan but they found themselves culturally more rooted in India. Under pressure, some decided to migrate to Pakistan, but many of them regretted their decision later as they felt alienated by the predominant Punjabi and Sindhi culture and the language there. Those who stayed behind to preserve their roots went through the trauma of accepting a minority status in their country of origin, despite having made a significant contribution to India's struggle for freedom. These factors still have an unfortunate effect on the rising fundamentalism which is pulling the community toward more conservatism and separatism.

Even after 50 years, I cherish the memory of the day when I was sitting in the Royal Albert Hall and my name was called out. It was an international gathering of students, most of whom belonged to the privileged classes, including the royal families worldwide. I got up to receive my degree from the British Queen Mother, Queen Elizabeth, who was then the Chancellor of the University of London. I could not help recalling my humble past as the daughter of a middle-class family who had an illiterate grandmother and a mother who had no schooling and was taught only Urdu at home; as a child whose return to school was threatened at the beginning of every academic year; one who was discouraged at every stage from studying abroad to become a professor; who was ridiculed for having such high aspirations. But there I was, sitting in those royal surroundings, receiving a degree from the University of London. It was no dream. Those reading it today, including my grandchildren, will probably say, "So what? It is no big deal." But given my circumstances, it was a very big deal for me. I have explained why an ordinary event like the distribution of degrees at a university convocation had such importance for me and gave me a sense of achievement, and I have placed my personal experiences and struggles in the context of the then prevailing socio-cultural setting. These accounts may be viewed as a brief cultural history of that time. The prevailing social structure of the time when I was growing up was highly feudal and patriarchal. The society was socially and economically segregated on caste, class, and gender lines. The social structure was far more rigid than it is now; it left little room for individual deviations which, whenever occurred, were more severally disapproved, making individual aberrations more difficult. Indian Muslim society was no exception to this situation.

Despite the Muslim claims of Islam having an egalitarian ethos, the Indian Muslim society has been highly influenced by the dominant Hindu social structure. It practiced caste system analogous to the Hindu caste system with minor regional differences. It adopted the Hindu customs regarding gender relationships, arranged marriages, gender discrimination, legal rights, disapproval of widow remarriage, and treating widows as accursed and placing many restrictions on their personal lives. Muslim society was harsh on women. It deprived them of education and kept them in seclusion, restricting any exposure to the outside world. It was considered to be virtuous to follow the prescribed social norms without any form of protest.

I have tried to record in some detail the functioning of the traditional social structure in the Oudh region, which was then the United Provinces of Agra and Oudh and now known as Uttar Pradesh (UP). The Oudh region of the erstwhile province was feudal and dominated by the Muslim landed gentry. Not only economically, but also culturally, that social structure started crumbling under the weight of the newly acquired ideas of social justice and socio-economic equality. I have been a witness to that process of change and my personal experiences and struggles to deal with that societal and familial environment reflect in the following narrative. By narrating my life experiences, I also wish to convey to my readers that it is important to have dreams and aspirations in order to grow, and have self-belief to pursue them.

Acknowledgments

I wish to thank Professor Pat Huckle, State University of San Deigo, California, for reading the earlier part of the manuscript and giving a positive feedback. I want to register my delight and thanks to my grandchildren, Daniyaal Khan and Layla Khan, for rescuing me whenever I got into trouble with the computer as I am not very computer-savvy. My eldest grandson, Arman Ghosh, while on a short visit to India, was also roped in to help nanna (grandmother) which he did with great patience.

Millions of thanks and a bagful of appreciation for my dear friend Dr Romila Thapar, for reading the manuscript and making suggestions despite her very busy life. I wish to thank Dr Saba Mahmood Bashir and am indebted to her for her detailed editing and positive suggestions to improve the quality of my manuscript. And last, but not the least, I thank Ms Sunanda Ghosh of SAGE Publications for offering the possibility of publishing it. I also wish to thank Ms Shreya Chakraborty for editing part of this manuscript and for further editing to Amrita, and record my thanks and appreciation to Elina Majumdar for being a great help in handling my somewhat imperfect manuscript, cheerfully and with patience.

I would like to record my appreciation and gratitude to a number of my friends and close relatives who kept my motivation alive, besides my daughters, Huma, Kiran, and Nikhat, for their continuous encouragement and support. I also would like to name my nephew Sohail Akbar, my sister Seemin, her husband Abdul Hai, my niece Kakul, and my friend and one-time colleague Dr Taisha Abraham whose support has been vital in my effort.

I sincerely apologize to all those who may have felt offended by any omissions or unintended remarks that I may have made in the memoirs. I wish to assure them that I did not intend to hurt or misrepresent anyone. In the end, I would like people to remember me as a woman who was a humanist by faith, sociologist by profession, and a feminist by conviction.

Zarina Bhatty
Mussoorie

1

The Background

My long journey from Lucknow to Royal Albert Hall in London began on 9 August 1933, when a baby girl was born to Faridul Haq and Mohammadi Begum, their firstborn. This baby was named Zarina (literally translated as 'golden'). She was so underweight that her survival seemed unlikely; she not only survived, but also thrived and is still living (though not kicking) as an 80-year-old overweight granny.

As a firstborn, I was fondly welcomed by my parents, and especially by my grandmother, unusual for an Indian family where the birth of a girl brings gloom, particularly more so if she's the firstborn. The reason for such an unusual welcome was because my grandmother did not have a daughter. She had become a widow at the tender age of 18, only two years after her marriage and did not marry again. My father was only six months old when my grandmother lost her husband. She yearned for a daughter. When my father got married and my mother became pregnant, my grandmother prayed for a girl child and her prayers were answered. My birth was a poignant response to her prayers. Although at the time of my birth my parents were living in Barabanki—a district town in UP—I was born in Lucknow, which had better medical facilities, as my mother was brought there for the delivery.

Both my parents belonged to the land-owning families of Rudauli, a Muslim-dominated *qasba*[1] in the erstwhile district of Barabanki. Former UP Chief Minister Mayawati had reorganized the districts during her first tenure in the year 2007, so Rudauli now falls in the district of Faizabad. Before Independence, UP was called the United Provinces of Agra and Oudh (now Awadh). The Oudh region was

[1] A small town.

ruled by a dynasty of Muslim nawabs until the British took over. The Nawabs of Oudh were famous for their leisurely, highly feudal lifestyle bordering on debauchery. Remnants of that culture persisted even till very recently in Lucknow and the *qasbas* of that region.

Iska to ulta dola wapas ayega,[2] my mother's oft-repeated refrain, because I was not at all inclined toward domestic chores, still echoes in my mind. Little did she know at that time that it would take 12 long years before my 'dola returned', when I divorced after 12 years of an unhappy marriage.

I do not have very clear memories of my early childhood but I do have this overriding memory that I never did anything right. My parents must have had a tough time bringing me up. During my growing-up years, there was much disapproval of any unconventional behavior, and a great deal of emphasis was placed on age-and-gender-specific socially prescribed conduct. This code of behavior was more rigidly applied to women and girls than to boys and men; society was more indulgent toward the deviant behavior of boys and men than toward that of girls and women and thus were the social sanctions less harsh for boys and men. I was forever corrected for what was considered unseemly behavior for girls, such as walking fast, jumping and running around, asking questions, talking loudly—"A woman's voice should not be heard in men's quarters" used to be the refrain—and so forth. I was constantly reminded that I was a girl and girls could not behave like boys.

Femininity was defined as having a delicate physique, a dependent nature, being quiet, docile, obedient, soft-spoken, unquestioning, non-argumentative, and accepting the gender-based code of behavior unconditionally. This conditioning of girls and boys started from almost infancy in India, indeed in the subcontinent. Little girls were fed on the ideal femininity model of being speechless, desire-less, submissive, obedient, serving, sacrificing, and pious persons whose entire purpose in life was to live and die as daughters, wives, and mothers, without even aspiring to have an identity of their own. On the contrary, boys were encouraged to play outdoor games, be aggressive, physically strong, have a big appetite, develop a commanding personality, and consider themselves to be superior to girls. We girls were even discouraged from having a healthy appetite for the fear of us getting fat, as slim figures were, even then, preferred in the marriage market.

[2] Her wedding palanquin will return the same day.

Girls were expected to eat one or, at the most, two chapattis and a fistful of rice, while boys were encouraged to eat at least three or four chapattis and two fistfuls of rice. I sometimes liked to have three chapattis, but would eat the third one with a strong sense of guilt. Luckily, despite this, I remained very slim throughout my youth.

One of the reasons for restricting food for girls may have been because we did not get much physical exercise. We were confined within the four walls of the house; even little girls were not allowed to go out of the inner courtyard to play. We girls were introduced to domestic activities from an early age and did not have much time to play around outdoors. The games that girls played were also different from the games that boys played. We mostly played with home-made dolls or with a skipping rope or played hop-scotch, mostly with female cousins. If a young male cousin joined us, he would be ridiculed and discouraged from doing so. Such gender distinctions would annoy me a great deal; I often wanted to join my male cousins in playing ball or in flying kites. Commercial toys were not as common as they are nowadays.

We girls were instructed to be more respectful toward elders, cover our heads in the presence of the older men of the family, which was considered as a sign of respect. We were also instructed to cover our bosoms properly when we started developing physically. The dupatta became mandatory and had to be worn in a crisscrossed manner to cover the bosoms. Unmarried girls were discouraged from wearing brassieres; it was considered shameful for a girl to buy a brassiere and tell the usually male shopkeeper her size. Some of us learnt to stitch brassieres at home and had to wash and dry them away from everyone's gaze. Different standards of modesty were applied to unmarried and married women—married women had more liberties and the dictates of modesty were less for them. Women acquired full, social status only after being married and then enjoyed a certain amount of societal indulgence. For example, married women wore *chikan*[3] kurtas, long shirts made of muslin, which is a see-through material with only a brassiere underneath and covered themselves with large dupattas. They wore ghararas.[4] The waist of the gharara was embroidered with colorful threads or *zari*[5]. This obviously must have been done to draw attention to a woman's waist. I suppose the idea was

[3] A form of delicate hand embroidery.

[4] wide-legged skirt-like pants covering the legs.

[5] Type of gold thread used for embroidery.

to make married women sexually attractive to their husbands, but unmarried women's sexuality was suppressed as their virginity, their most "precious asset," was to be protected.

Unmarried girls were discouraged from decking themselves with very bright clothes and heavy jewelry and wearing make-up or flowers was also disapproved. Dressing up or conducting oneself in a manner that attracted male attention was highly disapproved. Girls were not given any knowledge of the facts of life; on the contrary, every effort was made to keep them ignorant about anything related to sex, while married women were allowed to indulge in sexual conversations. In our region, it was a custom that on the morning after the nuptial night (Muslim marriages are supposed to be consummated on the very first night, as the marriage is not legally valid until it is consummated) the newly sexually initiated bride would be made to sit in a gathering of married women and professional singers would sing lurid songs to the enjoyment of the audience. Unmarried girls were not allowed to join this *mehfil*.[6]

Izzat

The concepts of izzat (honor) and shame also played an important role in socially conditioning girls. These were drilled into me during my growing-up years. These concepts were closely associated with a woman's sexuality. A woman was central to the concept of izzat, as she could bring down or enhance her family's izzat through her behavior; in particular, through her sexual conduct. For this reason, she was guarded and her sexuality controlled. An unmarried girl was also taught to suppress her sexuality. Nothing could sully a family's izzat as much as the loss of a daughter's virginity before marriage.

I was not allowed to go out or visit my friends. My socializing was confined to visits to relatives, accompanied by parents. Whenever we went out, we would be seated in a covered tonga,[7] wear burkas and be accompanied by a male escort, usually our father's peon, if our father himself was not accompanying us. The peon would sit in the front seat of the tonga and we would be seated in the back seat, segregated by a curtain. A similar arrangement was made if I was occasionally allowed to visit a school friend.

[6] Gathering.

[7] A horse-driven carriage.

A girl was expected to sacrifice her talents on the altar of family izzat. Activities that led to public exposure were denied to girls; any artistic talent, such as drawing, painting or music was discouraged.

Women did find some outlet for their artistic potential by dying dupattas in imaginative patterns and color combinations and by embroidering articles of daily use. Unfortunately, I was fond of music and drama. We lived not far from a famous music college in Lucknow and I expressed my desire to join that college to learn Indian classical music. But my family immediately disagreed. How could a girl from a "respectable" family even think of learning music? Only women from the professional singers' castes or prostitutes sang in public. Younger women and girls did sing folk songs at family functions as amateur singers, but learning music and singing in public was strongly disapproved of.

I was also fond of acting and would participate in school plays with certain riders from our parents. Once, in a school play, I was to play the role of a newlywed bride, which meant that I had to be dressed as a bride. My parents initially did not allow me to do so while still unmarried, but after a great deal of apprehension, they gave the permission. On another occasion, soon after Partition, a play *Dhani Bankein* (green bangles) written by a well-known Urdu writer, Ismat Chughtai, was presented in the Zenana Park (Ladies' Park) in Lucknow. I had the main role in the play, for which I was given the permission only after some discussion in the family and that too because it was to be staged in an exclusive women's park where the audience was going to be only women. The play was based on post-independence communal riots and depicted the plight of a young woman who had lost her husband in those riots. While lamenting over her misfortune, she was supposed to say that she was also pregnant and that made her sorrow even greater. How could an unmarried girl say that she was pregnant, even in a play? The director was advised to delete that sentence from my dialogues.

The play was highly appreciated. It was later decided that it would be presented in the bigger common open park. But my parents did not allow me to act in front of men. I was very frustrated and angry, which was partly compensated by the fact that Ansar Chacha—my uncle who was a journalist—published a review of the play in the local newspaper and praised my performance. I was thrilled to see my name in a newspaper, but my *abbujaan*[8] was not happy that my name

[8] Father.

was mentioned in a newspaper for public reading. Such was the invisibility of what women desired in society, in those days.

Rituals and Life-cycle Ceremonies

Islam traditionally shuns rituals, yet Indian Muslims performed rituals at all life events. In fact, certain persons were regarded as experts in ritual procedures and would conduct rituals in a precisely prescribed manner. The life-cycle rituals reaffirmed the strong patriarchy present among Indian Muslims. Right from conception, various ritualistic practices emphasized the supremacy of sons. It was suggested to the expecting mother that she should maneuver to conceive during moonlit nights as she would thus give birth to a son, while daughters were conceived during dark nights. After conception, the pregnant mother was advised to sleep on the right side to ensure that she gave birth to a son. Right side was regarded as more auspicious than the left. The birth of a son was received with joy and celebrations, while the birth of a daughter led to gloom. As late as 1968, when my third daughter was born in a hospital in Delhi, I myself experienced this discrimination. There were no ultrasound devices available at that time and the sex of the fetus was not known; so naturally, the moment my baby was born, I enquired about the sex of the baby. I noticed a complete hush in the delivery room and my repeated queries were received with silence. Finally, when I was taken to the ward, the doctor came to my side, affectionately pressed my hand and said in a low voice (as if she was about to deliver a death sentence) that I had given birth to a daughter. I was furious at her attitude. I pushed her hand away and said, "Have I not given birth to a human child, you are behaving as if I have produced a monster." She was embarrassed and replied that mothers generally broke down at the birth of a girl child and some even refused to take her home, so she had to be cautious.

Birth Ceremony

The scale of celebration also varied with the gender of the newborn. Among the Indian Muslims, the *chhati*[9] generally takes place on the sixth day of the birth when the new mother is given a purifying bath, the baby's hair is shaved, and a feast is given. In case of a girl child, the

[9] Sixth day.

celebration either did not take place or was toned down. According to Islamic belief, two goats should be sacrificed at the naming ceremony of a baby boy but only one for a baby Under the *Jajmani* system, the *kameen*[10]—like the nai or barber—who shaved the baby's hair and performed the circumcision for baby boys, the barber's wife who assisted the new mother in the purifying bath, the *mirasis* or the singing caste who sang on the occasion, and other castes who helped in organizing and executing the ceremonies, were rewarded in cash or kind. The value of their gifts also differed according to the sex of the newborn. The status of the new mother and her treatment depended on whether the child was a boy or girl as due to ignorance, the mother was believed to be responsible for the sex of the child. A woman's status in her in-laws' family would rise if she had a son.

Marriage Ceremonies

The most important event in a person's life was marriage. Marriages were arranged—a practice which has persisted to this day—but boys were more often consulted before finalizing the match and it was the girl's family which was expected to give dowry and bear the expenses of the wedding. Among Indian Muslims, certainly in the region of Oudh, no cash transactions or explicit demands for dowry items were made. It was, however, assumed that the girl's parents would give some items to the daughter according to their financial resources. Similar expectations were also held from the boy's family, for the *bari*[11] was brought by the groom's family. But nowadays, even among Muslims, huge demands are made by the boy's side among the rich and the poor alike. The law banning dowry was passed in 1961 and it regarded both receiving and giving dowry a criminal offence, but the custom of dowry instead of abating is becoming more common, often causing indebtedness and financial hardship for the girl's parents. Dowry has turned into a status symbol and a vehicle for laundering unaccounted wealth. Those who do not have unaccounted wealth try to keep up with the rich and consequently get into financial difficulties.

Marriage remains an absolute necessity for girls in all classes and boys take advantage of this to make huge demands. Aspirations have grown in India. The young want to start life with all the luxuries. If

---

[10] Serfs of service castes to their land-owning feudal patrons called Jajmans, received grains in lieu of their services.

[11] Gifts of clothes and jewelry for the bride.

they fail to make enough to achieve their desired standard of living, they try to fulfill their aspirations through dowry. Not many have the social courage to refuse dowry demands, for the fear of risking the chances of their daughters finding another match. The legislation banning dowry has remained ineffective.

Manjha

The traditional notion that a daughter is *paraya dhan*,[12] belongs to the in-law's family, and becomes a stranger to her natal family after marriage, was reaffirmed by the custom of Manjha. According to this, the girl to be married is physically separated from the natal family by lodging her in a separate part of the house where she is accompanied only by girls of her age. The Manjha is marked by a ceremony in which the girl is dressed in simple yellow or pink clothes (regional variation) without any jewelry except a bangle, to which is attached a little rice and fresh grass wrapped in a piece of cloth. Rice signifies prosperity and fresh grass signifies fertility. Friends and relatives are invited and *butna*[13] is rubbed on the body of the bride-to-be. The *butna* is supposed to make the body supple and fragrant. Widows are excluded from the entire ceremony. The *butna* is massaged twice a day during the Manjha stay. The girl is treated like a guest in her home and special snacks are provided for her and her friends who stay with her, sing romantic songs, and tease her during the stay. In the old days, Manjha would last from a week to two weeks, but nowadays, it has become a formality and may be observed for three days while the rituals attached to it continue to be performed.

Wedding Day

Traditionally, weddings would take place during the daytime. The *baraat*[14] would come to the bride's house late in the morning. The groom and his party would be received formally. After the initial introductions, the bride's family members and relatives would behave more humbly and courteously. Non-alcoholic drinks would be served. I do not remember snacks being served with drinks, but it has become

[12] Another's property.
[13] A herbal preparation.
[14] Marriage party.

a custom nowadays. Soon after these formalities, the *nikah*[15] would be performed and the completion of *nikah* would be announced by *patakhas*.[16] Relatives of the bride and the groom would congratulate each other, shake hands, and embrace as recognition of the newly created relationship between the two families. An elaborate lunch would be served, first in the *mardana*[17] and then in the *zenana*.[18] Interestingly enough, the *nikah* was preceded and followed by an atmosphere of joy in the *mardana*, while in the *zenana*, a kind of gloom dominated as the near and dear ones of the bride expressed mixed feelings of happiness peppered with uncertainty about the bride's future. These feelings were more explicitly expressed through actual crying by the relatives and the bride, both at the time of *nikah* and then at the *rukhsati*.[19] At the time of the bride's departure, male singers sang a typical song depicting the bride's sentiments: "*Kahe ko biyahi bides babul more, Bhaiya ko dihe mahle do mahle, Mere ko diye pardes*" (My dear father, why are you sending me so far away? You have given my brothers mansions and to me a far-off unknown place).

The bride was normally accompanied by a senior relative as a protective shield in her new home. She would return next day to her natal home. It was important that the bride spend the wedding night in her husband's house as that was when the marriage was consummated–a necessary condition for *nikah* to be legally confirmed. This event was celebrated by a *walima*.[20] Rituals marked the bride's entry in the groom's house too. Firstly, the groom's sisters would block the bride's entry into the house. The bride was only allowed to enter when the groom gave them money. This signified the fact that an outsider was entering into the domain of the groom's siblings. The bride was then made to sit among all the invitees. She was supposed to be very shy, her head and face would be covered. The groom would be invited inside and a platter of sweetened rice decorated with coconut slices would be placed between them. The groom would pick a little bit of rice and place it on the bride's palm and then give it away to a child. He would do this seven times; this ritual signified that he would be the provider. Thus, the husband's role as the giver and the wife's role as a receiver were established

---

[15] Marriage in Islam.

[16] Fireworks.

[17] Male quarters of the house.

[18] Female quarters of the house.

[19] Bride's departure from her natal home to her affinal home.

[20] A feast given by the groom's family.

right away. The bride would next be made to sit in the middle of the hall, assisted by an older relative, her face covered with the *ghunghat.*[21] One by one, relatives and friends—mostly women, except a few very closely related men with whom the bride would not observe purdah—would come close to the bride and the woman assisting her would draw the *ghunghat* up and reveal the bride's face. Comments would be made on her looks; often rude comments were whispered if the bride was not good-looking. Then each one would give her a gift, usually monetary. This was called *moonh dikhai.*[22] This was a very demeaning custom and most distressful for the bride if she was not conventionally good-looking. The women, while staring at the bride's face, would also scrutinize the jewelry that the bride would be wearing, which would have been given by her parents. It was only after these rituals were performed that the bride was accepted into her conjugal home. Next day, when the bride would return to her natal home accompanied by her husband, the ceremony of *salam karai*[23] would take place. The groom would sit, surrounded by his newlywedded wife's relatives and be introduced to them. Each relative would give him a gift of cash or kind. He would be teased by the bride's younger relatives, asked awkward questions, and even practical jokes would be played on him. After this introduction, the groom was fully accepted in the family. But his ordeal was nothing compared to what the bride had to go through.

[21] Veil worn by women to cover their head and often the face.
[22] Showing the face.
[23] Saluting the relatives of the bride by the bridegroom.

2

Introducing the Family

Faridul Haq, my father was more conservative than my mother and grandmother. He was only six months old when he lost his father in a plague epidemic in 1903, which had gripped the entire country. *Baji*[1] kept in touch with her in-laws so my father grew up in Rudauli under the guardianship of his youngest paternal uncle Siraj-ul-Haq. Although *baji* was very attached to her son, she valued education above all else and sent him to a reputed boarding school in Etawah, UP. After completing school, *abbujaan* joined the Aligarh Muslim University (AMU), which was regarded as the Mecca of learning for Indian Muslims in those days. His uncle, Siraj, had also graduated from there; in fact, he was the first graduate from Rudauli. After graduating from the AMU, my father decided to study law. He did not want to take up a salaried job, as for the landed gentry, working for someone else was considered to be somewhat demeaning. So, he decided to follow a profession which gave him independence. Later though, he realized that temperamentally, he was not suited for the legal profession. *Abbujaan* would handle all the legal cases of his relatives, who were endlessly involved in litigations regarding their landed assets. He not only refused to accept any fee from them, but would also provide them lodging. "Hospitality is my religion," *abbujaan* would say when my mother would sometimes get tired of entertaining guests. After struggling for some years in the legal practice, he finally took up a job with the Sunni Central Waqf Board in Lucknow. He did well in that job and moved up to be its director, at which position he retired.

[1] Grandmother.

Once *abbujaan* was settled in his legal practice, my grandmother decided it was time to find a bride for him. Uncle Siraj had a daughter of marriageable age named Arifa, and it was considered appropriate that she should be married to *abbujaan*. Marriage between first cousins is allowed and even preferred among Indian Muslims. However *abbujaan*, despite the fact that he was close to his uncle and felt highly obliged to him, politely declined to marry her. Arifa was average-looking and a year older to him. Unlike a girl's refusal, a boy refusing to accept an arranged match, even in those days, was not considered disgraceful. Fortunately, despite *abbujaan's* refusal, the uncle–nephew relationship did not sour and the two families continued to be cordial. Arifa was soon married off to another cousin. Later, my parents got married in an arranged match.

My parents were not overtly religious. My parents did not say their *namaz*[2] regularly. But *abbujaan* fasted during the month of Ramzan.[3] He would fast for all 30 days and would say his *namaz* once a day only after breaking his fast. My mother would fast irregularly during the month of Ramzan and that too when she was not pregnant or lactating. I do not remember *baji* ever saying her *namaz* or fasting throughout the month of Ramzan. *Abbujaan* would make a lot of fuss about *iftaar*,[4] organizing *iftaar* parties at home and visiting his friends' parties too. *Iftaar* parties have now acquired political connotations, as non-Muslim political leaders give *iftaar* parties with the intention of gaining Muslim votes. Earlier too, these parties were occasions for demonstrating social status. Who served what, was considered more important than who fasted or did not and who was invited to whose *iftaar* party and was not. We children were not pressurized to say our *namaz* or fast regularly or read the Koran. We did have an old copy of a Koran placed on a shelf, but no one in my family ever read it.[5]

---

[2] Prayer.

[3] During the month of Ramzan, a Muslim adult is required to fast and abstain from evil thought or actions, as a sign of self-purification. The fasting during Ramzan requires no intake of food, water or any eatable from sunrise to sunset.

[4] Fast-breaking snacks.

[5] The fasting lasts from sunrise to sunset and during that time one is not allowed to drink or eat anything. The month of Ramzan is followed by Eid, to signify the end of Ramzan when *zakat* (charity) is given to the poor. Ramzan is regarded as a holy month by Muslims, when every adult Muslim is required to fast as a purification exercise and lead a pious life. The rozaie, the *zakat* should be 1/40th of one's annual income.

Despite the fact that my parents were not religious, I was put through the ceremony of *Roza Kushai*.[6] It was customary in those days to give money at such occasions rather than gifts, so all the invitees had brought some money to give me for fasting. On the day of my fast, I did not go to school, but Soofya—my younger sister—did, and when she returned home around 4 p.m., she declared that she had also kept the fast, showing her uneaten lunch. It was too late in the day to make her break the fast. The end result was that the money I was to receive was divided between us. I was furious. Even now when we meet, I remind her of this and jokingly tell her that I have not forgiven her for "stealing" half my share of the money. After that first fast, she kept fasting while I did not. I would feel very hungry and simply could not survive without eating or drinking the whole day. "Look at the younger sister, she is fasting and you, despite being older, cannot tolerate hunger!" I did fast under pressure and suffered for it, but I never managed to fast for the full thirty days.

I also had to go through certain religious formalities like learning to read the Koran. I did not show any particular interest in doing so as it was written in Arabic, a language we did not understand. In fact, the entire exercise of teaching us to read the Koran turned out to be a farce. Iqbal, my cousin who was a year older than me, and I were entrusted to a *maulvi*[7] to teach us to read the Koran. The *maulviji* himself did not know the Arabic language. He also appeared to be more interested in the salary he was paid than in teaching us. He was an old man and had the tendency to doze off.

The Koran is divided into a number of chapters and every time we completed a chapter, our effort was appreciated and sweets were distributed. *Maulviji* was paid an additional sum of money apart from his salary. My cousin and I started competing with each other as to who would complete a chapter first. In order to get ahead, we would turn several pages together. *Maulviji* was never able to detect our naughtiness. It was in the interest of all of us that we finish a chapter quickly—we got our parents' appreciation and *maulviji* got his monetary gift.

Abbujaan used to cycle to his office and would have brunch before going to work. He was addicted to paan[8] with a little tobacco, so

[6] Celebration on the day when a younger fasts for the first time.

[7] Priest of a local mosque.

[8] Betel leaves.

a number of paans were prepared for him to take to office. If my mother did not have time, then *baji* would prepare the paans and put them in *gilouris*,[9] then into small rectangular containers. Interestingly, the paan containers also reflected social status—richer people used containers made of silver with fine filigree work on them. If there was more than one man who had to go out for work or for some other errands, a number of containers were prepared and this formed a major activity for women in the morning hours. Paans in fancy containers called *khasdanans* were also offered to visitors. These also had a similar status connotation, depending on whether they were made of silver or ordinary metal.

Abbujaan led a pretty disciplined life. He was fond of good Mughlai food but always ate in moderation. He loved to invite relatives and friends over, so we always had house guests. The only time he would indulge in excesses was when with guests, to make them feel welcome. *Abbujaan* kept in good health throughout his life, never had any major illness, and had a most peaceful death at the age of 83. Until his last day, he looked after himself and never became a burden on his children. Fortunately, he did not spend much time with us, which saved me from his disapproval of my unseemly behavior. He spent his evenings mostly with his male friends. He was more conventional than my mother and grandmother. I do not remember my father ever helping us with our homework. We would complete our homework on our own and help our younger brothers and sisters with theirs.

My Mother

After my father declined to marry his cousin, my grandmother had to look for another bride for her son. Her eyes fell on my mother, who was from the same village and from the same background. Aapa (we called our mother aapa, a term for older sister, as she was too young to be called amma, the usual term for a mother) was the youngest of three siblings and had lost her mother at the tender age of 6. She had been brought up by her oldest sister, who was 12 years older than her, with a brother in between. My maternal grandfather did not remarry and was devoted to his children. Aapa was very beautiful and

[9] Paan prepared and wrapped up in a conical shape, rolled with old papers and in red muslin cloth that is wetted to keep the paan fresh through the day.

childlike, a quality which she retained throughout her life. She was not sent to school—according to the custom of that time—but was given elementary education in Urdu at home and was taught to read the Koran. She was only 16 years old when she got married, and only 18 when I was born.

Aapa produced a child every third year throughout her reproductive life. She was overburdened by these frequent pregnancies and childbirths. In all, she had 11 pregnancies and nine surviving children–seven daughters and two sons. Once she had a stillborn and one child died as an infant. *Baji* provided a helping hand to my mother and practically adopted me to relieve aapa. *Abbujaan* was 12 years older than her and much more mature, patient, and sober. My mother was just the opposite in temperament—friendly, outgoing, and impatient. Despite the age difference, *abbujaan* was supposed to be a good match for her, since he belonged to the same caste and class with a university education, had an independent profession, and was regarded as a true gentleman. Though there were temperamental differences, my parents made an amicable marriage. There was a traditional division of labor in the family, so *abbujaan* was responsible for providing the finances and aapa for managing the household and bearing and rearing children. My father never shared any housework nor helped in rearing us, which was customary. I do not remember aapa ever questioning this division of labor, except the burden she had to bear on account of a large family and constant flow of house guests, which *abbujaan* encouraged. Aapa showed respect to *abbujaan* and, according to the custom, never called him by his first name. *Abbujaan* was kind to her and respected her. Their relationship was not overly formal though–aapa addressed *abbujaan* as *tum* as against the more formal *aap*. She was not servile to him either.

Although aapa was not highly educated, she was very secular in her outlook. As women in my family observed seclusion, there was not much social interaction between us and the neighboring Hindu families. Social interaction was confined to the men, but at each other's festivals, gifts and goodies were exchanged between us. I remember that we used to receive *poories*[10] and vegetarian dishes and sweets from our Hindu neighbors. Aapa used to look forward to having their curries as she believed that Muslims, being primarily nonvegetarians, could not cook vegetables as tasty as the Hindus did.

[10] Fried puffed bread.

We did not send any food items to them, instead we reciprocated by sending them firecrackers on Shabbrat[11] which is celebrated by serving halwa[12] and bursting firecrackers. I would ask my mother why we did not send halwa to our Hindu neighbors and my mother explained that Hindus practice *chhuva-chhuth*[13] and did not accept cooked food from us. She did not have even the slightest hint of resentment at this. At my further questioning, she would explain that it was their custom and that was that. Before Soofya and I were put in purdah,[14] we, along with other children, were sent to see the Diwali lights and also to the Dussehra mela,[15] dressed in our best clothes. We regarded them as Indian festivals rather than just "Hindu" festivals, and enjoyed participating in them. But after the Partition, my nephews and nieces no longer shared the same sentiments, because these festivals were now regarded as "Hindu" rather than "Indian". Similarly, we were taught to greet our elders by bending slightly and saying *Adab*[16] or *Tasleem*,[17] but now when I go to Lucknow, I find my sister's children saying "*Salaam alaikum*"[18] to which I am supposed to respond with the Arabic greeting "*Walai kum Assalam*[19]." It still does not come spontaneously to me, as earlier I used to bless them by saying *jeete raho*,[20] or something similar. Fortunately, my family still continues to be secular and well-integrated in the wider Indian society. Yet, I notice that a certain amount of exclusiveness is creeping into their lifestyle almost unconsciously.

My relatives and family friends saw my mother having seven daughters and only two sons as a great misfortune. But thankfully, my parents and grandmother never treated us girls as a burden. It was only when my brother, Khalid, was born after three daughters that we felt some change in our father's attitude toward us. My brother would have meals with *abbujaan* and they were served the best of what was cooked. Their choice in food was given preference over ours.

---

[11] Festival celebrating Prophet Mohammad's birthday.

[12] A sweet dish prepared with semolina and clarified butter.

[13] Untouchability.

[14] Practice of wearing an additional garment, covering head to toe.

[15] Fair.

[16] A secular Urdu greeting.

[17] Salutation.

[18] Peace be unto you.

[19] May peace be upon you too.

[20] A blessing, which means, 'have a long life'.

My brother's education was given much more importance than ours; his needs were promptly met, while we sisters had to often wait.

I loved sitting around with my mother, especially when her friends visited her. I would listen to their conversations and couldn't resist butting in with questions and comments. I could not fathom some things they said, for example, once aapa's friend said to her in a jocular mood, "Oh, so you have had a bath. Now you will be caught!" My mother blushed and replied "I hope not!" What on earth did that mean? Why should she be saved from getting "caught" because she'd had a bath? When I asked aapa, she dismissed my query, saying that I was too young to understand. It took me several years before I understood this mystery. Another mystery was that I never noticed aapa having her monthly periods. Apparently, she got her period only once in a year and nine months or two years and three months, depending on the sex of the child she was breastfeeding. Because she did not menstruate while lactating, she did not need to have a purifying bath, which is mandatory after menstruation. Soon after she would stop breastfeeding, she would have her period and take the purifying bath. Then she would conceive again. Thus, the bath signified having a period, in most cases followed by pregnancy.

Societal Pressures

My elders, as I have mentioned earlier, were always worried about "what people will say" at my deviant behavior. Public approval for one's lifestyle was eagerly sought. My mother would often scold me and say that I had inherited Wakeelan's genes. But when I would ask who Wakeelan was, everyone would avoid the question. My grandmother was forever worried that I would not get a suitable match if I built up a reputation of being argumentative and unconventional. I used to tell her not to worry as I did not want to get married (little did I know at that time that eventually I would marry not once but twice). To that she would retort, "You shameless little thing, girls never talk about their marriage. In fact, whenever your marriage is discussed, you must lower your gaze or walk out. These are matters determined by your elders." Even at the age of 8 or 9 years, I used to get furious that others would decide my future. During my growing-up years, I often had to hear the comment, "What will people say?" I would retort, "I don't care." In response I would hear, "If you don't care about people's opinions, then you become *badnaam*."[21] Societal pressure ruled our lives. In fact, societal control of individual behavior is regarded as one of the distinguishing features of traditional societies, and this control loosens as societies move toward modernity. In present-day India, we are experiencing this process of change, with all its pressures and conflicts. I feel that my generation had been caught between tradition and modernity—those of us who are in our 70s, grew up in a tradition-bound society but our children grew up in a somewhat modern society. As a young woman, I flouted many social norms and tried to carve out a life for myself and was regarded to be somewhat ahead of my time. My unconventionality earned me a great deal of social disapproval and caused a lot of embarrassment to my parents. I do regret having done this, but I also admire my parents' ability to understand my urge for change and their graciousness to forgive me. On my return from England, I persuaded *abbujaan* to allow aapa to shed her burka, which he graciously did. Finally aapa was also liberated from that unnecessary encumbrance.

Wakeelan: The Rebel

However, I was not the only rebel in our family. Wakeelan—my father's step-sister who had been disowned by the family—had taken many more daring steps than me. Wakeelan[22] was nicknamed so because since childhood she was very argumentative. She was made a victim of family politics but was courageous enough to denounce all social norms and carve a life of her own. My father, who lost his father when he was only six months old was, according to the Muslim Personal Law, declared *mahjoob*, which meant that my grandfather's title and property went to his nearest blood relatives—my uncles—as a son is closer than a grandson. My father's uncle, Siraj, urged his three other brothers to give a piece of their inherited property each to my father. One of his uncles did not like the idea of parting with even a small piece of his inherited property, but agreed to do so under the pressure of his brothers. Being a manipulative person, he thought of a scheme whereby he could get it back. He proposed marriage between his son and Wakeelan, as that way he could claim Wakeelan's share

[21] You will earn a bad reputation.

[22] The Urdu word for advocate.

of *abbujaan's* property (in Islam, a girl is entitled to half of what her brother inherits). His son and Wakeelan were no match for each other. Wakeelan was a very intelligent woman who had learnt Urdu on her own by reading the Koran in Arabic as the Arabic alphabets are very similar to the Urdu alphabets. Her cousin, with whom her marriage was proposed, was barely literate. Moreover, he was short in stature, very unimpressive with no personality, while Wakeelan was tall and well-built with a very imposing personality. Wakeelan did not want to marry him and expressed her rejection of the match in no uncertain way. Her refusal was regarded as sacrilege and was not given any heed. The marriage was finalized. Wakeelan was at her wits' end. She finally thought of soliciting the neighbors' support. She wrote "Please stop my marriage" on pieces of paper and pasted them on her neighbors' doors. She must have somehow managed to sneak out of the house and done so late at night. This was of no avail either. Her family regarded this public display of her refusal as even more shameful. The marriage took place as arranged; however, Wakeelan did not reconcile to the marriage and after a few months ran away to Delhi. How she managed such an escape has remained a mystery, because no one in my family would ever talk about it. Wakeelan was disowned and we never heard of her for a long time. Apparently, she earned her livelihood in Delhi by teaching Koran to girls and singing Islamic hymns at female gatherings. Later, she remarried and had two sons, but became a widow at an early age. All this news filtered through acquaintances travelling from Delhi to Rudauli and then to our parents' residence.

In her old age when her sons were posted in Lucknow, Wakeelan too went to live there. My parents were staying there as well. By then matters had cooled down, so she was forgiven for her "sins" and accepted back in the family. It was then that I first met her. I must have been 9 or 10 years old at that time. I was very impressed by her personality—a very interesting and knowledgeable person, who retained a deep love for her brother, that is, *abbujaan*, and was very affectionate to us nieces and nephews. I often think about how she must have suffered emotionally after being disowned by her entire family for establishing her right to choose her own spouse. She was very dignified and never showed any regrets or guilt about her past. After India's Partition, both her sons decided to migrate to Pakistan and she went along with them to Karachi, but she did not like Pakistan and returned to India after a couple of years. It was in Lucknow at our place that she died of a minor illness. I remember noticing then, that Wakeelan, despite being a rebel who had broken so many social conventions, wore only white and followed all the restrictions imposed on widows.

There was another brave aunt of ours who was also my mother's cousin and her best friend, who too suffered at the hands of convention but did not have Wakeelan's courage and succumbed to an arranged marriage, despite being madly in love with a cousin. For a girl to fall in love and express the desire to marry her lover was the biggest social crime. So the moment her family came to know of their intentions, they quickly arranged her marriage, though she kept protesting. My mother told me that until the wedding day itself, she kept protesting and declared that she would not give her consent to the *nikah*. Theoretically, the consent of both the bride and the groom is essential for a *nikah*. The practice is that two males, preferably related to the bride and accompanied by a lawyer, enter the *zenana* and ask for the bride's consent. The bride is not supposed to say out loud "I accept", as that would be regarded as shameful, so just a simple sound of "hoon" is accepted as consent. According to my mother, my aunt refused to give her consent and finally an aunt of hers said "hoon" on her behalf. She remained very unhappy in her marriage. She often used to visit my mother in Lucknow and always looked sad and lost. She died in her 40s. Her lover remained a bachelor all his life. After coming to know of her past, her husband did not take much interest in her, although he gave her three children. He kept himself amused with other women. Such were the social compulsions which denied even the basic human rights to women.

My Paternal Uncle: Ansar Harvani

I immensely admired both my paternal uncles and used to brag in school about their importance. However, my Ansar Chacha, who was involved in politics from his student days, was often "underground" or in jail, and I remember *dadi*[23] worrying for his safety. A couple of incidents made a huge impression on me, filling me with a deep sense of patriotism and strengthened my Indian identity. When Ansar Chacha would be "underground", the family would not know his whereabouts. There would be no communication with him, and Darus Siraj—his residence—was kept under strict surveillance. Once,

[23] Paternal grandmother.

we received an unsigned postcard saying that Ansar Chacha would be passing through Lucknow station on a certain train at a certain date and time. So the family, including me, went to the station, hoping to at least get a glimpse of him. He was, in fact, being transferred from one jail to another. We all waited impatiently for the train to arrive and located the compartment he was in. It was heavily guarded. When the train stopped, we rushed to the compartment. There were armed guards at the compartment door and the windows had iron rods. *Dadi* tried to put her hand through the iron rods to touch Ansar Chacha but her hand was rudely pushed away by a guard standing outside the window. I was shocked at the cruelty of the guard. The train only stopped for a few minutes but we were at least able to see him. He kept telling us not to worry for him and that he was well looked after in the jail. We returned home with tears in our eyes but ever more convinced that he was fighting for a noble cause.

On another occasion, Ansar Chacha was underground for a long time. A reward was announced for anyone who could inform the police of his hideout. When even that did not work, the British Police started harassing our family and said they would auction all the belongings of the family. This was used as a pressure tactic. A day before the auction, an inventory was prepared of all the belongings at Darus Siraj, including the children's things. The same was done at their village home in Rudauli. The actual auction was to take place the next morning, which would have stripped the family of all its belongings, but it so happened that Ansar Chacha was captured the previous night, so the auction was cancelled. I cannot forget the trauma that the family went through on that occasion. We were all against Partition and were willing to sacrifice whatever was necessary. We were not the only such family. There were millions of others, both Hindus and Muslims, who went through such sufferings. These incidents added to my admiration for Ansar Chacha as they reflected his patriotic zeal and courage.

I also vividly remember the fear my family went through during the Quit India Movement when its frenzy had spread all over the country. My cousin, Abbu Bhai,[24] was involved in it along with many other Lucknow University students. He was the only child of his widowed mother and she did not want him to be deeply involved in the freedom movement for the fear of his being arrested and sent to jail, like Ansar Chacha. There was going to be a students' demonstration

[24] Brother.

in the city in support of the Quit India Movement and Abbu Bhai was going to join it. It was feared that there would be violence and lathi charge and arrests would be made. So everyone tried to dissuade Abbu Bhai from joining the demonstration but he was adamant. He was forcibly pushed into a room and locked in with my aunt—his mother—saying, "We cannot lose my only son." I can still hear Abbu Bhai shouting and banging the door, pleading to be let out.

The Poet Majaz: My Paternal Uncle

My paternal uncle Majaz—we called him *ammujan*—was another person who inspired me a great deal. Besides being among the best Urdu poets of his time and a very good human being, he also had a very good sense of humor. Poet Josh Malihabadi, a contemporary of Majaz and a well-known Urdu poet, knowing Majaz's habit of excessive drinking, once said to him, "Yaar Majaz, to control drinking you should put a *ghadi*[25] in front of you." Majaz replied, "Why *ghadi* Josh Saheb, I am willing to put a *ghada*[26] in front of me." Another popular joke of his, which is often repeated, goes like this: One day Majaz met a gentleman who did not have a good opinion of him and had heard that Majaz smoked and drank heavily. The gentleman asked him if this was correct. Majaz retorted, "Of course not, I neither drink nor smoke." To this, the gentleman expressed his surprise and remarked, "You really do not have any vices then?" "Only one vice I have," said Majaz, "that I lie a lot."

Majaz was a total misfit in the highly traditional Muslim society, dominated by the land-owning class of feudal values. He was, by nature, carefree and did not abide by the social norms of his time. After graduating from the AMU, he was employed by the All India Radio (AIR) as an editor of its journal, *Awaz*. That was the time when his poetry was at its zenith and he was highly popular in the high echelons of Delhi society. During his stay in Delhi, he became familiar with Dr Ansari, one-time president of the All India Congress Committee (AICC) and a rich and highly respected Delhiite. Majaz was warmly welcomed in his family. Dr Ansari had a beautiful young daughter and Majaz fell head over heels in love with her. She too enjoyed the company of this tall, handsome, young man with a sharp sense of

[25] Clock.

[26] Pitcher.

humor, who was the most popular poet of Delhi. Majaz's passion for her became ignited to the extent that he confessed his love for her and even proposed marriage. But she outrightly rejected him and he was banished from the family.

In the 1950s, the Progressive Urdu writers and poets wrote personal narratives on each other in the form of small booklets. Ismat Chughtai wrote one on Majaz where she described Majaz's plight beautifully. She wrote that Majaz's life was like that of a gardener who had tended a beautiful garden for a princess. One day, the princess visited the garden and stopped and admired a red rose. The gardener felt very proud and offered the rose to the princess, requesting her to adorn her hair with it. To that, the princes replied, "No, no, I do not have to adorn my hair with this rose. I have flowers made of gold to adorn me." Unfortunately, it was also the time when Majaz lost his job in the AIR for writing against the British government. He also wrote critical verses targeting two well-known Urdu poets for supporting the government. Faced with personal and professional setbacks and being extremely sensitive, he lost his mental balance and took to drinking to drown his sorrows. The family then called him back to Lucknow where his parents had taken residence after his father's retirement.

When I was old enough to know Majaz, he was living with his parents. Though he did not marry and had no children of his own, he loved children. I admired him immensely and would hang around him whenever he was in the house. He was very popular among women and one of my school teachers had a crush on him. She had an unusual name—Hawwa Bai Rehman. She was often teased by her friends by being called "*Kawwa*[27] Bai." So one day, Majaz asked me if I was taught by Kawwa Bai. I protested and said, "No, she is Hawwa Bai." So in a very serious tone he said, "Oh, so your teacher hides her real name," and suggested that if I did not believe him, then I should ask her if she was known as Kawwa Bai. As a young girl, I used to brag about being brave and not being afraid of any of my teachers as were some of my classmates. So he pumped me up and said that if I was really very brave and was not afraid of my teachers, I should prove it by asking her if she is known as Kawwa Bai. I was in a fix but I also wanted to prove my claims. So the next time when Miss Rehman was walking out of the class, I stopped her at the door and told her that my uncle had told me that she was known as Kawwa

[27] Crow.

Bai and if that was her real name. She was very gracious and said that I should tell my uncle (she had guessed who was this uncle) that I should not ask such rude questions to my teachers. I still remember, I was so small that Miss Rehaman had to bend down quite a bit to be able to listen to me. I then realized my stupidity and felt embarrassed. The next day, *ammujan* asked me if I had mustered the courage to ask my teacher the question. I said proudly that I had. So he started laughing and teasing me further, saying, "You mean you really asked your teacher such a rude question? Oh dear! Dear! You called your teacher Kawwa!" I felt so silly that I burst into tears. He then affectionately hugged me and said that he was only joking and he was fully convinced that I was a very brave girl. I remember he used to play a lot with Jadoo (Javed Akhtar, the poet-lyricist) his nephew and my favorite cousin, and used to tease him a great deal too.

Despite having lived a short and sorrowful life (he died at the age of 42), he retained his sense of humor and positive attitude toward life until his tragic end.

Baji: My Paternal Grandmother

We all called our paternal grandmother *baji*,[28]—as my father had been instructed to address her as *baji*—because she was considered too young to be called amma. In fact, she became *baji* to the neighbors and relatives and even the domestic servants called her *baji* instead of the usual, Begum Saheb. *Baji* practically brought me up and has been much more influential in my socialization than my own mother. For a long time, I even regarded *baji* as my mother. In her youth, she must have been a beautiful woman. She was tall and slim with classical features and was very intelligent. She was only 16 years old when married to my grandfather who was much older than her. He was a widower with a daughter from his first wife, who was the same age as *baji*. I have always been curious to know how *baji*, despite being young and beautiful and belonging to a respectable family, was married to a person much older than her. As bad luck would have it, my grandfather died only two years after his second marriage, leaving behind a 6-month-old son. *Baji* was never remarried, which was contrary to Islam as it recommends that a widow should be remarried

[28] Another term used for addressing an older sister.

soon after the prescribed period of *iddat*.[29] The logic behind this mandatory period was that, within that time if pregnancy had occurred, it could be easily established. But like many other Hindu customs, the ban on widow remarriage prevailed even among Indian Muslims.

The influence of Hindu culture was so strong among the Indian Muslims that *baji*, after losing her husband, was regarded as accursed as Hindu widows were. A number of restrictions were placed on her according to the prevailing Hindu customs of the region, including, being barred from participating in joyous occasions. She had to wear only simple white clothes all her life since the time she was 18, the age at which she became a widow. She could not wear any jewelry, not even simple bangles or flowers, and could not use *ittar*.[30] How frustrated she must have felt being denied all the pleasures of a teenage girl, only on account of losing her husband, for which she was not responsible! I remember how resentful I used to feel when I was old enough to notice her sorrowful plight. *Baji* also had to stay away from ceremonies and rituals at all joyful occasions like engagements, weddings, and births, although she could contribute her skills and labor in their preparation. She hated the color white and would not allow us to wear anything white, although it was fashionable in those days to wear white dupattas. While we would be away in school, *baji* would dye our dupattas in whatever colors she chose, which often did not match with our clothes. We would be frustrated and grumble, but she believed that by wearing white we might face a fate similar to hers and become young widows.

Baji was an excellent cook and very good at stitching clothes. In those days, girls and women stitched their own dresses. It was considered immodest to give measurements to tailors—who mostly used to be men—with an exception where in some places, a widow or an abandoned woman of a lower class may learn to stitch to earn money and provide the stitching services to richer families. *Baji* was known to be very good at cutting and stitching ghararas. Ghararas required special skills to cut and stitch as they were made with six yards of material. Some women took pride in stitching ghararas and using the material economically. For weddings and other functions, women used to sit together to cut and stitch ghararas. *Baji* was usually invited as a consultant.

---

[29] Period of waiting a woman must observe after the death of the husband or divorce from her. It is for four months and 10 days.

[30] Perfume.

Purdah or Women's Confinement

Confined as women were within the four walls of the *zenana*, they seldom went out to shops. But traders often visited our homes and I remember, there used to be Chinese traders who brought special silks. There were also Afghan traders who used to bargain very hard. Their goods were sent inside to the *zenana* by a servant boy. Arguments and bargaining was done through a third person or from behind the curtain. Women had no other entertainment besides the life events which called for celebrations. There was no television in those days and no cinema houses in villages and small towns. So, these celebrations and religious festivals provided some entertainment and kept the women busy. These occasions also provided scope for their organizational skills and to show off their fine clothes and jewelry. One of the ways women showed their natural talents and creativity was by dyeing dupattas in exotic color combinations and created intricate designs called *leheriya*.[31] They used to crinkle dupattas at home too. According to one saying, "Keep a thing long enough and it will be in fashion again" and this has proved right. Nowadays *leheriya* and crinkled muslin dupattas are in vogue once more.

Women then had skillful hands and would make beautiful covers for *khaasdans*[32] and *paandaans*.[33] These artistically prepared covers formed a part of a girl's wedding trousseau. Managerial skills were also utilized in organizing these events. Above all, women grabbed the opportunity to order the men around to provide money and goods for expenses. Had *baji* been born in these days and educated, she could have managed a multinational organization. She would have certainly been a successful event organizer. But alas, *baji* was illiterate!

I grew up under the care of my grandmother. She would dress me up like an adult in shiny, gaudy clothes, which I would resent and even throw tantrums at. She used to make stuffed dolls for me, both male and female. She would organize the dolls' weddings and would invite children from the neighborhood and provide a feast. I remember often resenting such events. But she, in her own way, was preparing me for my future role as a housewife and a mother. Understandably, this used to irk aapa a great deal as my grandmother never had the time to indulge in such elaborate dolls' play for my other sisters. As

[31] Brightly colored clothes with distinctive wave-like patterns.

[32] Containers for ready-to-eat paan or *gilouris*.

[33] Containers for various ingredients needed to prepare paans.

a reaction, aapa leaned more toward Soofya. *Baji* meant well but her over-indulgence damaged my relationship with the rest of my family to some extent because everyone saw me as being more pampered than my younger siblings.

In later life, *baji* suffered from hypertension to which she finally succumbed to at the age of 62. My love and closeness to my grandmother's plight made me aware of the cruel ways in which women in general and widows in particular were treated in all Indian communities. This awareness created resentment in my mind against such traditional customs from an early age. I rejected most of them in my personal life. So, when my daughter was getting married, I had requested *khala*—my maternal aunt who also had been widowed at a young age and had to follow all the culturally prescribed restrictions on widows—to initiate the wedding rituals, as she was the oldest relative around. Eyebrows were raised at this. *Khala* also rejected my request initially but on my insistence and with the approval of some of the more enlightened guests, she finally conceded. I could see that she felt good after being released from the stigma of widowhood.

However, I must admit that despite the cruelties widows were subjected to, the traditional system also provided some solace in their bleak existence, as they were absorbed within the joint family and did not suffer the pangs of loneliness. For example, *khala* ran my maternal grandfather's home who was also a widower. The household chores kept her well occupied. She had, more or less, brought up my mother who was 12 years younger to her. But *khala* became bitter despite having her father's protection. We girls did not like her much as she would nag us and pick on us for every little thing. *Baji*, fortunately, did not have such bitterness in her, partly because of her happy temperament and partly because she was not financially dependent on anyone as her father, who was a rich God-fearing man, had distributed his wealth among his daughters too. According to the Islamic principles, daughters can inherit their parental property but only half of what the brothers would. However, girls were generally denied any share in their parental property in those days, as Muslims, like the Hindus, were governed by what was called the "Customary Law" which deviated a great deal from the Muslim Personal Law. In keeping with the Customary Law, *baji*'s father did not give his daughters any land but compensated them in cash, which was very unusual in those days. This was an example of unconventional generosity.

My Siblings

In matters of looks, Soofya was regarded to be the most beautiful among us sisters as she met the standards of beauty prevalent in those days. She had classical features, very fair complexion, big eyes, oval face, and thin lips. She was also very obedient and accepted everything quietly. I was placed as number two in physical appearance as I had a rather roundish face and small eyes and, unlike Soofya, I was a brat who questioned everything. But some relatives and friends were inclined to find me more attractive because I had a warm and vibrant personality. Soofya and I had to wear the burka, though the younger sisters did not. They also studied at the IT College (now Isabella Thoburn College), which by then was not considered as "modern," as it was in my days. They even studied at the University of Lucknow, which was co-educational.

Our third sister, Sehba, was not considered too attractive as a child because she was neither fair in complexion nor had big eyes or oval face and, above all, was the third daughter in succession. But Sehba grew up to be the most attractive young woman with a good height, interesting personality, and intelligent looks. She is now regarded as beautiful according to contemporary standards. We sisters presented an attractive combination of qualities, good looks, and traditional Muslim *tahzeeb*,[34] plus the right dose of modern education, qualities valued in the marriage market. We were taught stitching, embroidery, and knitting, in addition to cooking; skills required in a good wife and a daughter-in-law. All my sisters were good at these skills. I liked knitting, which I still do, and embroidery, but hated ordinary stitching and cooking. This was terrible because as the oldest sister, I was to be the role model for the younger ones. My fourth sister, Shahla, was particularly good at cooking and stitching. She now keeps herself busy in social work and teaching Urdu in Lucknow. Sehba was also pretty competent in domestic chores along with being academically inclined. She continued to study after getting married. Fortunately, her husband was posted in Washington, so she took advantage of her stay in USA and procured a PhD in Linguistics from the University of Chicago and taught Linguistics and English Literature in USA and Canada. She has published her PhD thesis and also produced a compilation of the poetry of our uncle, the poet Majaz. Sehba is now

[34] Culture.

trying her hand at writing poetry too, a talent which remained latent all these years. My fifth sister, Yasmin, worked as a librarian in Lagos, Nigeria, where her husband was posted. Among us seven sisters, it has been only me and my youngest sister, Resham, who pursued long-term careers. Resham moved to Toronto, Canada, with her husband and worked as a supervisor of day care centers. Soofya did a course in baking and kept herself busy with social work. My other sisters, though graduates, enjoyed being homemakers.

Soofya had to move to Pakistan with her husband; she is the only one from my family to have moved to Pakistan. She remained my mother's favorite as she managed to do everything "right." She was docile by nature and happily became domesticated. My two brothers, Khalid and Shahid, were not very ambitious and after acquiring a moderate level of education, were satisfied with living a somewhat leisurely life and earning a modest income. Khalid, who arrived after three sisters, was pampered by my father, who also tried to impose some discipline on him. But it did not work because Khalid is a little wayward and very imaginative. He has inherited the family genes for poetry and a collection of his poems has recently been published. He is settled in Ottawa with his South Indian dentist wife and daughter. Shahid, my younger brother, acquired some moderate level of computer skills, married a Pakistani girl, and lives in USA. They decided not to have any children. It may be noted that we, nine siblings, have produced only 13 children among us.

Two of my sisters, Seemin and Resham, were born while I was away in London and they saw me for the first time when they were six and eight years old. One of my brothers was sent to Pakistan—to Soofya—as in those days, Indian Muslims could live in Pakistan for a certain period of time and yet retain their Indian citizenship. I did not meet him for many years. After returning to India from London, I lived in Delhi, so I never shared a home with the youngest three siblings. We made up for the distance to a large extent later, but never fully.

All my siblings married within the fold, that is, to Muslims. I broke the convention and not only had a divorce, which was most uncommon in those days and no one until then was divorced among my relatives or family friends, but also married a Christian later, another rarity at that time. My parents welcomed my Christian husband in the family, as did my siblings and other close relatives. Their ability to change with the times was remarkable.

Women's Education in My Family

My family had a number of firsts. My aunt, Safia Akhtar (poet-lyricist Javed Akhtar's mother) was the first female from Rudauli to get a graduate degree. For a Muslim woman from a *qasba* to be a graduate was such a unique event in the early 1930s that a close family friend, Chamru Baba, a great supporter of women's education, came to Lucknow to congratulate her. But he did not know her exact residential address, so he asked the neighbors in the locality about the address of the "house where a girl has recently graduated." He was directed to the correct address. Safia also took up a teaching job in Aligarh, another first to her credit. But my aunt still donned a burka and observed most of the social restrictions imposed upon women.

Aunt Safia was my mother's age. My mother had been married off at the age of 18 without any proper schooling, but Aunt Safia had the good fortune to not just go to school but to university as well. Circumstances were created to make this possible. As luck would have it, Safia's father was transferred to Aligarh at a time when Muslim girls' education was getting a great deal of attention and a Muslim girls' school was started in Aligarh. My uncles, Ansar and Majaz, being older to my aunts and having liberal views, influenced their parents to send Safia and Hameeda to the newly established girls' school in Aligarh. Despite starting late, both my aunts did extremely well and always topped the class and later, the university, at the graduate and postgraduate levels. They always impressed upon me that I should follow their footsteps and get high grades.

My younger aunt, Hameeda, also went to the IT College in Lucknow in a burka. This synthesis of tradition and modernity was highly appreciated. My aunts chose their husbands too, but all the trappings and the pretense of arranged marriages were observed. They conformed to the customs of the time more closely and did not openly protest against the gender discrimination that was so blatantly practiced. I suppose that the first generation of educated women must have thought that despite purdah and restrictions on their freedom, at least they were allowed to pursue education and even have a career. At that time, it was a radical act for an Ashraaf woman to not only study but also to earn a living, which both my aunts did. But I insisted on greater personal freedom. When I audibly expressed my protest, I earned the disapproval of my family and relatives. I remember being advised even by my educated aunts to accept the prevailing social norms without protest.

3

Ancestral Homes

Amethi: My Grandmother's Native Village

Baji's ancestral home was Amethi, a *qasba* in the district of Lucknow (not the Amethi that is the Nehru-Gandhi family's constituency). Her father was a *talukdar*[1] and had owned large tracts of agricultural land in addition to a number of mango orchards. He had built a huge mansion to accommodate the families of his four sons, two of whom had married twice (Muslims are allowed up to four wives at the same time, an archaic law which is still valid in India), so the house was divided into six apartments as the co-wives did not live together. In fact, there was intense jealousy between the co-wives. One of my father's uncles had married a woman named Masooman, allegedly from a *dhobi*[2] caste, who therefore, was regarded as "unclean." She lived in a separate apartment on the first floor of the house. Except *baji*, no other member of the immediate family interacted with her. Fortunately, *baji* accepted her, so whenever we visited Amethi, we were warmly welcomed by Masooman and we preferred to stay with her. Although the other great-aunt avoided all contacts with Masooman, strangely enough, she had adopted her co-wife's first child—a daughter—and brought her up with love and affection as her own. But it was understood that this girl and other children born of Masooman would never be able to get spouses from high-caste families. The three girls and a boy were married into a caste below their father's.

[1] Landholding gentry.

[2] Washerman.

My grand uncle treated both his wives "equally," according to the Koranic instruction, which allows up to four wives as long as all four receive equal treatment from the husband. How this was possible is another question. However, my grand uncle tried his best and spent an equal number of nights with each of the wives and provided identical clothes and jewelry for both. Masooman was allowed to come down to the main house during ceremonial occasions. The first wife had the status of being the main wife and officiated at ceremonial occasions. I remember on one such occasion, when during a family wedding, Masooman came down dressed expensively and bejeweled like the first wife. When lunch was served, she too sat down with the other guests. But the moment she did so, all the high-caste ladies stood up and refused to have the meal alongside her. Masooman had to retire to her apartment, humiliated and distressed. After that, she would always go to her apartment at meal times and her food would be sent to her. That event added to my resentment of caste-ridden practices in India. Masooman's distraught face has stayed in my memory to this day.

Caste System Among Indian Muslims

Among Muslims, there are two major sects: the Sunnis and the Shias. The difference between the Shias and Sunnis has mostly been a political one. The Shias claim that Prophet Mohammad designated Ali—the fourth Caliph and the youngest of the four main Caliphs—to take his place, but by political maneuvering, Caliph Abu Bakr, the oldest, replaced the Prophet. Over time, some minor differences in the manner of *namaz*[3] procedures and personal law have come in. Shias celebrate Moharram,[4] which Sunnis do not.

Zaat or *jaati*, as caste was called in the vernacular, played an important role in social relationships among Indian Muslims, despite Islamic teachings against socio-economic inequalities. During my growing-up years, the caste system was fully functional and we were exposed to it whenever we visited our *nana*'s[5] place in Rudauli. Although Muslims claim that Islam preaches social equality,

[3] Ritual prayers prescribed by Islam to be performed five times a day.

[4] Annual celebration commemorating the death of Hussain, the grandson of Prophet Mohammad.

[5] Maternal grandfather.

the Indian Muslim society never followed the Islamic ideal and an elaborate system of socio-economic differentiation still exists among Indian Muslims on the model of the Hindu caste system. The Indian Muslim society is divided sharply between two major groups, known in North India as Ashraaf or Shaireef and non-Ashraaf or Kameen. The Ashraaf comprise of four sub-castes: the Sayyads, who occupy the highest place in the social hierarchy and claim to have descended from Prophet Mohammed; the Sheikhs, who are supposed to have been descended from the four Caliphs who followed the Prophet; and the Mughals and Pathans, who are considered lower in social status and regarded to be the descendants of the Mughal rulers and their Indian chieftains, respectively. The Sayyads and the Sheikhs intermarried and inter-dined without any prescribed restrictions, as did the Mughals and the Pathans. The latter two castes were allowed to inter-dine with the Sayyads and Sheikhs but marriages between them were not approved. My uncle, Ansar Harvani, married a Pathan girl as he did not believe in these caste-based divisions. Eyebrows were raised as my family claimed to be Sheikhs. I remember my grandmother's remark, "My luckless son should have married a Hindu rather than a Pathan." My daughter, Kiran, married a Pathan too but by that time, my parents had passed away and such differentiations had lost their significance, particularly in urban-educated Muslim society.

The Kameen were supposedly locals from the Hindu population who had converted to Islam. They continued to follow their traditional occupations and did not change their lifestyle after conversion. These non-Ashraaf castes adopted a few Islamic practices such as *nikah*, but retained their caste panchayats, which regulated their day-to-day social behavior. The Kameen mostly comprised the occupational castes, such as the *nai*s (barbers), the *kumhar*s (potters), the *dhobi*s (washermen), the *manihar*s (bangle sellers), the *mirasi*s (singers) and so on. They too had a hierarchical ladder, similar to the Hindu concept of ritual pollution associated with one's occupation.

The Ashraafs and the non-Ashraafs did not dine together and did not intermarry. Both the Ashrafs and the "cleaner" castes of the non-Ashraafs also avoided physical contact with the untouchables from Hindus and "unclean" Muslim castes. The criteria to determine "cleanliness" or "uncleanness" was similar to that used by the Hindus. I remember that a *chamar*[6] woman who carried the faeces

[6] One of the untouchable communities in India.

and cleaned the toilets had to stand a few steps away from us. When she was paid her salary, she had to cover her palms with a cloth to receive the money so that while the money was being transferred, even the slightest contact with her did not occur.

Nau Muslims

Another category of Muslims were the Nau Muslims, the new converts to Islam. They mostly engaged in commercial activities and mainly belonged to the western Indian states, such as Gujarat and Maharashtra. They were regarded to be lower than the Ashraafs in social status. The land-owning Ashraaf gentry did not enter into marriage alliances with the Nau Muslims. One of my father's maternal uncles, while on a visit to Mecca, befriended a Nau Muslim, a fellow Hajji from Bombay (now Mumbai). To strengthen their friendship, the uncle promised to give one of his daughters in marriage to his Nau Muslim friend's son. This gentleman was a businessman of considerable economic means, his son was educated, and the uncle's daughter was a very beautiful girl. But when my father's uncle disclosed his intention of marrying his daughter to this Nau Muslim friend's son, his two older brothers, who had allegedly married low-caste women, protested and almost forced him to desist from such a marriage alliance. Their argument was that, their children from the low-caste wives would not get high-caste spouses in any case, so why should the children of high-caste parents "pollute" the blood. Finally under pressure, the engagement was broken and the poor cousin was married to her second cousin who was not a good match. In fact, she led quite a miserable life.

Qasbatis versus Shahris

During my growing-up years, a distinction was made between the *qasbatis* (people who belong to *qasbas*) and the *shahris*.[7] The *qasbatis*, who were mostly landowners, considered themselves more cultured and sophisticated than their *shahri* counterparts. The *shahris* were mostly salaried persons or traders—professions that carried low prestige—while land ownership was regarded to be more prestigious.

[7] City-dwellers/urbanites.

Shahris were regarded as uncultured, unsophisticated, and money-minded. Most *Shahris* were either traders or salary earners as against the land-owning zamindars or *talukdars*. Land ownership was viewed as far more prestigious than trading and salary earning. While arranging marriages, this factor was given prime importance. A family living in a city but having its origins in a *qasba* was preferred over the one that did not have origins in a *qasba*. "We are *qasbatis*, we do not marry among the *shahris*" was often said. A *qasba* was not only a geographical area but also a cultural unit having its own cultural identity. The predominantly Muslim landowning gentry nurtured this identity. Despite having lived mostly in towns, our family considered itself *qasbatis* and our lifestyle adhered to that rather than to the *shahri* ways. The only major break from *qasbati* tradition was that, we girls were sent to school. Purdah and the use of burka continued in our families even while living in Lucknow. We, in effect, exhibited a mix of urban and rural cultures with heavy doses of *qasbati* traditions. Our social interaction was confined to *qasbati* families, as were marriage alliances. A few exceptions, when a *qasbati* girl may have been married to a *shahri* or vice versa, were sneered upon.

Language was another factor that distinguished the *qasbatis* from the *shahris*. The *qasbatis* spoke a regional Urdu dialect called "Awadhi," that of the Oudh region, whereas the *shahris* spoke proper Urdu. I grew up speaking Awadhi because my mother, grandmother, and all other Rudauli relatives used to speak it. It was only when I started going to school that I learnt to speak in Urdu. But I became so conditioned that I would speak in the language I was spoken in, that is, in school I used to speak in Urdu with my friends but at home I used to speak in Awadhi. Despite socio-cultural stereotyping and minor religious differences like the fact that Shias were mostly *shahris* and Sunnis were mostly *qasbatis*, amicable relations existed between the two groups and open conflicts did not take place, reflecting a tacit understanding of different belief systems and lifestyles.

Qasbati Tahzeeb

The landed gentry, to which my parents belonged, took pride in being *qasbatis* and not *shahris*. The *qasbatis* and those who lived in the neighboring areas were conscious of their sophisticated lifestyle. They made a virtue of gracious living called *takalluf*,[8] which included

[8] Extreme politeness.

a correct way of greeting by saying *adaab*, speaking chaste Urdu, correct pronunciation of Urdu words, eating food in a manner that one's fingers beyond the first three digits should not be soiled, the proper way of declining food or any eatables when offered, and also eating small quantities when invited as guests. There were jokes about certain families who would eat so little that they would have a second meal after returning home. Another characteristic of *takalluf* was that you always put the other person first, for example, while at a dining table, you always asked the person next to you to take the food first or when you entered a house or a building or even a train, you had to request your companion to enter first. *Pehle aap*[9] was always the refrain. There were stories about how when more than one person would travel, each would request the other to enter the train compartment first and would keep saying *Pehle aap* to each other till the train left. Great pains were taken to preserve this *takalluf* or *tahzeeb*. Our mannerisms were monitored in great detail. Girls especially, had to meet the prescribed standards as we were to be judged in our *sasural*[10] on these things. Having grown up in Lucknow, it was very important for me to teach my children the Lucknowi *tahzeeb*, especially the correct way of saying *adaab*. We were taught to cup our right palm slightly and bend slightly while saying *adaab*. I have been at pains to first teach my children and now grandchildren the Lucknow culture and Urdu language and its correct pronunciation. I must confess that I am rather chauvinistic about it. I have often lamented the fact that my daughters have not fully internalized our *tahzeeb*, having grown up in Delhi which has a North and South Indian composite culture and is somewhat dominated by the refugee Punjabi culture. One day, my youngest daughter Nikhat, who was studying at St. Stephen's college, came up to me and said "Mummy, you will be very happy today, because yesterday our Vice Principal M. Ameen called me and asked me where I came from. I told him I have been born in Delhi but my mother belongs to Lucknow. To which he replied, 'I should have thought so, that Lucknow *tahzeeb* is reflected in the manner you walk and talk'." It certainly made my day.

Extreme delicacy of behavior was the hallmark of the erstwhile Lucknow culture that was part of my upbringing. But today, I cannot claim to meet those standards in my behavior and lifestyle as my

---

[9] You first.

[10] Husband's home.

extensive travels, both within and outside India, and my exposure to various cultures has diluted my way of life, some for the good too. Elements of every culture, over time, become redundant as society moves on; certain cultural practices need to be rubbed off. So, I am not unhappy that during my lifetime, I have discarded some elements of conventional behavior and adopted others. However, despite changing times, all is not lost. Even now, when I get down at the Lucknow railway station, I sense a lack of aggressiveness of the kind that one experiences in Delhi. The coolies and *tangewallahs*[11] are more polite than the ones in Delhi and continue to speak refined Urdu. A few *tangewallahs* still ply in the old part of Lucknow. Lucknowi *tangewallahs* have been known for their sense of humor. Once, a very fat gentleman hired a tonga in Lucknow and the *tangewallah* quoted twice the usual rate to take him. At the occupants' protest, the *tangewallah* very politely said, "sir, in consideration of your 'good health', I will have to take you in two lots." I am often reminded of the poetic chants of Lucknow hawkers who used to sell ice by shouting "Take the ice for your sherbet,[12] it is melting away in love" or "Huzoor, (Sir) take some cucumbers, as thin as Majnun's ribs," referring to the great Laila–Majnun Persian epic.

The Jajmani System

The *Jajmani* system was practiced among the Muslims prior to the land reforms that were legislated in 1961. It was essentially a patron–client relationship, whereby the zamindar or the *talukdar*, known as jajman, gave land to the non-Ashraaf castes called kameen, to till. The praja had to share the produce with the landlord on an agreed basis, in cash or kind. In addition, the landlord also provided sites to them for building their houses. These castes were attached to the sarkar's family in a hereditary relationship. The Ashraaf and the non-Ashraaf castes were organized economically according to the *Jajmani* system.

A number of occupational castes, such as the nai, the *mirasi*, the potter, etc., were attached to different landlords, to whom they provided their specialized services. These services were not paid for

[11] Horse-driven carriage drivers.

[12] Home-made cold drinks.

on a normal basis but payments were made generally in kind, on ceremonial occasions and on festivals, etc.

I have vivid memories of how different kameens, such as the barber's wife and the bangle-seller's wife, would come to serve us during our visits to Rudauli or Amethi. These castes have been mentioned in previous chapters but not in much detail. The barber's wife especially, would insist on bathing us and cutting our nails. We would not allow her to bathe us but we sometimes allowed them to wash our hair and cut our nails.

After the land reforms took place, most of the occupational castes either started charging for their services or moved to urban areas. With the collapse of the *qasbati* social structure, the *Jajmani* system was bound to collapse. Maybe it was for the good, as the lower castes were perceived by the upper castes to be uncivilized and of lowly character. The word '*kameen*' means low caste and is still used as a derogatory term. I observed this casteist attitude even within my family during my growing-up years and it left me with a deep sense of injustice. I often protested against it, only to be rebuffed.

One such incident took place during my school days. Two girls had joined our school in my younger sister's class. Soon we found out that their family also belonged to Rudauli and her mother sent a message saying that she would like to visit my mother. So she was invited over. When she came to our house, my mother realized that she was from a *kameen* caste. As our guest sat on the charpoy beside my mother, aapa in an angry voice said, "How dare you sit with me? You may be rich enough now to send your daughters to a school, but that does not change your caste." We were shocked at our mother's behavior; we had never noticed aapa being so caste-conscious earlier. The poor visitor moved herself to the lower part of the charpoy without any protest. Social hierarchy was so strictly observed in those days that even the charpoy had a lower and an upper part. The lower section of the charpoy, which was uncomfortable as it was not properly strung, would normally be assigned to lower-caste visitors.

Jinnats and Superstition Among Indian Muslims

I loved my visits to Amethi but I also suffered from the constant fear of being confronted by the Jinnat Baba lived on each apartment's roof. Although Islam condemns superstition, Indian Muslims are as superstitious as their Hindu counterparts. *Jinnats* were supposed to be celestial bodies who were invisible to ordinary humans. They were kind and protective to the families and everyone was to be very respectful to them in terms of taking care of the areas in the house where Jinnat Baba was supposed to tread. In case those spots were disturbed or defiled in any way, Jinnat Baba would express his displeasure through certain signs. I remember a couple of instances when Jinnat Baba's displeasure was expressed. Once, my *baji*, out of a desperate need to relieve herself (the only toilet in the apartment was occupied), sat at the end of a rickety staircase in a dark corner of the courtyard. She later discovered blood on her gharara. She showed it to her sister-in-law, mystified as to where it could have come from, as she had attained menopause and had no wound which could have bled. I still remember that red stain on her white gharara. She washed it off but the very next instance, the same red blot appeared on the other part of her gharara. Again, everyone was surprised. Then *baji* suddenly realized that she had defiled the staircase which Jinnat Baba would use for climbing to the roof. The moment she realized this, the stain disappeared.

In the event that Jinnat Baba got offended, instant amends would be made by getting sweets (Jinnats were supposed to be fond of sweets) and performing *Fateha*[13] on the spot which was regarded to be his domain. The strange thing was that the sweets would disappear after a while and it was believed that Jinnat Baba had consumed them and thus, accepted the penance. Who used to consume the sweets is a mystery to me! It now sounds so ridiculous but to the residents in *baji*'s ancestral house, it was absolutely real.

In another instance, we youngsters were sleeping in a room where there was an oil lantern in a corner. Suddenly the lantern flew out of the room and crashed on the floor. We all woke up. I almost froze with fear but the eldest amongst us understood the sign and shouted, "Who put the lantern at the spot where Jinnat Baba says his *namaz*? See, it has angered him." In the morning, the same ritual of offering sweets was repeated. After that, I would sleep with *baji*.

There were also stories about Jinnats in my parents' ancestral home in Rudauli. But for some inexplicable reasons, they had left their abode and gone away, no one knew where. I enjoyed listening to stories about them and was relieved that they were not there anymore. I could visit Rudauli without the fear of encountering

[13] Reading of Koranic verses.

them. One of the stories went back to our great-grandfather's days, when a Jinnat Baba lived in the residential compound at Rudauli in a small room in one corner. Interestingly enough, this Jinnat Baba was very romantic and temperamental. According to the story, one day a bride was found unconscious in Jinnat Baba's room. It was believed that Jinnat Babas liked beautiful women, so at weddings, special precautions were taken to protect the bride from their gaze by reciting special verses from the Koran. The unconscious bride was assumed to have been secretly brought there by Jinnat Baba. On hearing this, the children of the house started peeping into the room and making rude remarks. It is said that Jinnat Baba got annoyed at that and cursed them, saying that from then onwards, in every generation, there would be a male who would have a wayward personality and would cause embarrassment to the family. Strangely, since then, there has been a wayward kind of man in our family since the last few generations. My grandfather's younger brother; in my father's generation, our uncle Majaz; and in my generation, my brother, who is intelligent but unconventional. So far, we have not yet identified any such male in our children's generation; hopefully, the curse has died out.

Nowadays, one does not hear of Jinnat Baba. After the Partition, most young men migrated to Pakistan while the old ones passed away. The huge mansion in Amethi has almost been erased due to misuse as the occupants migrated to Pakistan and those who remained, were financially unfit.

Rudauli: My Mother's Ancestral Home

I spent many happy summers in Rudauli and Amethi.

We loved visiting Rudauli and virtually spent all our summer holidays there, playing with our cousins—our *khala's* and our *mamu's*[14] children. They were about our age. *Nana's*[15] house was very large. It had a huge courtyard that had a well in one corner from which water was drawn for the use of the household. A man from a lower caste was employed to draw the water from the well which was stored in clay pitchers, as there were no refrigerators in those days. Women of the

[14] Maternal uncle.

[15] Maternal grandfather.

household observed purdah from the man, so when he came inside—usually once or twice a day depending on the daily consumption of water—we would go inside the rooms.

There were three sets of verandas in our *nana's* house on three sides of the courtyard and a large room behind each of them. On the fourth side was the kitchen and a large storeroom that contained grains, rice, dals,[16] etc., which was produced on *nana's* land. One of the three sets was allotted to *khala* and her family, the other to *mamu* and his family, and the third was kept for the guests. My *nana*, who was a widower, had a separate apartment outside the main house. The concept of individual rooms was not known in those days. Small children slept in their parents' room and as they grew older, they were shifted to the veranda which, in winter, was covered with *chics*.[17] Old houses used to have a small anteroom between the inner courtyard and the main outside door. The purpose of this anteroom was to stop male outsiders from entering the inner courtyard directly. The anteroom was also where the *doli*[18] would be kept for the women whenever, which would be very seldom, they had to go visiting. Once they were seated, the *doli* would be covered with thick cloth from all the four sides; the *kahaars*[19] were then called in to carry it. I have happy memories of sitting in my mother's or aunt's lap in the *doli* and opening the cloth curtain a wee bit to peep out.

Our *nana's* big house was one of the several houses within a huge compound where *nana's* first cousins and their families lived. In addition, there was a common men's area in the huge compound with a large double verandah with 12 pillars called a *baaradari* (*baara* means 12). Almost every *talukdar* had a *baaradari* in those days. This common *baaradari* was used for wedding receptions and other festive occasions. *Nana's* apartment was attached to the *baaradari*. He had a very loyal personal servant who looked after him. *Nana*, although a young widower, did not remarry because he was attached to his three young children and did not want to impose a stepmother on them. He was a tall, well-built man with a very impressive personality and generated a lot of aura around him. *Nana* was highly respected in the family and the community. He provided a helping hand and

[16] Pulses.

[17] Hanging bamboo curtains with cotton lining.

[18] Small palanquin.

[19] Doli bearers.

protection to the widows and the children of the extended family and led a very disciplined life. *Nana* was an "absentee landlord" and owned a considerable amount of land in the villages around Rudauli, as well as several mango orchards which brought in a good amount of seasonal income. As was customary in those days, he did not work the land himself but let it out to farmers who tilled it for him, kept the produce, and paid him with a certain percentage of the products and some cash, known as *malguzari*.[20]

Nana would wake up early to say his morning prayers. His servant would give him a cup of tea, then *nana* would go for a walk and would have his breakfast in his apartment, prepared and served by his servant. He was very particular about his tea which was prepared in a *samovar*,[21] while in the inner household, tea was prepared in the usual manner by boiling water in a saucepan. We children used to be very intrigued by his *samovar*. After his breakfast, *nana* would walk into the *zenana* and my *khala* would inform him about whatever was happening inside the house, such as which guests were coming, or any wedding, or other functions which would take place in the near future, how much *newta*[22] was to be given and the money she needed for those and other domestic expenses. *Nana* would provide the finances for running the household, then would go back to his apartment and again come to the *zenana* for lunch. Everyone had to be on their best behavior when he entered the house. He would clear his throat upon entering, as a kind of alert of his presence. *Nana* would have his lunch in the main house accompanied by younger grandchildren. He would occasionally invite a visiting son-in-law to lunch with him and this was considered to be a privilege.

Nana would go for an evening walk every day that would end in a village meeting. Every evening the men of the village, mostly senior ones, would gather in a central place called *tipai*, which literally means a bench. At that place, a number of benches were placed in a rectangular manner and at the head would sit the senior-most member of the land-holding family. There, the daily Urdu newspaper would be read and discussed, in addition to village affairs. *Nana* would enter the house again after his evening walk, just for a few minutes, to enquire if all had been well during the day. His dinner would be sent to his apartment.

We were pampered by our *nana* because we visited him only once a year, while his other grandchildren were there all the time. We

[20] Money collected by levying taxes.
[21] A specially designed tea-pot with a double boiler.
[22] Monetary gift.

enjoyed our special status as *shahris;* we felt one up on our cousins and would impress them with stories about the facilities we enjoyed while living in a city, such as electricity, cinema houses, pukka roads, and the fact that we went to school while our female cousins did not. Our female cousins would particularly enquire about city fashions and films.

There were a considerable number of Muslim *talukdars* and zamindars in Rudauli who led a leisurely, feudal style of life. A differentiation was made between *talukdars* and zamindars on the basis of landholdings. *Talukdars* had bigger landholdings and led a more luxurious lifestyle. Besides these, Rudauli's population consisted of Hindu and Muslim farmers, traders and occupational castes. What I wish to point out here is that the Hindus and the Muslims of all castes and creed lived harmoniously in the *qasbas* without communal feelings. The Hindus accepted the Muslims' economic and cultural supremacy and the Muslims respected the Hindus' way of life and caste system. I well remember the feelings of camaraderie that existed in the pre-Partition days in the *qasbas*. Neither did the sound of the conch in the temples disturb the Muslim nor did the sound of *Azaan*[23] annoy the Hindus. During Moharram, Hindus and Muslims walked shoulder-to-shoulder, reciting *marsias.*[24] Unlike now, such occasions did not cause any communal tension; even the slaughter of animals during Bakra Eid[25] did not lead to conflicts. This was the environment in which I grew up.

Rudauli Cuisine

Rudauli was not only larger in area, but compared to other surrounding *qasbas*, it had a special place in terms of the sophisticated lifestyle. Among other things it took pride in, was its cuisine. Food played an important part in the feudal lifestyle. Rich Mughlai dishes soaking in ghee and highly sweetened desserts formed their food. There were several dishes which were unique to Rudauli, such as *boot ke laddu*—sweet balls made from green grams—and *andarse ki goli*, another specialty that was prepared from rice paste mixed with *til*,[26] then

[23] The call for Muslim prayer.
[24] Mournful songs dramatizing the Battle of Karbala.
[25] Festival of sacrifice. Also called Eid al-Adha.
[26] Sesame seeds.

shaped into small balls which were filled with *khoya.*[27] *Rasawal* was another favorite dessert, somewhat unique to the Barabanki District. My *abbujaan* was very fond of *rasawal* and it was served as one of the desserts at my aunt Hameeda's wedding feast. *Rasawal* was prepared during the sugarcane harvesting season and was made with rice and sugarcane juice. Elaborate arrangements were made for cooking it, as it had to be cooked for the whole night on slow fire and had to be constantly stirred. This very sweet preparation was then enriched with nuts and coconut, cooled and stored in earthenware *handis*[28] which were tightly covered with red muslin cloth. *Rasawal*—like mangoes—was sent as a gift to relatives and friends living in cities away from the *qasba.* Some enterprising *talukdars* would also send it to politically influential persons with a view to oblige them. Now, some of these specialties have become almost extinct as both the *halwais*[29] who used to prepare them and the *talukdar* and zamindar families have migrated to Pakistan. Those *halwais* who are left behind do not find many buyers for *rasawal* among the modern health-conscious lot.

Chewing paan was another habit of *qasbatis,* men and women alike, particularly in landholding families. Unlike these days when a guest visits for a short time, tea or coffee is offered, in those days paans were given. The lady of the household was always seen with the *paandaan,* the size of which expressed the social status of the family. The *paandaan* had two compartments: the lower compartment held condiments like the lime, *kattha,*[30] crushed betel nuts and small cardamoms, and the upper part held the betel leaves. The condiments were placed on the betel leaf in correct proportions and then wrapped into a conical shape called *gilouri.* The *gilouris* were presented to visitors in beautifully filigreed silver or metal *khasdans* (depending on the financial status of the family). Crushing betel nuts and making paper coverings for *gilouris* formed an important activity of the leisured-class women who had maidservants to cook and do other household chores.

Rudauli also takes pride in having produced a number of poets, writers, and politicians of renown. My paternal uncle, Majaz, was a well-known Urdu poet; his brother Ansar Harvani was a freedom

---

[27] Highly reduced milk.

[28] Pots.

[29] Cooks who specialized in making sweets.

[30] Acacia catechu.

fighter who gave his entire youth to the freedom movement and was a Member of Parliament in the first two parliaments of independent India. One of my mother's uncles was an educationist who established the first girls' school in Rudauli.

Makhdoom Mian: Rudauli's Sufi Saint

Rudauli has its own shrine of a Sufi saint, popularly known as Makhdoom Mian. His death anniversary or Urs (among Muslims, a revered person's death is commemorated because at death, a person gets liberated from the worldly bondage and mingles with God) was celebrated annually with great gusto. A fair took place at the time of the Urs. The saint was revered by the Hindus and the Muslims alike and the fair provided an opportunity for traders to set up shops and sell their merchandise. Our annual visits to Rudauli also coincided with the Urs which occurred in the month of June. It used to be a very special occasion and brought a lot of activity and cheer in the otherwise sleepy *qasba.* Almost a mile around the shrine, stalls were set up, selling all varieties of consumer goods. The shops were set up by merchants not only from nearby *qasbas* but also from distant cities like Faizabad and Lucknow. The major attraction, besides the merchandise sold, were the *qawwali*[31] sessions for which the *qawwals* or singers came from different parts of India. Bamboo curtains cordoned off a part of the hall, for women, where the performance took place. Young girls and boys specially looked forward to these occasions. *Qawwali* sessions provided opportunities to them to get a glimpse of their beloved. The more daring even exchanged gifts–small articles of personal adornments like colorful silk braids, earrings and *ittar.* Cold drinks were also sent to the beloveds through young servant boys. In those days, aerated drinks were not available, so cold drinks were made from seasonal fruit extracts and a lot of crushed ice. There used to be one special drink called "glass" which was very rich with kulfi,[32] fruit pieces, and *falooda.*[33] It was the costliest drink and if a girl received a "glass," it meant that her boyfriend was really serious about her. She would accept the "glass" with giggles and would feel one up over the others. However, most of them were innocent fancies and only indicated a natural interest in the opposite sex.

[31] Sufi songs.
[32] Frozen dairy dessert, especially ice cream served in the shape of a cone.
[33] Rose-flavored beverage.

Strangely enough, a few years ago, I was strolling along the Juhu Beach in Mumbai and came across "glass" being advertised. To my utter surprise, I found exactly the same "glass" of my childhood being sold there.

My female cousins lived much more restricted lives than me but love always found a way of expressing itself. Rudauli girls were famous for their romantic temperament and innocent love affairs were common there. Strict purdah was observed even between the first cousins, so opportunities of seeing or meeting each other were very limited. Therefore, love letters were exchanged, sent through a servant boy who would be lured by a handsome tip to maintain the secrecy. Occasionally, at a wedding or some other festive occasion, the lovers would try to catch a glimpse of each other from behind the curtains. There would be secret love affairs mostly between cousins, sometimes even imaginary ones. I had a cousin, the same age as mine, with whom I was very friendly. A room on the first floor of her house had a window which opened on to one of the few streets of Rudauli. She had the habit of sneaking upstairs and sitting near the window just to gaze at men, especially younger men strolling on the street. I am sure she even imagined herself to be in love with one of them. She would bring me up to date with the prevailing love affairs, during my visits to Rudauli. Most of them were temporary and the moment the parents would get even a hint of it, the girl's marriage would be arranged and she would live happily ever after. It is an irony that my friend who followed these affairs so closely and hoped that one day she might find a lover too, neither found a lover nor a husband. In fact, a number of young women from my *qasba* remained unmarried. This was very unusual among Muslims as due to marriage between cousins being preferred, girls were absorbed within the extended family itself.

The Rudauli fair lasted a week but on the main day, with the melodious tunes of specially arranged *qawwalis* playing in the background, the male and direct heir to the saint called Sajjada Nashin, had to don the saint's robe (claimed to be the original one) that was kept in the *zenana* of Sajjada Nashin's house. Sajjada Nashin would go inside the *zenana* to put on that robe and then make an appearance in the shrine. The devotees would touch the robe as a sign of their devotion to the saint and his heir. Rudauli ladies would gather in the *zenana* and make cash offerings called *nazrana*, to the wife of Sajjada Nashin while the men would do the same to Sajjada Nashin himself in the *dargah*.[34] All Rudauli girls who were married outside Rudauli or within, were expected to attend the ladies' gathering at the Urs, especially in the first year of their marriage. The *mirasis* would sing *qawwalis*. Women and girls used to look forward to the Urs which provided an occasion to display their clothes and jewelry too. The economically well-off would prepare several sets of clothes for different occasions like the *qawwali* sessions held at different places and finally, the gathering at the Sajjada Nashin's residence. It was an occasion to show off one's economic status through one's finest attire and jewelry.

Once *dadi*, our aunt Safiya Akhtar's mother, was very keen that *manjhli phuphi* (as we called our aunt) goes to Rudauli for the first Urs after being married and offers *nazrana*. *Manjhli phuphi* was at that time teaching in the Training College in Aligarh, so she did not want to undertake the long journey to Rudauli just for that occasion, but she finally agreed on *dadi's* insistence. *Dadi* also insisted that *phuphi* deck herself in expensive jewelry and wear a heavily-embroidered gharara, and in particular, wear gold *payals*.[35] *Manjhli phuphi* was not at all interested in this but for *dadi*, there could not have been a better occasion to impress her village folk with their economic status. Finally, *manjhli phuphi* yielded to her mother's request and dressed and decked herself up and offered a heavy *nazrana* to Sajjada Nashin's wife. Status consciousness was so prevalent that even religious occasions were not spared from demonstrating one's economic status.

When in Rudauli, as mentioned earlier, we would visit our relatives in *dolis*. When we travelled by train, we went to the railway station in *dolis* too. The train would stop only for two minutes at Rudauli. There used to be a separate compartment for women. The moment the train came into view, the *kahaars* would pick up the *dolis* and start running toward the ladies' compartment. It used to be quite a funny sight as the *dolis* were lifted to the level of the compartment door one by one and the invisible occupants would jump into the compartment. Women were not to be seen entering the compartment, even in a burka. Inside the compartment—while the train would be moving—we could peep out from the window, but when a station approached, we would have to pull down our veils. I also remember

[34] Islamic shrine built over the grave of a revered religious figure.

[35] Anklets.

how the poorer women, without a burka but with the veil drawn over their faces, would start wailing the moment the train was sighted, as they were going to leave their natal village for their husband's village or town. Their wailing would stop abruptly the moment the train left the platform.

Another reason why I looked forward to going to Rudauli was to visit Chamru Baba. His actual name was Chowdhry Mohammad Ali. He was the leading *talukdar* of Rudauli and very liberal in his outlook. He was a great supporter of women's education and had his daughters educated up to college level. In fact, his daughters were among the first students of the Karamat Husain Muslim Girls' College (now Karamat Girls College) in Lucknow. After losing his first wife, he married a woman from Lucknow who was alleged to be the daughter of a prostitute. He defied his family and the existing social prejudices of that time and insisted that full respect be accorded to her. Chamru Baba was a family friend and would invite me and my sister to his home and encourage us to study seriously. He would tell us about courageous women from Indian history and also about contemporary women active in the freedom movement.

Mangoes formed an important part of the *qasbati* culture in Oudh. The landholding families, particularly the *talukdars*, used to own mango orchards and took pride in having a large variety of mangoes. Mango-eating parties were regularly held, often in the orchard itself. Elaborate arrangements were made for the guests. Separate women's mango parties also took place at night. Gasoline burners were used to provide light. Mangoes would be soaked in cold water for several hours as there were no refrigerators in those days. Gifts of special varieties of mangoes were exchanged between friends and relatives.

My father was extremely fond of mangoes and considered himself to be a mango connoisseur. The only shopping he ever did was for mangoes. I remember a mango-related incident which reflected his honesty and integrity and left a lifelong mark on us children. My father's job offered many opportunities for *balai amdani*, the accepted term for bribery. But he was meticulously honest and never accepted favors of any kind from his clients. However, his fondness for mangoes was well known. Once *abbujaan's* peon brought inside the *zenana,* a basket full of choicest mangoes; *abbujaan* was busy with a client in the men's quarter. We assumed that he must have bought them so we children started eating. We had already consumed a few when *abbujaan* came inside and seeing the mangoes asked us where they had come from. My mother said, "Your peon brought them, did you not buy them?" He said, "No," and called the peon to enquire where those mangoes had come from. The peon replied, "The Saheb that you were talking to, gave the basket and asked me to take it inside." *Abbujaan* was furious and made us count the seeds of the mangoes that we had eaten. He had the same number of similar mangoes bought and sent back along with the uneaten ones to the client.

Chamru Baba was a connoisseur of mangoes too. His mango orchard had a variety called *Sundarya*[36] because this mango had a double-colored skin, red on one side and yellow on the other. He used to offer this variety, particularly to us children, and would tease us by asking the color of the mango skin. If we said red, he would quickly turn it around and say, "But see, it is yellow!" Our visits to him were such fun.

Mangoes were not eaten as dessert with a few pieces being served after a meal but in bulk. In my childhood days, they were not sold in kilos either but in *saikdas,* that is, price quoted per hundred mangoes or according to a *dheri,*[37] which contained 33 mangoes. So one bought at least a *dheri,* if not hundred mangoes at a time.

I have fond memories of mangoes being soaked in buckets of water and after the afternoon nap, us eating them. *Abbujaan* would sit on a chair with the bucket of mangoes in front of him and we children would sit on the floor around him. He would pick a mango from the bucket, admire its shape and color; he would smell it, then give it to one of us to smell too and ask our opinion if it smelled sweet or not. After this ritual, which was repeated for every mango, he would cut a slice and offer it to one of us, while the rest of us waited impatiently for our turn. In this way, a dozen or two mangoes were consumed in each sitting. It is very befitting to *abbujaan's* fondness of the fruit that he is buried under a mango tree and every season, mango blossoms fall on his grave. It is a pity that mangoes are not allowed to ripen on the trees anymore. Nowadays, traders from big cities come and buy mango orchards for the season, pluck the unripe mangoes and ripen them with chemicals. We find that these days, we cannot digest mangoes beyond a few slices. Probably because of the chemicals used for ripening them.

---

[36] Beauty.

[37] A heap.

Moharram

Shias observe the festival of Moharram to commemorate the Battle of Karbala when—according to the legend—hundreds of years ago, Prophet Mohammad's grandsons, Hasan and Husain, were tricked into the Battle by the ruling king, Yazid. Being unprepared for an armed conflict and having very limited resources, Hasan and Husain's army was defeated and the brothers, along with their troops, were killed. The Shias of India, to this day, commemorate that event over 10 days of mourning. They make effigies of the tombs of Hasan and Husain—called *Tazias*—display them in their homes and in their prayer homes called *Imam Baras*[38]. Then on the 10th day, these effigies are taken out in a procession and buried, similar to a human burial. During the 10 days of mourning, collective, mournful singing takes place, dramatizing the Battle of Karbala. These songs are known as *marsias.* Some *marsias* are composed in the highest literary quality of Urdu poetry. Sunnis do not observe Moharram but to respect Shia sentiments, they avoid any form of festive activity during these 10 days. Though not common, Shia–Sunni marriages did take place; my *baji*'s mother was a Shia. *Baji* and her siblings were brought up as Sunnis according to the patriarchal system but there was a healthy tolerance of my great-grandmother's faith. She would go to Rudauli to her natal home to observe Moharram.

In Rudauli, there was a separate locality where Shias congregated and observed Moharram, kept *Tazias* and sang *marsias.* A Shia *talukdar's Tazia*—the largest and the most beautifully decorated—would lead the procession in which Sunnis and even Hindus mingled to share the poignancy of the occasion.

The Lucknow Moharrams were famous, both for the *marsias* and for the quality of their *Tazias.* Two Lucknow poets—Mir Anees and Dabeer—were famous for writing heart-rending *marsias* of high literary quality. The *Tazias* were made of colorful paper and decorated in silver and gold material. But the most sought-after *Tazia* in Lucknow used to be the last in the procession. After all the *Tazias* were taken out in a procession amongst the singing of *marsias* and chanting of Hasan and Husain's names, the last one would be the one prepared by a Hindu devotee. Without changing his religion, he had developed great reverence for the legend of Karbala and to express his reverence,

[38] Shrine built by Shia Muslims.

he would make a *Tazia*, display it in his home, and include it in the procession. It was made of clay and had fresh grass grown all over it. It was awaited with curiosity by the spectators of the Moharram procession. It was called "Doob ka Tazia" (*Doob* means fresh grass). It must have required a great deal of preparation and expertise in watering and caring for the grass to make sure that the grass grew evenly and remained fresh until the day of the procession. We used to go to a Sunni relative's house on the 10th day of the Moharram to watch the procession. I can visualize the *Tazia* and its fresh green grass waving in the breeze, even now.

Strangely enough, Lucknow never had Hindu/Muslim riots, not even in the days of Partition when many parts of UP were affected. However, despite the cordial relations at a personal level between the Shias and the Sunnis, Shia/Sunni riots often erupted in Lucknow. To counter the Moharram procession, Sunnis in Lucknow would take out a procession on the birthday of Prophet Mohammad, singing praises about the Prophet and his first predecessor, Caliph Abu Bakr. These songs were called *Madh-he-Sahaba*, which means "in praise of the Caliphs." The Shias contested Abu Bakr being the First Caliph and so they felt offended by his praises being sung and would protest by throwing stones at the Sunni procession. This would often result in physical fights and in disruption of the procession. I remember on one occasion, when we were living in the nearby town of Barabanki, my family and some friends and relatives together, hired a bus and went to Lucknow to watch the procession and listen to *Madh-e-Sahaba*. But the moment *abbujaan* felt that some trouble was brewing up, we quickly drove back.

4

School and Burka

My first school was a government primary girls' school in Barabanki, a small town where my father had started his legal practice. I used to go to school in a wooden cart known as *thela*, which was curtained from all sides and pulled by one man in the front and pushed by two men from the back. There were wooden seats inside. The older girls would wear burkas and the younger ones would not. One of the cart-pullers used to go from house to house collecting the girls. The older girls were brought in *dolis*. The *dolis* were raised to the *thela* and the girls would jump inside. I was later forced to wear a burka and hated it. Yet at that time, I yearned to go in the *doli*, like the other grown-up girls. I once told the cart-puller to bring the *doli* for me because I had started purdah. This was a lie as I was too young to have been put in purdah. For a few days, I felt great going in the *doli* instead of walking to the *thela*. But my happiness was short-lived. One day, the cart-puller saw me in the market walking without a burka and that ended the luxury. It is amazing how strongly children wish to be treated as grown-ups!

Our Shift to Lucknow

When *abbujaan's* legal practice did not yield sufficient income, he decided to take up a salaried job in Lucknow. It proved beneficial to us girls as our parents decided to send us to a well-known Muslim girls' school–the Karamat Husain Muslim Girls' School. It was within walking distance from our house and my sister and I used to go escorted, either by my father's trusted peon or by our old *bua* (maid).

I was nine years old when we moved to Lucknow. About that time, our grand uncle and *abbujaan's* guardian—Siraj—had retired and decided to settle in Lucknow. He bought a bungalow close to our house named Dar-us-Siraj and it was also within walking distance from our house, so I was able to frequently interact with my educated aunts, Safia and Hameeda, which I greatly enjoyed. I owe a great deal to them for encouraging me to do as I wanted to. They would even coach me during the long holidays.

Karamat Husain Muslim Girls' School

My father accompanied me to the school for admission. Fortunately, in those days, there were no waiting lists for admission. I went properly dressed in a gharara and dupatta and was instructed to keep my head covered while at school, as my dupatta was somehow in the habit of slipping from my head. My father wrote my real age on the admission form but the admission officer advised my father to reduce it at least by a couple of years, as was customary in those days, because almost all parents aspired for their children to join the government services which had an age limit. My father objected to this suggestion and rather said angrily, "My daughter is not going to work for a living!" Little did he know at that time that his daughter would end up being a highly qualified professional woman. My father also wanted my name to be registered as Zarina Khatoon. Surnames were not commonly used in those days for Muslim girls and suffixes like Khatoon, Bano or Nisan were used after the first names. But the admission officer insisted that my name should be registered with my surname as Zarina Farid. After some hesitation, my father accepted his suggestion.

Karamat Husain Muslim Girls' School was essentially a boarding school, established for the daughters of the *talukdars* of the region by an enlightened lawyer named Justice Karamat Hussain. The nineteenth century was a time when general awakening for modern education took place in the Indian Muslim community. Indian Muslims felt threatened about losing their identity in the wake of the English ascendancy. A few enlightened Muslims identified their educational and economic backwardness as a cause for that situation. Sir Syed Ahmad Khan—a great advocate for modernizing the Muslim community—established the Mohammedan Anglo-Oriental

College for Muslim boys in Aligarh, UP, on May 24, 1875. But even a reformer like him gave no importance to women's education. In fact, he considered it inadvisable in the prevailing social environment of the times to educate Muslim women; he felt that education may amount to cruelty and push them into a life of suffering and unhappiness as they would become misfits in society. Sir Syed's negative attitude toward Muslim women's education was attributed by his admirers to Sir's dependence on the financial and moral support from the Muslim gentry of the time, which was conservative. It seems he did not want to antagonize them.

However, modest beginnings toward women's education were being made, particularly under missionary influence. Awareness was also brought about by a few Muslim individuals who had studied in British universities and were influenced by Western liberal ideas. Among them was Karamat Hussain, who had gone to England for legal education. During his stay in England, Hussain was exposed to liberal ideas and realized how backward the Indian Muslim community in India was. Karamat Hussain identified the lack of education among Muslim women as one of the reasons for the community's backwardness. He believed that ignorant, uneducated mothers could not bring up enlightened children. Therefore, it was important to educate women and expose them to modern ideas. He decided to promote education among Muslim women and was able to win a few supporters too. He persuaded a prominent social reformer, Mr Ghulam-us-Saqlain, who had built a good reputation in the Muslim community, and urged him to introduce his ideas to the broader Muslim community. They soon found an occasion in 1891 when a Muslim Educational Conference was held in Aligarh. Ghulam-us-Saqlain took advantage of the occasion and presented a scheme at the conference for Muslim women's education. Despite considerable opposition, he managed to get an approval. Luckily, they also found a supporter for their scheme in the then Governor of UP, Charles Crosthwaite. With his support, a girls' school was started in Allahabad in the year 1833. The school was named after Crosthwaite. Karamat Hussain was appointed secretary of the school's governing body. Thus, a concrete beginning toward women's education was made in as early as 1883.

In 1911, Sir Raja Mohammad Ali Khan, the Raja of Mahmoodabad and another enlightened Muslim, visited the girls' school in Allahabad. The Raja was so impressed with the school that he suggested that Karamat Hussain start a similar school in Lucknow too.

Thus, on November 21, 1921 a Muslim girls' school was started in Lucknow, later christened Karamat Husain Muslim Girls' School. It has now grown into a flourishing degree college and is affiliated to the University of Lucknow. It was initially situated in the house of Choudhary Nusrat Ali, another liberal *talukdar* of Oudh who was also the secretary of "Anjuman-e-Talukdarane Oudh" (the Association of the Talukdars of Oudh). Miss Amina Pope, a Christian convert to Islam and an ardent supporter of women's education, was appointed the headmistress of the school. The school had started with only eight students, all daughters of the neighboring *talukdars*. The first few headmistresses of the school were either British or Anglo Indians. The medium of education was Urdu but English was taught as a subject and some rudimentary education of Islam was also on the curriculum. When I joined the school in 1944, an Anglo Indian, Miss Myles, was the headmistress. After India's independence in 1947, Muslim women were appointed as headmistresses and Hindi was made as a compulsory subject. I studied up to intermediate as did all my other sisters. In those days after 10 years' schooling, a High School Certificate examination was conducted. After that, there would be two years' intermediate, followed by two years of BA which was known as graduation.

I started wearing the burka when I was 13 years old, which was late for a girl. But my resistance could not last longer. I disliked going to school in a burka and considered it old-fashioned. I also felt oppressed and hot. In school, I was in the company of upper-class girls, many of whom had studied in convent schools, spoke English fluently and did not wear a burka. The Lucknow burka—which women in the gentry wore—came in two pieces, one was the flared garment worn from the shoulders, covering the body until the feet and the other consisted of a long skirt and a separate top which covered only the head and shoulders. A netted veil at the top covered the eyes and functioned as an opening for visibility. This restricted the vision, as one could only see straight in the front. To view one's right or left, one had to keep turning her head from side to side. I always found this most awkward and idiotic. Once I got off the *thela* at some distance from my home, I would uncover my face. I wonder who invented this peculiar design of Indian burka used in the subcontinent as in other Islamic countries, this kind of burka is not used. He must have been a male chauvinist of the highest order. It is not mentioned in the Koran or Hadith[1].

[1] Collection of reports claiming to quote what Prophet Muhammad said verbatim on any matter.

Wearing a burka could be an advantage too. For example, my sister Soofya often wanted to borrow my clothes to wear at school and I would refuse absolutely. So she found a solution–she would quietly put on my clothes, cover them with her burka and go to school. Once there, she would remove the burka and I would discover that she was wearing my clothes. I would get infuriated and utterly frustrated. But there was nothing I could do at that stage.

At the school, we were taught in Urdu. The teaching methodology was very conventional. Most teachers belonged to middle-class Muslim families who themselves observed purdah, including my aunt Hameeda, who had studied in IT College and later the AMU. In both those places, she wore a burka. She kept a strict eye on my behavior in school, which often irritated me. But I accepted it because she helped me in my homework and encouraged me to do well in studies.

Mrs Usuf Zai—my Maths teacher—stands out in my memory as the best teacher I had in school. I always looked forward to Maths classes. It must have been her way of teaching and my admiration for her that I did very well in Maths, even securing a distinction in Maths in my High School Certificate examination. Mrs Usuf Zai was a Christian married to a Muslim, unusual in those days. That added to my respect for her, as from an early age I had secular leanings. Other teachers that I remember fondly include our Urdu teacher whom we called *Ustaniji*.[2] She was an elderly lady, short and stout, chewing paan all the time; in fact, she carried a *paandaan* to school. She would wear old-fashioned ghararas and brightly colored *leheriya* dupattas as well as some jewelry too. Her method of teaching was almost archaic. She would make students stand up and read a paragraph from the textbook, one by one, while she dozed off under the influence of tobacco in her *paan*. We would often skip lines while reading and shout, "Ustaniji, I have finished reading," then the next girl was made to stand up and read. The following day, she would give a dictation on that text and dictate what she considered to be the most difficult words, to judge our spelling skills. Her favorite word was *Kustuntuniya*—the Urdu word for Constantinople—the earlier name for Istanbul. This word and the way she used to dictate it, buzzes in my ears till today. It created in me a fascination for and desire to visit the town of *Kustuntuniya*. Finally, I had the good fortune to satisfy this curiosity in 2007, when I visited Turkey at my daughter Huma's invitation, a visit I enjoyed enormously.

[2] Teacher ma'am.

As our school was essentially a boarding school, all extra-curricular activities took place after school, so we day scholars could not participate in them. Since I lived within walking distance, I often persuaded my parents to allow me to go to school in the evenings or to hang around in the after-school hours and participate in some of the extra-curricular activities. I was never good at sports but I had a great deal of exposure to Urdu poetry, nurtured by my uncle Majaz. I took the initiative of forming a literary society in our college and served as its secretary. Besides organizing a few lectures and discussions on literary topics, *baitbazi*[3] or *antakshri*[4] used to be its major activity. In *baitbazi* sessions, unlike *antakshri* these days, film songs were not allowed; we only recited verses from Urdu poetry. I had a good memory then and had memorized a lot of works by the most celebrated Urdu poets like Ghalib, Iqbal, and Faiz; not to speak of my uncle Majaz's poetry, which I would recite with great pride. I usually won those *baitbazi* competitions and my competitors would find me intimidating. I was also the teachers' favorite as I mostly topped the class in examinations because I was greatly motivated to do well for the fear of being taken out of school. Although I was very good at Urdu, my knowledge of English was elementary. I was very keen to learn to speak English. The English we were taught at school was not enough to enable us to converse in the language. We had a few girls from English-medium convent schools who could converse beautifully in English. I used to envy them and aspired to learn sufficient English to be able to talk like them.

Early Teens

Like other adolescent girls, I was totally ignorant about the physical changes that were taking place in me. Any mention of a woman's sexual self, or for that matter of a man's physical organs or their functions was taboo, both at home and in the school. General newspapers and magazines did not refer to sex as explicitly as they do now. I had no access whatsoever to anything related even to menstruation, let alone sex. As I was the oldest girl in my family and my mother had periods so sparingly and was so discreet about it, I did not know

[3] Verbal game and a genre of Urdu poetry played by composing verses of Urdu poems.

[4] A spoken game in which each contestant sings the first verse of the movie song that begins with the Hindustani consonant on which the previous contestant's song ended.

about how and when menstruation took place. I neither knew how one got pregnant nor how a woman knew that she had conceived. Hundreds of questions would rise in my mind but there was no one to answer them. Once in a while I tried to ask the older girls in my class. Some girls had started school late, so I had classmates older than me. Instead of answering my questions, they would feel shy and tell me to shut up, saying that I had a "dirty" mind. I think they themselves probably didn't know the answers to my questions.

In school, twice a week, Koran reading class was taken. I noticed that sometimes, the older girls would shyly tell the Koran teacher that they would not read the Koran on that day. The teacher would not insist that they do. During menstruation, women are regarded as "impure" so they should not even touch the holy book. I suppose, those girls looked grown up enough to have periods, so the teacher understood their reason for not reading Koran on certain days. I was unaware of this and did not enjoy reading the Koran because it was in Arabic, a language I did not know. So one day, I also told the teacher that I did not want to read the Koran. However, she scolded me and sternly ordered me to get the Koran and read it. For some time, I did not understand this discrimination.

Fortunately, as my curiosity about sex and sexuality was growing, my cousin got married to a girl a little older than me. Apparently, she too was ignorant about the physical relationship between men and women and resisted her husband's sexual demands. So my cousin bought two manuals written in Urdu titled *Hidayat Namah Khawind* (Instructions for the Husband) and *Hidayat Nama Zauja* (Instructions for the Wife) for his wife to read and understand his desires. Curiously enough, even the book meant to inform the wife about gender-related duties only such as dressing up pleasingly, putting on ittar to attract the husband, and serving the in-laws etc. It concentrated on how she should be obedient to the husband and in-laws and dress up nicely, apply *ittar,* and decorate herself with flowers to make herself alluring to the husband. But the book meant for the husband had all the information about sex, describing male and female physiology, and how to draw the most pleasure from sex. I naturally got hold of the men's manual and read it, although secretly.

As a middle-class Muslim girl, I was considered to be overambitious and almost a lunatic to have such high aspirations like studying abroad; I had a special fascination for teachers who also wrote books because none of my teachers in India had written books. I had such dreams at a time when, at the end of every academic year, my return to school was questionable. For me, writing books was the ultimate academic achievement. My ambitions did not stop there; I wanted to learn to drive. This was considered to be absolutely crazy too, as none of my relatives owned a car. I also wanted to swim. While I did not know any woman who knew swimming, I had heard that the IT College in Lucknow had a swimming pool. For this reason, I applied for admission there after passing high school but I was not allowed to study there. It was considered to be too modern and Westernized for girls from "respectable" families like ours. My younger sisters were lucky enough to have studied at IT College as after I shed the burka, my sisters did not have that encumbrance.

Many years later, it so happened that my parents visited Canada and stayed with my sister Sehba. Her house in Ottawa had a swimming pool and Sehba had learnt swimming in IT College. I also visited Sehba while my parents were there. One day, *abbujaan* and I were sitting by the poolside watching Sehba swim. *Abbujaan* asked me why I also didn't swim. I reminded him that I could not swim as he had not allowed me to join the IT College where Sehba had learnt swimming. I could see that he felt bad about denying those opportunities which he later provided to my younger sisters. He asked Sehba to get me a swimming suit and teach me how to swim. Since my stay in Ottawa was very short, I did not learn swimming from Sehba there.

Although my high aspirations were laughed at, I did finally achieve most of them, including the ability to swim, though rather late in life. I learnt to speak English in my late teens when I went to England with my first husband (I was a teenage bride). I also wanted to drive and swim which were almost unachievable desires, considering my class and circumstances. I learned to drive when I was 42 years old and to swim when I was 51 years old. My second husband, Idrak, and I had moved into our flat in Delhi, opposite a five star hotel which had a swimming pool. I could see the pool from my bedroom window and this heightened my desire to swim. Idrak had been a champion swimmer; he had won a number of swimming championships at home and abroad. I requested him to teach me swimming and also to our teenage daughters, Kiran and Nikhat. After some initial resistance, Idrak agreed to teach all three of us to swim. The pool manager was very amused to watch a woman in her 50s learning to swim, as were the other young swimmers. If sometimes Idrak could not accompany me to the pool, then one of the young swimmers would offer "Auntie" his or her help. My swimming was regarded as very "daring" in Zakir Bagh which was predominantly a middle-class Muslim locality and where no woman swam, and that too in a regular swimming costume, like I did.

My ambition to drive was fulfilled when Idrak and I bought our first car. I requested him to teach me how to drive. Very few women drove in those days. He resisted, saying that driving requires good reflexes and I was too old to learn because with age, reflexes become slow. And also the usual refrain, "I do not want to lose my car and wife at the same time." I knew it was only an excuse for his chauvinism. However, when my eldest daughter Huma turned 18, she asked Idrak to teach her to drive and used his argument about good reflexes in her favor. Willy-nilly, he arranged for his office driver to teach her. A young girl could not be left alone with a driver, so I used to sit with her and thus learnt to drive along with her, without my husband's knowledge. One day, the driver said to me, "Madam, today you drive Saheb to office" and asked me to sit behind the wheel. When Idrak got into the car and saw me sitting there, he was very surprised. The driver told him, "Sahib, Memsahib drives very well now because without your permission, I taught her to drive too along with Huma baby. Saheb, you must forgive me for that. I shall sit with her in the front; you may sit at the back. Then you will know how well she drives and that she is ready for the driving test."

Idrak was put in a tight spot since he could not argue against his wife's abilities with his driver. When he saw me drive quite well even during the rush hour and take him and the car safely to his office, he had the graciousness to allow me to go for a driving test. Later, it was I who taught my other daughters how to drive.

I achieved my ambition to publish my writings at the age of 27 when my first publication, an article, "Caste System Among Indian Muslims," was published in 1962 in the *Economic and Political Weekly*. But I had to wait for another 18 years before my book, *Women's Contribution to Household Budget: A Case Study of Women in Beedi Industry,* was published by the International Labour Organization (ILO), Geneva, in 1980.

5

Exposure to the Freedom Movement

Dar-us-Siraj

Dar-us-Siraj—my granduncle Siraj's home in Lucknow—used to be the hub of political and literary activities as my uncle, Ansar Harvani, was fully involved in the freedom movement and my uncle Majaz was part of the Progressive Writers' Movement. In the late 1930s and early 1940s, the political activity in India was at its zenith. Political leaders were always coming and going and I would, from behind the bamboo curtain inside the house, peep at them and listen to their conversations, though I did not fully understood the political reasons for that frenzy. All I knew was that it was about getting rid of the "*goras*"[1] and about freedom.

Political consciousness in my family, generated by Ansar Chacha's involvement in the freedom movement was such that even my *baji* and *dadi*, Ansar Chacha's mother, who were illiterate, were involved in the day-to-day political happenings. They were strongly opposed to the idea of a separate Muslim State and did not like Jinnah and his western style of life. I remember *baji* singing the lines related to the Khilafat movement: "*Boli amma Liaqat Ali ki, jaan beta Khilafat pe dena*" (Liaqat Ali's mother said to him, "My son, sacrifice your life for the Khilafat Movement"). These two old ladies admired Nehru and Gandhi and did not like Mohammad Ali Jinnah who wanted to divide their country. They were strongly opposed to the idea of a

[1] Whites, that is, the British.

separate Muslim state. I remember *dadi* often repeating an incident which she had probably heard about from someone else that once a reporter went to interview Gandhi and Jinnah. When he met Jinnah, the latter was enjoying his evening whisky. When the reporter went to Gandhi, Gandhi was spinning on his charkha. "See!" she would say, "The Muslim leader was a *sharabi*[2] and the Hindu leader a devout teetotaler and khadi wallah." An uneducated aunt of mine, Khadeeja *Phuphi* and her family, wore only homespun khadi. When her only son got married, she spun khadi for her daughter-in-law's wedding dress. Such was the political involvement of even the uneducated and the illiterate Muslim women of Rudauli and the region. It was an irony of fate that Khadeeja *Phuphi* had to migrate to Pakistan after Independence, as her only son decided to migrate. We were told that she was very unhappy in Pakistan and passed away after only a few years of a miserable life there.

Besides being exposed to political activities just prior to Independence, I was also exposed to the literary movement in support of the freedom movement. The Progressive Writer's Association comprised well-known poets and writers like Sajjad Zaheer, Ali Sardar Jaffery, Krishan Chander, my uncle Majaz, and many others. I was, however, too young to be allowed to interact with them. The Association brought out a journal, *Naya Adab*.[3] Majaz Chacha was on its editorial board and copies of *Naya Adab* used to be sent to Dar-us-Siraj. I would be glued to them and enjoyed reading the articles and poems printed in them. I was only 10 or 11 years old at that time and there was a lot which I did not understand like the meanings of words and even ideas, but I would still read and then ask my aunts to explain. The politically and educationally rich atmosphere at Dar-us-Siraj attracted me so much that soon after coming back from school, I would go there. My mother used to get angry with me as instead of staying at home and helping her with the household chores, I would run away to Dar-us-Siraj. Since I was the youngest in Dar-us-Siraj and very curious to learn, my uncles and aunts would take a great deal of interest in me and encourage my curiosity. My parents though always felt that I was aspiring too high. They also feared that I might not accept their choice of spouse and bring disgrace to the family like my aunt Wakeelan. However, it was decided that I would be allowed

---

[2] A man who takes too much alcoholic drinks.

[3] New Literature.

to study up to high school which was regarded as a decent level of education for a girl. With good looks and a high school degree, a decent educated young man could be found for me. My aunts, Safia and Hameeda, were however, able to convince my father that I should be allowed to continue my education.

We had no electricity at home in those days, which was not uncommon, and I used to study under a kerosene lamp. So, my aunt Hameeda would invite me and even give me her room to study in at night under the electric light as they had an electricity connection. I owe a great deal to my two aunts for my intellectual growth. During the long summer holidays, I would move to Dar-us-Siraj. Aunt Safia, who would come home to Lucknow from Aligarh during the summer holidays, would tutor me in English and Aunt Hameeda would tutor me in Mathematics. I was given English lessons in the morning after breakfast and Mathematics lessons in the afternoon after the midday siesta. I loved doing Maths and could not sleep during the siesta, waiting for everyone to get up so I could get on with my lessons. On one such day, I could not wait any longer and decided to play a prank. I advanced all the clocks and watches and woke up everybody. They were surprised that they had overslept and were still sleepy. They also noticed that the sun was still very high but I assured them that it was half-past four, the usual time to be up and have sherbet. In summer, instead of tea, we had cold drinks. I even had the audacity to tell them to check the time. Sure enough, every watch indicated the same time. So everyone got up and the servant too was scolded for sleeping late and ordered to serve the drinks, while I got ready for my Maths lesson. Just then my aunt noticed a stool near the mantelpiece in the drawing room and wondered what it was doing there. My cousin, Abbu bhai, remembered that he had seen me climbing on it and doing something on the mantelpiece. I was, in fact, advancing the hands on the clock since I was too short to reach it. Thus, my mischief was discovered and I was given a good scolding.

The result of extra coaching by my aunts was that I passed high school examination with flying colors. I secured first division with distinction in three subjects. The marking system in those days was very different. 60 percent meant first division and 70 percent was regarded as so high that a distinction was awarded. I am amazed how these days 98 percent and 99 percent marks are awarded even in Social Sciences.

My aspirations rose and I quietly applied to the IT College for admission in the Intermediate. IT College was situated at the same walking distance from my home as was the Karamat Husain Muslim Girls College. It was regarded as the best women's college in Asia in those days and students came to study not only from all over India but also from neighboring countries like Afghanistan and Nepal. But IT College did not have high walls like the Karamat Husain College and the girls there did not observe purdah. So, my father did not find it suitable for girls from "respectable" families like ours. Although my aunt Hameeda had earlier studied there, she used to go in burka which I refused to wear. Besides, my parents feared that if I went to IT College and interacted with girls who did not observe purdah and was taught by Christian teachers, I might become more "modern." So finally, to my utter disappointment, I was sent back to the Karamat Husain College for Intermediate.

Independence Day

I consider myself fortunate to have been old enough to understand the significance of political freedom and to participate in the rejoicings on August 15, 1947, the day of India's independence. Sweets were distributed in schools and tricolor flags were hoisted all over the city. Lucknow was abuzz with patriotic songs, including "Vande Mataram," without any negative feelings from Muslims toward the song, though much is made about it by fundamentalist Muslims these days. The entire city was lit up and we all went out to see the lights, except aapa who was pregnant. But alas, the rejoicings were short-lived. The very next day, we were summoned back from school earlier than usual because the news of communal riots in Punjab and its spread into Western UP had filtered into Lucknow. However, we were lucky as riots did not occur in Lucknow. The ages-old Hindu–Muslim unity and mutual trust sustained the peace in the city.

Impact of Partition on Rudauli's Muslims

Rudauli's gentry was very secular and most zamindars and *talukdars* had opposed the Partition. My father too was against it, as was my maternal granduncle, Latif Nana, who was actively involved in the freedom movement. Those secular Muslims who called themselves "Nationalist Muslims" found no contradiction in being Muslims and

Indians. But as the news of the massacre and brutal atrocities spread, joy was turned into gloom and a deep sense of insecurity gripped the Muslims who had decided to stay behind in India, the country of their birth. As a result of these brutal killings, even die-hard nationalist Muslims started having fears about their safety and planned to migrate to Pakistan. It was a time of much political uncertainty for Indian Muslims who suddenly felt that their loyalty was being suspected despite their full participation in India's freedom movement. Our expectations of a free and secular, prosperous India, were busted like a balloon. Our relatives and Muslim friends started leaving for Karachi or Dhaka. Every day, we would hear that some uncle or cousin of ours had left, leaving behind old parents and women to be invited later to Pakistan, once they secured jobs there. Muslim youth felt insecure in India, fearing discrimination in jobs and began seeing Pakistan as a "land of opportunity." But soon after arriving there, they realized that it was not so. They were not welcomed and even faced hostilities from Punjabis and Sindhis who viewed them as "outsiders." These immigrant Muslims had become a minority in their country of origin; now they were *muhajhirs*[4] in their country of adoption. Religion—the basis for truncating India—did not play an integrating force in Pakistan as was expected; language and culture proved much stronger binding forces than religion.

Older persons left India with heavy hearts under the pressure of their children. Many missed the Indian varieties of paan and found the mispronunciation of Urdu words by Punjabis and Sindhis jarring to their ears. The UP gentry found the loud, exuberant Punjabi culture "vulgar" compared to the sophistication and subtleties of the Oudh culture. In the second round of migration, after hearing of the plight of their relatives who had migrated earlier, many Indian Muslims decided to stay in India, fearing they would be cultural misfits in Pakistan. It was not easy for Muslims who were born and brought up in undivided India to change their loyalty overnight and forget the symbols of their pride such as, Muslim architecture, the Taj Mahal, the Qutub Minar, the Red Fort, and all the shrines of their revered saints. They missed the mushaira[5] sessions and the classical music of Ustad Allauddin Khan, Pandit Ravi Shankar, and Vilayat Khan, among many other renowned musicians in India. They

[4] Outsiders.

[5] Recital of Urdu poetry in front of an audience.

missed the typical North Indian Mughlai cuisine like the *nihari*[6] of Jama Masjid in Delhi, *seekh kebabs*[7] from Tunda of Lucknow, the Hyderabadi biryani and so on. They missed revering the graves of their ancestors and the hundreds of years' old havelis depicting the Muslim presence in India. They also missed the wide varieties of mangoes like the Langda of Banaras, Dussehri and Samar Bahisht of Lucknow, Safaida of Malihabad. Punjabis and Sindhis were as unfamiliar with the subtle nuances of UP culture as were the UP Muslims with their culture. Therefore, many Indian Muslims decided to stay back despite the hardships caused not only by being separated from their dear ones who had migrated earlier to Pakistan but also by financial hardships as the property and other immoveable effects of those who migrated to Pakistan were taken away by the government or given to the immigrants from Pakistan.

This unfortunate situation had some unexpected consequences for young women and girls. The young men migrated to Pakistan for better career prospects while girls stayed behind with their parents, holding on to their ancestral property. It created a shortage of marriageable young men for Muslim girls in India. For some time, boys of Indian origin in Pakistan took brides from India but as the political tensions between the two countries grew and visa restrictions became more stringent, flow of boys coming to India seeking brides slowed down. As a result, many Muslim girls remained unmarried. Spinsterhood among Indian Muslims was almost unknown; the custom of marrying one's cousin would absorb girls within the family. Several girls of my age, among my relatives too, remained unmarried as the standards of suitability did not change overnight with Partition. Caste and class considerations continued to be important. It was considered preferable for a girl to remain unmarried than to be married below her caste and class. Forced by circumstances, some unmarried girls passed High School privately and took up teaching jobs in Rudauli itself or in the adjoining villages. This was a revolutionary change for them. Young girls who were not allowed to step out of their homes except in *dolis*, were walking—albeit in burkas—to nearby villages to earn a living. With growing communalism in India, further "liberating" changes took place and some

---

[6] South Asian curry consisting of slow-cooked beef or lamb along with bone marrow.

[7] Indian cuisine consisting of a mixture of minced meat and spices, wrapped around a skewer and grilled in tandoor.

parents even allowed their daughters to discard the burka for the fear of being recognized as a Muslim.

Land Reforms

The Zamindari Abolition Act was passed in 1951 which struck a further blow to the landholding class and to those who subsisted only on the income from their land. Being absentee landlords, they lost their land under the land reforms legislation that gave land entitlement to the tiller. My father was one such absentee landlord. Our family resources were depleted not only because the *malguzari* he used to receive from the cultivators stopped but he also lost a share in the produce. I remember how we used to get pure ghee, jaggery, and mangoes etc., from his village; all that stopped too. *Abbujaan* did receive some monetary compensation from the government like the other zamindars and *talukdars* but not a large amount. Even that was paid in installments which did not help much. Fortunately, my father also had his legal practice, so we managed to survive. The Act adversely affected a majority of *talukdars* and zamindars in Rudauli who did not have a secondary source of income. Some of them were too old to take up employment. Even the younger ones were used to a leisurely life and were not educationally qualified to take up salaried jobs. My *mamu* was one such person. He had never worked and had led a fairly luxurious life. Being the only son, he had inherited all of my *nana*'s land. *Mamu* led a miserable life after the land reforms. After *nana*'s death, our cherished visits to Rudauli became more and more infrequent and finally stopped.

6

India to England

When my parents' anxiety was growing to get a husband for me, an interesting thing happened which almost changed the course of my life. Just after my High School results were out, one afternoon, I happened to walk into the *mardana* where an unopened envelope addressed to *abbujaan* was lying on the floor. The postman had probably dropped it into the room. I had a strange curiosity to open it. I did precisely that. It was a proposal for my marriage from a *talukdar* family whose son had graduated and taken up a government job which was considered very prestigious in those days. I still remember this sentence, "We hear that your daughter Zarina is beautiful, good-natured, highly domesticated, and *Mashallah*[1] has just passed her high school. My son, who himself is a graduate, wishes to have an educated wife. I therefore, ask for your daughter's hand for my son." I walked straight into the kitchen and threw the letter and the envelope in fire. I still do not understand what had come over me. My parents never knew about this until I told them after many years. I knew then, that if my parents even had an air of this proposal, they would have jumped at it and I would have been married straightaway. My life would have taken a totally different course.

Just as I turned 18 and entered the final year of Intermediate, the anxiety of finding a suitable match for me gripped my parents. I knew that my parents' standards of suitability would not match mine. To begin with, I had ambitions to study further and was not prepared to be married and lost into domesticity forever. But what choice did I have? Even my educated, economically independent aunts were reluctant to

---

[1] Arabic phrase to show appreciation, joy, praise, thankfulness for an event/person.

oppose my parents at that point. Around the time when discussions about my marriage were getting more heated, Hayat—a much younger cousin of my father who was already married—took fancy to me. He was unhappy in his marriage that was purely out of convenience. He had graduated from AMU, then moved to the University of Calcutta for a Master's in Psychology. There, he stayed with a devotee to his ancestral shrine who strangely enough belonged to the very famous and highly educated Suhrawardy Family of Calcutta. Hayat was very keen to go to England for further studies but had no financial means to fulfill his desire. His host in Calcutta, appreciating his keenness to study further, encouraged him by giving him an ancient manuscript which he could sell for enough money to last him for the initial few months in London. A friend of Hayat from Lucknow, Anwar Ansari and his wife Ghazala, had already gone to London and were earning their living by broadcasting in the newly established Urdu and Hindi services of the BBC. There were very few Indians in London in the early 1950s and even fewer knew both Hindi and Urdu. The Ansaris were earning a decent living from broadcasting alongside their studies. They encouraged Hayat to do the same. Hayat decided to do so, not realizing that his very feudal, lazy habits, would not meet the requirements of the hard life of a working student in London. He managed to gain admission for PhD in the University College of London.

Hayat Enters My Life

Hayat did face one problem. He fancied himself to be in love with me and could not go far away from me. He feared that I may be married off in his absence and knew that he could not approach my parents for my hand as he was already married. He was also 12 years older than me. So he tried to win my favor. During his holidays, he would be in our house. Since he was closely related, I did not observe *purdah* from him. He would take me out along with my younger sisters to coffee house and even to see a movie; entertainments that we were normally not allowed. Since Hayat was much older and married, my parents did not suspect his intentions. My sisters and I too enjoyed going out. When he returned to Calcutta after the holidays, he started writing love letters to me. After a few letters that I did not reply to, he sent me a passionate one, proposing to marry me. Then I got really frightened and wrote back, telling him that he must not write to me and that

I did not love him and had no intentions of marrying him as he was already married. Moreover, I wanted to study further. Apparently, the moment he received my refusal, he started for Lucknow and arrived at our place unannounced, looking totally famished and almost half dead as he had not eaten for two days. He threatened to starve himself to death if I did not agree to marry him. He convinced me that I was no more a virgin (my ignorance was such about matters of sex that I did not know what virginity exactly meant). He even tried to physically molest me and threatened to tell everyone that I used to meet him secretly. Then no one would want to marry me. I believed Hayat and thought that I was not fit to be married to anyone else. Thus, he coerced me into marrying him. I went through an extremely traumatic time and even had a nervous breakdown.

Hayat went to his village the next day and his parents sent a marriage proposal. I was devastated, frightened to death. For several days, I could not eat or sleep and kept crying. My parents could not understand what had happened to me. I could not tell anyone about my plight and suffered alone. When the marriage proposal came, my parents were furious. They did not approve of Hayat as he was already married. At my parents' refusal to the marriage proposal, his parents replied that my parents did not know that their daughter was an "immoral" girl and had been having an affair with their son. Under the spell of their daughter, he had already divorced his wife. My parents did ask me if it was true that I wanted to marry him. They were devastated when I said I did. They then had no choice but to marry me off as quickly as possible to save the family from further disgrace. I was totally isolated in my family and had to live under the disapproving, almost hateful gaze of my parents and grandmother. I spent days as an outcast in my own home. It was heartbreaking to see my parents and grandmother so distraught as they could not understand why I was insisting on marrying Hayat. But I had to marry him for the fear of being socially disgraced, although I did not love him. The only silver lining in this unfortunate situation was that he decided to go to England for further studies and promised to take me along.

Wedding

At the age of 18, I was reluctantly married off to Hayat on November 25, 1951. No one could have imagined what that fateful day had in store for me. But it certainly changed the entire course of my life, beyond my wildest dreams and expectations. My parents met their obligations and provided a modest dowry consisting of a few sets of clothes, mostly ghararas and some jewelry. Hayat sold the jewelry a day after our wedding to collect the fare for our journey to England. At that time, I found it heartbreaking to part with the jewelry as according to my upbringing, it was a young married woman's prerogative to deck herself in fancy clothes and jewelry. It was worse because in my region, unmarried girls were not allowed to wear fancy, heavy silk dresses and heavy jewelry. I felt a sense of deprivation but it was compensated for by the prospect of going to England and being taught by those who "wrote books." I was the first woman from my village and my family to go abroad, and finally, even for my parents, this provided some compensation for the "dishonorable" behavior of their firstborn. My parents were particularly worried about my limited, if any, domestic skills and I was hurriedly given a course in cooking before my marriage.

Exactly a month after getting married, Hayat and I travelled by train from Lucknow to Bombay to catch a boat named Batory, a Polish luxury liner which used to run between Bombay and London during the off-season. My uncle, Majaz, had a good friend in the passport department who helped us get passports within a very short time as well as some small amount of foreign exchange. I was totally ignorant about what it meant to go abroad. Neither had I ever seen a passport nor heard of foreign exchange as no one had ever gone abroad among my relatives or friends. My entire family—except *baji* who could not bear to see me leaving—came to the station to see me off. As the train whistled and started and I looked out of the window, I noticed that *abbujaan* had tears in his eyes. For the first time, I felt that he really loved me. He had always kept away from us daughters and in the months prior to my wedding, he had been very angry and had hardly communicated with me. But seeing the tears in his eyes assured me that he had forgiven me and he did love me, an assurance that helped me emotionally and reduced my sense of guilt. I had very mixed feelings on leaving home; this was going to be the first time ever that I was going to live away from my family. Leaving *baji* was particularly heartbreaking for me as I felt that I may never see her again. She did die while I was away in London. I was moving into a very uncertain future and that too with a man with whom I had no emotional attachment. If anything, I resented him for tricking me into marriage. However, I had accepted my fate with the silver lining of going to the land of prosperity, modernity, and scholarship. Such was my perception of England in those days!

Bombay to me was like a foreign country as I had not travelled much. In fact, besides Rudauli and Amethi, the only other place I had travelled to was Allahabad where I was sent after a lot of crying and begging to attend my best friend's wedding. I found myself walking on Bombay's streets with my eyes wide open. I had neither seen so many cars nor such wide streets. Even the traffic lights were such a novelty. We had no money to stay in a hotel, so for three days, we stayed in a furniture godown owned by a friend's uncle who was kind enough to let us lodge there free of cost.

Leaving for England

Finally, on 25 December 1951, the Christmas Day, the Batory left the shores of Bombay for Manchester, England. Thus, the first phase of my life ended. How strange has been my life that there was a time when I did not even know that 25 December was celebrated as Christ's birthday, and now, having been married to a Christian, I have been celebrating Christmas for over 50 years. Since we had bought the cheapest ticket, we were in the lowest deck, but we did have a two-berth cabin. Was it a deliberate decision on the part of the ship's management to ensure privacy for a newly married couple, or just luck? However, we spent most of our time on the upper deck and were served the same food and enjoyed all other facilities, irrespective of the cost of the ticket. For me, everything was new: the ocean, the ship, people traveling with us, the food, the use of cutlery, and above all, the alcoholic drinks, served openly. To prove his "masculinity," my husband also had a drink one day. Not only did I strongly disapprove, but also felt scared of going into the cabin with him. I thought he might beat me up or do something totally wild. Having grown up in a Muslim family, I considered drinking alcohol immoral and a sinful habit. We believed that even a drop of "*sharab*" could make a person a drunkard. To see my own husband drinking alcohol was a shocking experience. My uncle Ansar, who was a political worker, had invited a number of Hindu and Christian friends to his wedding, and possibly he served *sharab* to them. One day I was going through the bookshelf and found a bottle with yellowish liquid in it, hidden between the books. I wondered what it was and called my older cousin Abbu Bhai and showed it to him. He looked at it and in a superior knowledgeable manner, said, "You silly girl!

You do not know what it is! It is *sharab*!" It was a half-empty bottle of Black & White whisky. I had never seen any *sharab* so how would I have known what it was? My cousin challenged me to taste it. I refused to taste it and told him that neither should he. Just to show off, he brought the bottle to his lips. Just then my aunt called us and we rushed to the bathroom and with trembling hands poured *sharab* in the toilet and emptied the bottle. Learning that Ansar uncle was a "drunkard" lowered my esteem for him quite a bit. Such was my ignorance and attitude toward as common a thing as alcohol. It took me quite some time to accept having alcohol as a normal practice and later I even ventured to take a drink or two in parties where everyone would be drinking.

It was a 17-day journey from Bombay to Manchester. I had severe seasickness, especially when the ship entered the notorious Bay of Biscay. Our tables and chairs were screwed to the floor. The sea was so turbulent that at times it felt as if the sky was under our feet and we were floating up above. Half the occupants were sick. Hayat was the lucky one who did not suffer any seasickness, but I could not keep any food or liquid inside and kept vomiting. My condition was absolutely miserable. I was advised to drink some brandy, neat. But how could I? I considered myself a God-fearing Muslim girl. Then how could I stoop so low as to drink *sharab*? My health condition went from bad to worse. Everyone on the boat scolded me for being so stubborn and old-fashioned. Finally, I was persuaded to take a few sips and I reluctantly took, but instantly vomited it out. My mental resistance was so intense that even my stomach could not accept it. However, I did survive the journey, but it was a horrendous experience and dampened my enthusiasm about going to England. Finally, the Batory docked at the Manchester Dockyard on 17 January 1952, and when we finally stepped out in the open, my agony ended. Among the other things we had carried was a "*lota*."[2] It used to be and continues to be a culturally distinguishing feature of Muslims. They use a *lota* for washing, while Hindus use a mug without a spout instead of toilet paper. For a Muslim, a *lota* was essential for existence. My parents advised us to take one with us as it was unlikely that English bathrooms would have the one. But it became an object of ridicule. When we arrived in Manchester, we were advised to get rid of it, which we did for fear of further ridicule.

---

[2] A small pitcher with a spout.

With a heavy heart, I threw it in the sea. It took us time to get used to toilet paper. Our Indian host in London understood our problem as he had gone through the same traumatic experience himself, so he advised us to dip a piece of toilet paper and wipe to give an illusion of having washed with water. We had a Muslim friend from Bangladesh who refused to use toilet paper. He often used to miss his morning lectures if he could not manage to "go" in the morning. He had managed to smuggle in a *lota*. Despite all the ridicules and jokes, we refused to part with it.

Culture Shocks

There was no end to the culture shocks that I underwent like other Indians who had come to England for the first time. Some couldn't survive and returned home. The tougher ones survived but all had to modify their perceptions about the "heaven" that England was going to be. Hayat and I were, to begin with, stupid enough to have arrived in London in the middle of the university term and on top of it during the coldest time of the year, without having any idea of what English weather would be like at that time. We also did not inform the Ansaris of our arrival date and time and landed up at their place all of a sudden. We somehow had to be accommodated in their one-bedroom apartment for the night. I received my first culture shock when it was announced that Hayat and I would have to sleep under one *razai*,[3] as there were not enough *razais* to give us one each. I thought it was most immodest of Anwar Mian to suggest that. How could I sleep with my husband under the same comforter in the presence of others? I was squirming with shyness and wondering how even Indians could lose all decorum and how was I going to live there, devoid of all modesty. However, the following morning, we were taken out to Oxford Street, the main shopping center, to purchase appropriate warm coats. I had carried two long coats, especially stitched for London, but those were not warm enough to protect me from the cold of the January month in London. The same was the case with Hayat's warm clothes. So we both bought thicker, warmer overcoats. Then we were taken to a place where advertisements were pasted on the shop windows for

[3] Quilt.

renting accommodation. My main concern was to find a bed-sitter that had two separate beds. We finally found one on the road next to where the Ansaris lived, with their brother Athar Mian, Anwar Ansari's younger brother, who lived with him. I was again surprised and unhappy to realize that we were going to live in just one room that had a cooking stove in one corner and a washbasin in the other. The third corner had a round table, to be used both as a writing and dining table, and to my relief, alongside the table was one single bed and the other bed was next to the bay window in the fourth corner. This was going to be our "home." I was told that most students lived like that, as a complete flat would be out of our budget. Mrs Ansari, I called her Ghazala Aapa, then took me to a huge store to buy the basic pots and pans and some groceries. I was impressed by the store that had everything one would need, from groceries to furniture and household items. At last, something looked more like the London of my expectations. At the same time, I was disappointed to learn that as a consequence of the World War II, even in 1952, food stuff was rationed. Each person was allowed only one egg a week—similarly, very small amounts of sugar, cooking oil, etc. English people mostly eat boiled food, but we Indians like to fry onions and need much more oil in our cooking. How was I going to manage; my cooking lessons at home had not prepared me for such austerity. It dawned on me then that life was going to be hard. On top of all that, we had meagre financial resources. We had arrived in London with only an ancient manuscript that was sold for 100 pounds, out of which 60 pounds had already been spent on buying essential articles and paying one week's advance rent. Now, we had to urgently look for some paid work.

The Ansaris again came to our rescue, and we were taken for an audition to the British Broadcasting Corporation (BBC). Hayat failed the audition and was disqualified, while I passed and started getting assignments immediately. Thus, I became the bread earner for the family from the start of our married life, a burden I bore for the remaining 12 years, a role that Hayat did not object to. V.K. Krishna Menon at that time was the Indian High Commissioner in London and he used to encourage Indian students to go there for higher studies while working alongside at the High Commission. After failing the audition at BBC, the only option open to Hayat was to apply for a job there. He did get a clerical job there. On the basis of his masters, Hayat had already secured admission in the PhD in

Psychology at the University College of London. But my high school and intermediate diplomas had no value in England. Therefore, I was required to pass the General Certificate in Education (GCE) from the University of London to qualify for admission in a BA (Hons.) course. For that I needed to pass in four subjects, including English. I hardly knew any English; I had to be proficient enough in the language before I could start preparing for the GCE. So I took admission in a tutorial college that used to teach English to foreigners. Luckily, my work at the BBC did not require long hours, but I still had to do all the housework, which I regarded as my duty as a wife, and Hayat was also demanding. He did not use to take English food and wanted a full Indian meal every day. After six months of learning English, I dared to take the GCE examination. Not surprisingly, I failed in English, which was a compulsory subject. During my time of stay in London, that is, in 1952, one had to pass four subjects at the advance level to gain entry into the university. It did not discourage me, though, and with gusto, I started preparing for the second attempt. Fortunately, the exam used to take place twice a year. Therefore, within the next six months, I appeared again and cleared it successfully, which enabled me to get admission in the London School of Economics (LSE), for a BA (Hons.) degree in anthropology. I had no idea which subject I should take; I had no one to advise me. But I was greatly fascinated by the idea of graduating from LSE. I was inclined toward history, which was also one of my subjects for the GCE. But LSE did not offer history; it only offered social sciences. Finally, after some discussion with the Ansaris, I settled on anthropology. Two considerations favored the choice. First, my interest in history led to an interest in studying societies, although tribal societies, which was part of anthropology. Second, it was an up-and-coming subject that would open up job possibilities for me. I took sociology as the subsidiary subject.

London School of Economics (LSE) 1953–1956

I joined LSE in October 1953. Thus, one of my ambitions, of being taught by teachers "who wrote books," was fulfilled. According to the system at LSE, each student was allotted a tutor, who took tutorial classes. Dr Maurice Freedman, a highly embittered emigrant Jew, was designated as my tutor. He had an aura of arrogant aloofness around him. I suppose that it was a kind of protective shield. However, I was very scared of him. At that stage, I could hardly speak proper English and avoided communicating with him as much as possible. I vividly remember the first tutorial we had with him, when he briefed us on what was expected of us as first-year students. He then gave us a topic to write an essay on and bring it for the next tutorial. We were 10 students in the class, and I was the only Indian. After we were dismissed, the boys were very angry with Dr Freedman's arrogance and blurted out, "The bastard, are we going to be stuck with him for next three years?" It was another culture shock for me. Having grown up with the sanctity of the *guru–shishya*[4] relationship in India, I had been taught that no matter how unpleasant your teacher might be, students must respect him or her.

During my time, the system at LSE was to have only one final exam consisting of 10 papers at the end of three years. Only the subsidiary subject had to be cleared at the end of the second year. The sociology lecturer, Dr McCrae, was a funny person. He had this bad habit of not facing the class but walking sideways on the lecturer's podium while lecturing. He also would, every few minutes, pour a little water from a glass pitcher that always used to be on the lecturer's table. His rather dramatic way of picking up the pitcher mid-lecture, pouring a little water in the glass, and then sipping it used to distract and annoy us. So, one day we conspired and collected some money, bought some gin, and filled the pitcher with it. Since gin looks like water, he did not detect the difference and as usual went through the ritual of pouring and sipping. While sipping he realized the difference, but did not suspect us. He walked out of the room with the pitcher and blasted the peon, who was supposed to fill water in the pitcher. He came back, red-faced, and continued the lecture.

Another culture shock was waiting for me when the next tutorial took place and we presented our essays that were then discussed in class. Dr Freedman invited comments from the students and then gave his comments on the essays. One of the students whose essay was commented upon, Robin Fox, who later became a very well-known anthropologist and works and lives in the USA, said very boldly to Dr Freedman, "I do not agree with you." I froze in my seat—did he

[4] Teacher–student.

contradict his teacher? Now what would happen to him? But instead of getting angry, Dr Freedman smiled and encouraged other students to challenge his remarks. That incident was an eye-opener for me, and I admired Dr Freedman's generosity. The "bastard" became a friend to his students thereon. I was also in awe of this system of education that encouraged the free expression of views even from younger students, a crucial difference from our Indian system of education. Despite culture shocks that I kept encountering I realized, to my delight, that I was in the right place.

7

Ups and Downs

Things were not working out well for Hayat. He displayed zero ability to adjust to the English culture and started going into a shell. First, being used to a very comfortable life in India, he found the work and the discipline required at the High Commission, and at the same time having to take courses at the university, very difficult. He also discovered that his knowledge of psychology was totally inadequate for conducting a PhD-level research, so he declared that he did not want to continue with psychology and would rather study sociology at the London School of Economics (LSE). So, he applied for admission in Sociology (Hons.), but as he had not studied sociology before, he was required to qualify by taking two papers in the subject. By that time, I was already in the second year of my three years' course. That year, I also had to pass my two sociology subsidiary papers. Therefore, it so happened that Hayat and I both took the same papers at the same time. As luck would have it, Hayat failed and I passed. So he was denied admission at the LSE. Now what? He had also given up his job at the High Commission because he found that he could not cope both with studies and work at the same time. He then decided to study English literature and applied for a Masters. There too, he had to take a qualifying exam and again failed to qualify.

By then, we were in the fourth year of our stay in London and during that time, I had cleared the General Certificate of Education (GCE), acquired enough proficiency in English, and was heading for the final BA (Hons.) exam. But Hayat had nothing to show and no income. My income from the BBC was erratic and barely enough to pay for our university fees and to run the household. He did not like English food and hated the sandwiches which most students there had for lunch. He demanded three, full Indian meals. So I had to find ways of supplementing my BBC income. My Intermediate certificate had no value there so I could only take up a manual job. I took up work in the LSE canteen—washing dishes from 2 in the afternoon till 9 at night—which meant that I had to skip my morning lectures. At the canteen, I was also provided a meal. This was the single big meal in the day for me and the one I most welcomed. Besides that, I also worked in a number of other places during the holidays for my tuition fees. After the Holocaust in Germany, a large number of Jews from Poland and other affected European countries had migrated to England around that time. London had a considerable number of them. They provided cheap labor; those more enterprising had put up tailoring factories, mostly makeshift arrangements. I used to work in one such factory and stitch four to five dozen aprons a day on electrically operated sewing machines. The working conditions were appalling; no labor laws applied to them and the machines were almost joined to each other due to limited space. Minor accidents were not uncommon. We were paid a pittance of £3 a week without any other benefits. I found the work very taxing and looked for alternatives.

British Society in the 1950s

I had arrived in London in January 1952 and the first political meeting that I attended there was a gathering of mostly Indians who were addressed by Rajani Palme Dutt—the then Vice President of British Communist Party—to talk about the newly adopted Constitution of India. We Indians felt proud of the fact that we belonged to a free country and were no more subservient to the *goras*. The political environment was also more congenial to us Indians and Africans who had come from newly independent countries. After a prolonged Conservative Party rule in Britain, the Labour Party came to power and there was an emergence of the New Left movement which was supportive of the freedom movements of the colonies. The socio-political environment had begun to change in Britain, triggered by the collapse of the Colonial Era. The loss of India as "the brightest jewel of the British Empire" was widely felt in Britain. We felt both the trends among the British people, those who were sympathetic to us Indians and those who were still struggling to come to terms with their racial prejudices. One overt expression of racial prejudice was refusal of accommodation to colored persons, which included Indians too. Even social interaction between us Indians and the Britishers was very limited. However, I did not feel being discriminated against on the university campuses. Most students and our professors were cordial to us Indians, with minor exceptions. We stayed in a flat in West Hampstead throughout our stay in London and our landlord who was an emigrant Jew who was very good to us. He preferred Asians over Europeans because he would say that Asians paid their rent regularly and were not troublesome. I never felt that we, "native" Indians, were ever differentiated on the basis of our religion.

Gender Prejudice in England in the 1950s

I decided to learn typing so that I could do secretarial work; there were no computers then. I took typing lessons but I needed a typewriter to practice. So, I decided to buy one on easy monthly installments. I had nothing to show as security and besides, I was told that as a married woman, I could not buy the typewriter in my name as the loan could not be sanctioned to me. It had to be in my husband's name. I told them that my husband was unemployed and I was the earning member of the family but even then, it was against the law. A married woman had no identity of her own. Such was the women's status even in England in late 1954. Finally, I did manage to buy a second-hand typewriter by borrowing money from a friend whom I repaid in installments. Equipped with this new skill, I applied for a job as a typist in a Chinese news agency. A communist friend had recommended me and I got the job. But within a week I was sacked. I still looked very young and no one believed that I was married. I also did not wear a wedding ring and could not provide a marriage certificate as I had none. I had been married by a verbal *nikah* which did not require registration in those times. I had also conceived by then and my pregnancy was visible. So, my communist employer thought that I was going to be an unmarried mother which was considered to be "immoral." Therefore, the news agency sacked me in order to uphold its high standards of morality. This was a setback because being pregnant, I was in no condition to work from 8 a.m. to 6 p.m., sitting in the same position for such long hours in the factory. It was also a minor shock to my idealism; I had regarded communist ideology as liberal and progressive. Even if I was going to be an unmarried mother, I had expected more support from them. However, some good friends advised or rather insisted that Hayat share the financial burden and work for money until I delivered the baby. So, he worked for a few months in Batchelors Peas factory where many Indian students used to work on a temporary basis. But I continued to wash dishes until I was eight months pregnant. This took its toll later.

I worked in all kinds of other places during my vacations like making sandwiches at bus stops, picking fruits on farms, and modeling at the Institute of Fine Arts where I had to stand for half an hour for each sitting without moving, while the students sketched me. But the most lucrative of these vacation jobs was working in the post office during Christmas. In those days, there were no computers or internet, so Christmas greetings were sent by post and the load at the post offices would increase manifold. Therefore, students were temporarily employed and overtime rates were paid as we often had to work round the clock. Four times the usual rate was paid for working on Christmas Eve and Christmas Day. For non-Christian students, it was a boon as the Christian students did not work on Christmas Eve and Christmas day. On Christmas day, there used to be only one delivery early in the morning, so we were required to report at 6 a.m. to start sorting out the letters and greeting cards.

A very funny thing happened one year. Hayat and I had worked till late on Christmas Eve, came home tired, set the alarm for 5 a.m., and hit the bed. We got up with the alarm's buzz, still feeling tired and very sleepy. It was also dark outside. It happened to be one of those rare clear nights and we saw stars twinkling in the sky. We were puzzled. First, we felt as if we had just gone to sleep and did not understand why we were so sleepy. Second, it still looked like the middle of the night but we convinced ourselves that we had not woken up at such an early hour before, so we really did not know how dark it was at that hour. We quickly got dressed, wrapped ourselves as warmly as possible and started walking toward the post office because on Christmas day no buses plied. On a December night, with almost freezing temperatures, we had to walk for 20 minutes. When we arrived at the post office, we found the gate closed. We were further perplexed. However, we rang the bell and after a few minutes, the night peon opened the door and surveyed us with utter surprise; two shivering souls wanting to come in. He asked us what we were doing there at that hour. We, as gleefully as possible, informed him that we had come on duty. "What?, On duty?, At midnight?" Saying this he pointed to the clock on top of the gate which showed the time as 12:10 a.m. and shut the door on us, saying we had had too much to drink so we should better go home. We just could not figure out what had happened and kept blaming each other for setting the time wrong. We had to walk back home in that cold night and report on duty again at the post office after five hours. We discovered afterwards that when we had set the alarm clock, we did not check the time and the clock was running fast.

At that time, doing unskilled work for very small amounts used to depress me but looking back now, I feel working in those places provided tremendous experience to me. I met a large variety of people from drivers and cleaners at the bus stops where I prepared packed lunches for the passengers to budding artists at the London School of Arts. It gave me a deeper understanding of life and of people who helped me in dealing with the adversaries in life and maintaining a positive attitude despite the hardships I had to endure.

When Hayat again failed in qualifying the examination for Master's in English, it further added to his frustration. The fact was that he was not suited for an academic career and his ability to cope with a different culture and environment was almost nil. He was a highly pampered person, used to a leisurely life with his mother, wife, and sister doting on him. He had overestimated his capacity to deal with the demands of higher education and a different way of life. Meanwhile, I had come to England totally raw. I had no idea of my abilities except that I had been a bright student and was highly motivated to learn and achieve success. I handled life in London well and enjoyed learning new things besides the academic learning. This irked my husband and the prospects of his wife getting a degree from England while he did not achieve anything bothered him. He decided to hamper my success and forcibly got me pregnant.

Pregnancy and Childbirth

It was during my final year at LSE that I was forced into pregnancy. I was totally unprepared for motherhood. The timing could not have been worse as having saved some money, I was about to leave my paid work and wanted to concentrate on my preparation for the final examinations. I was also scared as hell. I knew nothing about childbearing or rearing, plus I was alone in a foreign country with no money, no one to advise me, or help me with the baby. Hayat insisted that I focus on the baby and postpone taking the exam to the following year. I went to my tutor and told him so. He knew my circumstances and advised me against this. He rightly convinced me that with a baby and financial problems, I would not be able to study next year and that in the remaining three months to the exams, I must put all my energy into studying and take a chance. Hayat opposed my decision but I was convinced that without help and with a baby, I would never be able to pursue my studies. I went ahead and took the exams while I was six months pregnant. With a bulging belly and under everyone's gaze, I wrote the exams for six hours a day continuously for over five days. Such was the system in those days. Ten papers to be taken over five days—Monday to Friday—in two sittings of three hours each. It was very difficult for me to sit for three hours at a stretch and write while bending over the desk. I also had to solve another problem. If I ate a full lunch, I found bending over the desk uncomfortable whereas if I ate less, I felt hungry during the second session. I had a very sympathetic lady teacher—I forgot her name now— who advised me to eat less at lunch and munch a chocolate in the second session as I would also need energy. It worked and I managed to sit for the entire duration of the exams. It was a miracle that I did pass.

I had severe pregnancy-related sickness for the first three months and became dehydrated, so I was hospitalized. In the hospital, the matron in our ward understood my dilemma and provided me psychiatric help. She also tried to help me accept the pregnancy. While talking to me about my interests, she found out that I liked knitting, so she got me some wool and a knitting book to knit for my baby. I wanted a daughter so I knitted a little frock in lemon-colored wool. When I completed it, the matron held it up, saying, "Can you see the little girl in it who is growing within you, my darling?" That moment onwards, I accepted my pregnancy and my entire attitude changed. My sickness also subsided. I came home having fully accepted my pregnancy and looking forward to be a mother. But my financial anxieties did not end as we had no resources to deal with the maternity expenses and to buy essential goods such as a stroller, a crib, nappies and so on. But I had a good circle of friends in my class who pooled in money and bought all the things that were required. They were also excited about my pregnancy as I was the only student who was going to have a baby. I must admit that throughout my life, so far, I have had very good, sincere friends. Without their affection and moral support, I would not have survived.

I also found out that the British Health Service (called National Health Service) would provide for medical expenses related to my pregnancy, childbirth, and post-natal care. I was entitled to that as we were “British by birth”, technically, having been born during the British rule in India.

I delivered a normal seven-pound baby girl on October 24, 1956. I was overjoyed as I had yearned to have a daughter whom I could provide all those facilities which my circumstances had denied to me. My mother named her Huma, a legendary Persian bird that is believed to bring prosperity, which we certainly needed.

I had to start working just after six weeks of the delivery as Hayat was now contemplating another change of subject for his degree and had settled on History. He could enroll himself for History (Hons.) without having to write a qualifying exam.

Supply Teaching

Britain had an excellent system of crèches for infants. I put Huma in a government-run crèche when she was six weeks old and started “supply teaching.” According to the British educational system, every London county has a central education office which, among its other responsibilities, has to provide short-term teachers called “supply teachers” to schools. After graduating from the University of London, I was qualified to teach. Every morning, those of us seeking work would go to the central education office which received calls from schools where teachers were absent. One or more of us waiting would be sent to these schools according to the requirement on that day. The assignment could be just for a day or for several days, depending on how long the regular teacher was away. After an assignment ended, we would come back to the same office. We could get an assignment the same day in a different school, depending on the demand, or we might have to wait. We were paid on a daily basis. The payment was pretty reasonable and if I had work even for four days a week, we could survive. I had myself registered in an East London county where teacher absenteeism was frequent, so there was more possibility of my getting work.

It used to be tough going to a different school each time and dealing with a different principal, and different students of different grades. The education officer, a woman, in the county where I'd registered, somehow had taken a liking for me. She would try to assign me the better schools. I was lucky as a couple of times I was sent to schools where I was absorbed even for a few months. I remember one such school, which was in a very poor area. The principal, Miss

Henderson, was a very kind woman, had liberal views, and took such a liking for me that she even created work for me even if there was no vacancy. One of the ways she kept me there for several months was by giving me a small class of children with reading difficulties. Many children there had reading difficulties. They came from homes where both the parents had to work in low-paid jobs and had no time for children. I remember a sweet girl who one day, very excitedly told me that her family had moved into a flat and said, "a real flat, madam, it even has a bathroom." Obviously, until then, she and her family had been using public bathrooms. Strangely enough, individual bathrooms were a rarity in England; sharing bathrooms with other families was the norm. In middle-class areas, the common architecture was to have a row of houses with three stories and a basement. Each floor had two rooms and a kitchen but no bathrooms. The residents of three flats shared a common toilet and a common bathroom. Such houses still exist in London. I once had an interesting experience. I visited the home of Member of the British Parliament, Mr Sydney Silverman. He was the Labour Party MP and was hosting a party for a visiting Chinese delegation. It was an elegant, fairly spacious bungalow. I needed to go to the washroom so a maid showed me one, remarking very proudly, "Here madam, this is one of the several washrooms in this house." No wonder, the British in India started having bathrooms attached to every bedroom.

However, I was not always lucky. Once I was sent back from a school immediately as the principal did not want an Indian. Racist feelings were prevalent among many people then. I had a frightening experience too when I was sent to a school that was full of "Teddy" boys (disgruntled young boys not interested in schooling). They were tall, rowdy young men, sitting with their feet on desks; a couple even smoking who blew smoke on my face. As I entered, they showered me with rude questions but fortunately one of them asked me where I came from. It was obvious that I was an Indian as I was wearing a sari but he wanted to know which place in India. Strangely enough, they knew a few things about India. So, I told them that my hometown was Lucknow. The moment I uttered this, there was a big roar in the class. "Ma'am, tell us more about Lucknow. Tell us about the Dilkusha Gardens[1] there." I was totally taken aback by their information and at the same time, relieved, because they suddenly became friendly. When I asked how they knew so much about Lucknow, they shouted,

[1] A military suburb of Lucknow.

"Oh ma'am, don't you know that Cliffy (Cliff Richard—the singer—who was a craze in those days) was born in Dilkusha Gardens? Tell us more about the place." So, I talked to them about Lucknow for the rest of the time and never went back to that school.

As mentioned earlier, I had to go back to work after six weeks of my delivery. My health, therefore, started failing. I had to get up at 6 a.m., sometimes not having had enough sleep. Huma still needed a midnight feed and I had to get up and prepare the formula for her. She was unusually slow in suckling milk. I would be sitting in the cold room, dozing off while she would consume only three ounces of milk in 30 to 40 minutes. In the mornings, I would get ready, prepare her for the crèche, and take her there. It was a 15-minute walk. I would deposit her in the crèche, then walk another 20 minutes to the Tube station to go to work. I followed the same route on the way back with the additional chore of picking up vegetables and other daily food-stuff (we did not have a fridge then). The moment I would enter, totally exhausted, Hayat would declare that he was hungry and that I should quickly cook a full Indian meal for him. In those days, before my exposure to feminism, I considered cooking to be a wife's job.

Tuberculosis

Until the early 1950s, tuberculosis was considered the most dreaded disease. When I was still studying, Britain had decided to eradicate the disease and launched a nationwide campaign to detect the early onset of tuberculosis in the population. Miniature X-rays were taken in all neighborhood factories and educational institutions. One such X-ray team had also come to LSE and I, along with other students, was X-rayed. A random sample of those miniature X-rays was enlarged and mine happened to be one of those. A spot was detected on my right lung which indicated that I had been infected with tuberculosis. I was examined further and fortunately, it was found that though I was infected with the disease, it had remained dormant and I was not infectious. I was advised not to have a child for the next five years and also to abstain from heavy physical work. But my husband was not convinced that such precautions were needed as according to him, I "looked so well," and soon after he tricked me into pregnancy, the latent tuberculosis re-emerged. I started noticing some spots of blood in the morning while brushing my teeth. When it persisted for a few days, I told Hayat that I feared it might be because of tuberculosis.

He dismissed it saying that my tooth must be bleeding. But when it continued, I decided to go for a checkup. Surely enough, it was found that the lesion which had remained dormant, had become active. I was advised immediate hospitalization.

Hayat remained unconvinced, saying that how could I look so well if I had tuberculosis? Somehow I never appear unwell, no matter how sick I may be. However, I could not take a risk as tuberculosis was considered a dreaded disease and highly infectious. I had already lost an aunt a few years ago to it. I had to be hospitalized and was admitted to a sanitorium. This was such a setback. We were financially a little better off; supply teaching was bringing in a reasonable income, Hayat had finally moved to the second year of his degree, we had a sweet little daughter, and I had also taken admission in MA at the School of Oriental and African Studies (SOAS). I knew that without a postgraduate degree, I would not get a university lectureship. And then suddenly this happened. What would happen to Huma; who will pay for my medical expenses? Hayat would have to work full-time and may not be able to cope with his studies. I even believed that I was going to die.

The British Health Service again came to our rescue. We found out that there was a students' tuberculosis eradication organization. It gave a grant to Hayat to continue his education on this plea that his wife was the earning member of the family and was in the sanitorium. So, unless he received financial support, he would be forced to discontinue his education. The grant was not very lucrative. Therefore, he applied and received a long-term loan from the Indian High Commission to be repaid after his return to India and became financially comfortable. The organization also arranged for Huma to be sent to a residential nursery and that too free of cost. At that time, the British Health Service was the best in the world. Unfortunately, I was admitted to a sanatorium outside London and Huma was sent to a residential nursery on the opposite end. We had no alternative but to follow this course. It broke my heart to send Huma away to an unknown place among unknown people. We took her to the nursery after her first birthday where she was to spend the next six months. She was not walking but could stand by holding on to something and spoke sort of gibberish. After dropping her there, I was taken to the sanatorium. Hayat was left to his own. It was the saddest day of my life when I parted with my child. I howled and howled in the car; I was convinced that I would never see my baby again.

I was kept in the sanatorium for the next six months. I was fortunate to have responded to the treatment well and fast. Hayat was allowed to visit me once a week. But I yearned to see my child and often cried for her. The doctor in-charge of the sanatorium was particular that her patients did not fret and felt happy. So after three months, when I started showing good results from the treatment, she allowed me to go out for a day and visit my child. When I arrived at the nursery, a nurse brought Huma in. She walked in, took a cursory look at us and walked back. This was the first time I had seen her walk. Her indifference toward me as she did not recognize us, broke my heart and I burst into tears. The nurse consoled me and explained that at that age, little ones have a very short memory span and I should have patience. She again brought Huma back to the room and we tried to play with her and gave her the chocolates and toys we had brought for her. In a while, she became familiar with us and we took her out for a walk. We were so thrilled to walk with her. During the walk, she pointed to a cat and said, "Look, pussy." It was again heartbreaking to realize that I had not been with her when she took her first step and spoke her first words. But I had to be thankful for small mercies, to find that she was well looked after, and was growing normally. We had to leave her after a couple of hours and return back to the sanatorium.

Hayat was allowed to come and visit me once a week. He found it very cumbersome and often missed the visiting days. Apparently, he was too busy with his newly acquired freedom and had even made girlfriends.

I progressed well with the treatment and was declared cured after six months. It was a day of great joy for me when I was told that I could go home. I was particularly happy because I could bring home my child. I had seen when other patients were discharged, their families came with flowers and even music was played. So, very joyfully, I called Hayat to give him the good news. He did not sound particularly happy and advised me to take the Tube and come home. He was not even at home to receive me when I came. The next day we brought Huma home. It was such a joy for me to have our child with us again.

Political Involvements in London

LSE was very politically active in the 1950s because of Harold Joseph Laski's legacy, as he had left-wing leanings. The common persons regarded LSE as a communist institution. Most Indian students in Britain at that time had grown up during the Indian Independence Movement and were politically conscious. They had formed an association called the London Majlis which was very active in articulating India's aspirations for political freedom. Indian students' political activities were encouraged and supported by V.K. Krishna Menon—the first Indian High Commissioner in London—who himself had formed an association called the India League, which during the pre-Independence days had lobbied for India's freedom. I had also grown up in a politically charged environment, as mentioned earlier.

One incident ushered me into the Indian students' movement in London. In the 1950s, the Indian students' population in England was dominated by Bengalis, most of who came from rich backgrounds and professed communism. However, majority of them settled back in their aristocratic families on their return home, except a few. A large number of Bengali students had joined the Communist Party of Britain. Membership to the British Communist Party—unlike the Indian one—was very easy. All you had to do was to fill in a form and pay your small dues. Among the more prominent communists during my stay in London were Taruna and Dilip Bose, who went to London to study and stayed on for several years, becoming more politically than academically involved. They lived on the same street as we. London Majlis had called a meeting to discuss the newly framed Indian Constitution and had invited Rajni Palme Dutt, who was the then Vice President of the British Communist Party, to chair the meeting. I used to meet Taruna and Dilip at the Finchley Road Tube Station from where we used to take the train for the city. In fact, she had introduced herself to us and asked us where we lived, etc. She informed us of the meeting and urged us to go to it, which we did. There Taruna Di came to me and requested me to give the floral bouquet to Palme Dutt. I suppose she chose me because I was the youngest in the crowd. From then on, she kept us informed of various students' activities and we soon became a part of the left-wing Indian students' group. She also suggested that I take some lessons in Marxism which were organized for newcomers. I did so and was inducted into Marxism. Both Hayat and I enjoyed being a part of that group but soon he fell out of it, while I continued my interest and also realized that I possessed some leadership qualities. It was a very exciting time in England. After many years, the Labour Party came back in power and a new Left movement was emerging, welcoming students from newly independent countries. We Indians felt proud of having come from an independent country. But, in order to get the benefits of British citizens, we enrolled ourselves as "British-born," which was a fact. In all official forms, there used to be a column "Origin of Birth" where we would fill in "British." There used to be another column, "Race," where we would write "Homo sapiens."

In my second year, I was elected as the General Secretary of the Students' Union of LSE. I had, by then, also joined the London Majlis and took part in its activities too. Hayat regarded these activities as "childish" and mostly kept away from them. But I must admit that he did not stop me from participating. He made friends who were all from backgrounds similar to his, that is, UP Muslims and Urdu-speaking, except one, a rather unusual Englishman by the name of Denis Greenstreet, who preferred to hang around mostly with Indians. Denis even wanted to marry an Indian girl but it did not work out. He finally ended up marrying a very attractive black girl from Ghana and made a good marriage of it.

Distinguished Indians in London

One of the activities of the Students' Union used to be to keep in touch with prominent Indians and to invite them for lectures and to interact with us. This helped us in keeping in touch with the happenings in India. I enjoyed meeting these personalities. During my long stay in London, I met some interesting and distinguished Indians, visiting or living there. One such interesting person that I had the privilege to know and work with was Attia Hosain, the author and broadcaster. Attia aapa—as we called her—was a remarkable woman who came from the same *qasbati* background as I. She was born and brought up in a *qasba* in Barabanki district of UP. She decided to live in London after Partition, when her husband opted to migrate to Pakistan. Besides her intellectual and creative qualities, she was regarded as the most beautiful Indian woman of her time. It was said that there were two most beautiful things to see in India, the Taj Mahal and Attia Hosain. She had a very charming personality and was a perfect combination of beauty and brains. Attia aapa was an excellent broadcaster and I, very often, had the privilege of broadcasting with her in the BBC. She not only dressed well, which used to impress me as a young woman, but also kept her home tastefully decorated. In fact, one of the British women's magazines, *Women's World*, had featured her flat in London as a model home.

Qurratulain Hyder, the celebrated Urdu novelist, was in London in the 1950s too. I frequently interacted with her. In fact, her Jnanpith-winning novel *Aag Ka Darya*[2] is based partly on her experiences in London. Later, on our return to India, I had the privilege of living in the same condominium in Delhi as hers. It used to be a great delight to talk to her as she was a perfect storyteller. It is such a pity that in her later years, she developed some eccentricities, one of them being her devotion to a Muslim *pir*[3]. She believed that this young man, the *pir*, had spiritual powers and controlled her life.

Zia Mohyeddin—now a celebrated theater personality of Pakistan—had come to London as a young struggling actor. I remember him as a talented, interesting personality and like any young aspiring actor, trying to establish himself and wanting to make an impression on Indians and Pakistanis through his acting abilities.

Dr Romila Thapar, now an internationally acclaimed historian, was also my contemporary in London. We became good friends and our friendship has endured over half a century. She lives in Delhi now, so we have the opportunity to meet often.

I consider it a great privilege to have seen Pandit Jawaharlal Nehru from very close quarters. Whenever Panditji visited London, he would address the Indians there. I fondly remember an instance when Panditji addressed us at the Indian High Commission. The High Commission had a moderate-sized hall with a small platform. A chair was placed on the platform while the audience sat on the floor below. When Panditji came, he folded his hands and looked around, saw the chair placed for him on the platform, and said, "Why am I being made to sit there, higher up, to look down at you? I am going to sit with you." He picked up the chair himself, brought it down, and sat among us. He talked to us just like a man next door. When he finished talking, a woman raised her hand and shouted, "*Pandit Nehru ki jai*!"[4] Panditji became furious and said, "Why *Panditji ki jai*, you should say *Bharat Mata ki jai*."[5]

---

[2] River of Fire.

[3] Sufi saint or spiritual guide.

[4] Hail Pandit Nehru!

[5] Hail Mother India!

On another occasion, Panditji was scheduled to speak at the Indian club in Osterly, London. A huge crowd of Indians and non-Indians had gathered there. He started speaking and then remembered the previous occasion when that Indian lady had said "*Panditji ki jai*" and recounted the incident. He then bent down, picked up a little mud from the lawn, and with tears in his eyes said in an emotionally charged voice, "You should all say *Bharat Mata ki jai*, Bharat is *mahan*,[6] her *mitti*[7] is *mahan*, not me." He then wiped his tears and continued his speech. Imagine a great leader—the prime minister of a country—shedding tears in front of a crowd without any qualms. This was the man–emotional, very human, self-effacing, and full of love for his country and countrymen. What a towering personality he was, so full of humanity and charm; and what a privilege for me to have seen and heard him.

I also joined in his funeral procession, several years later, in 1964. No man or woman in Indian history would have had such a surging, sobbing crowd, following a funeral. The news of his passing away had spread like wildfire. It was the month of May. Villagers came in their bullock carts from the neighboring areas. Young and old, men and women, rich and poor, of every community and religion were there to pay their homage to the beloved leader. And yet there was no violence at the immersion of his ashes in the River Ganges.

One of the most remarkable characteristics of Panditji was that he was extremely approachable. When, on my return from England, I was knocking at every door for a job and not succeeding, a friend suggested that I write to Panditji as he could fix a job for us. I laughed it off; after all, he was the prime minister of the country and had a billion tasks to take care of. But at my friend's insistence and in my desperation for a job, I sent my biodata to his secretariat, marking it as "personal." Believe it or not, I promptly received an acknowledgement informing me that on the PM's instructions, the secretariat had sent my biodata to an appropriate institution. After sometime, I was even offered a job at the Archaeological Survey of India. Such was Panditji's concern for every citizen of the nation. Panditji also had the remarkable quality of maintaining enduring relationships. Dr Z.A. Ahmed—a respected communist leader of

---

[6] Great.

[7] Soil.

India—had entered politics along with Panditji in the earlier days of formation of the Indian National Congress. Panditji and Dr Ahmed had become good friends but later, they differed on political ideologies and Dr Ahmed left the Congress and joined the Communist Party of India. But, on a personal level, they remained friends. When Dr Ahmed's daughter Saleema got married, Panditji was invited to the wedding but due to his busy schedule, he could not grace the occasion. But he invited the newlyweds to his residence as soon as he had a little time, treated them with tea and snacks, and spent some time with them.

Indira Gandhi

Indira Gandhi—Pandit Nehru's daughter— too inherited this quality of maintaining friendships. My uncle Ansar Harvani, as mentioned earlier, was a freedom fighter and was elected to the first two Parliaments. Later, under Mrs Gandhi's leadership, he developed differences with her policies and retired from active politics. Even after his exit, when his three daughters got married, Uncle Ansar invited Mrs Gandhi to each wedding and she attended all of them. I remember that she came in from the back entrance with an inconspicuous security person just like any ordinary guest, talked to the bride and groom, had a cup of tea, got a photograph taken with the couple, and quietly left. I also had the privilege of seeing her on other occasions and was amazed with the ease with which she upheld her position. Once, when my second husband Idrak was heading a prestigious economic research organization, we were invited to a luncheon hosted by Mrs Gandhi at the Rashtrapati Bhawan in honor of the Minister of Economic Affairs from one of the Gulf countries. The entire cabinet was there along with a few noted economists. We arrived earlier than the time scheduled for the Prime Minister's arrival. I was naturally rather nervous but I also noticed a kind of nervousness and tension among most of the guests who were waiting for her. When she did arrive, she entered with such an ease that all the prevailing tension just vanished. We all felt relaxed in her presence. It was a "sit-in" lunch and she was chatting away, offering dishes to the guest of honor and to the other guests sitting close to her while relishing the meal herself. It was an amazing experience.

8

Experiencing the Communist Regime

The 1940s and 1950s were the days of the "Iron Curtain" when travel by individuals to the Soviet Union was banned and only officially invited persons or groups could travel to that country. But the Soviet Union was also very keen to advertise its achievements to the rest of the world. So every two years, a Youth Festival was organized in one of the communist countries to which young women and men were invited. Their board and lodging were free and the travel was also highly subsidized. The idea behind it was to enable the youth of the world to interact with the communist youth, who themselves had no opportunity to travel abroad, and also to impress the world with the socio-economic progress of the communist countries. The first such festival was held in Bucharest, Romania, in the summer of 1953. By that time, I was well-integrated in the Indian students' movement in Britain. A delegation of Indian students was selected, who were required to pay a travel cost. I could not afford it, although I was very keen to go. There was a delegation going directly from India, and the London delegation was going to be part of it. As the Indian Communist Party had received some money, the party decided to share it with Indian students residing in England; so at the last minute, in recognition of my active involvement in the students' movement, I was offered a free ticket to Bucharest. It delighted me no end. It was a wonderful opportunity to meet young men and women from all over the world and also be united with our Indian compatriots. It was also the first time that I was going to a foreign country other than England. So I quickly and most excitedly packed my suitcase. But on the day of departure, I suddenly lost my enthusiasm and started feeling very low, even wanting to cancel my trip. I could not think of any reason for such behavior. However, it was too late to cancel; besides, it would have caused some offence to the Festival Organizing Committee who were kind enough to have provided the funds for my travel. So I went and boarded the train for a small port in Germany, from where we were to proceed by ship. The train mostly carried delegates from different parts of England, Ireland, and Scotland. Everyone was cheerful, joking and singing away and amidst all this merrymaking, I was sitting at the window, looking outside, trying to conceal my tears. By the next day, I started feeling better and finally got into the spirit of the festival. I had heard of persons having "premonitions" about current or coming events, and here I was experiencing one. Apparently, my *baji*, to whom I was very attached, who had practically brought me up, had died that day in India. I was told of this only when I returned to London after the festival.

The festival was indeed a wonderful experience. This was the first time I was travelling out of England, and I was so thrilled to be united with those coming directly from India. As usual there were very few women in the delegation, but the one from India included the reigning Miss India, Indrani Rehman. We from London were particularly curious to meet her and were delighted to find her very amiable, without any trace of arrogance. She was also an accomplished dancer and proved to be an asset to the Indian delegation as, to the delight of the international participants, she gave several performances. Until then, not many Indian women had travelled to that part of the world, except for a privileged few who had gone abroad for the higher studies. Not every country had a full-fledged Indian High Commission or Embassy, as it was only six years after India had become a Republic. Delegates from smaller countries, including Rumanians, had not even seen women in colorful sarees or *Sardarjis* in their elegant *pugrees*. So we Indian women and our Sikh delegates were highly admired, and the Sikh men even received marriage proposals.

The Bucharest trip opened my eyes about the prevailing communist regimes. I had not joined the communist party until then, and had a very idealistic view of the regime. This first exposure to it was disappointing. We noticed a total control over people's lives through a very rigid and hierarchical system. From the moment we arrived in Bucharest, even our movements were controlled. For example, we were taken on arrival to a room in an office-like building, and were told that later we would be transferred to a hotel where the rest of the Indian delegation was already put up. We were naturally keen to join our Indian compatriots and requested our guide to take us there to meet them. But he very firmly and rather unpleasantly kept repeating, "No, not until I get my leader's permission." We had nothing to do there and were getting bored, but he did not allow us even to stroll outside the building. We were in a way imprisoned in that building, waiting for the leader to give instructions. However, finally we were united with the other Indians and were comfortably lodged and well fed. Every morning we were given our program of the day. A large variety of cultural programs and trips to interesting sites were organized for our entertainment, and each individual was assigned to one such trip or program. We were not allowed to change our visit from the assigned venue. It often happened that our interests differed from what was assigned to us and we would have liked to make a mutual exchange, but it was not allowed; we had to go to the event that the "leader" had allotted to us, without consulting us. We did not like this imposed discipline but had to accept it.

The communist countries at that time were completely isolated from rest of the world and there was acute scarcity of consumer goods there. People craved for foreign goods. Men would ask us for foreign cigarettes and women for stockings and lipsticks. A couple of unfortunate incidents happened to me, which caused embarrassment to our Romanian hosts. I, along with two other Indian delegates, lost my dollars from the hotel. American currency was very much in demand there. Balraj Sahni, the actor, a very fine person and himself a communist, was the head of the Indian delegation. He was embarrassed too, because it was obvious that some Romanian had stolen our dollars. We did not make a fuss and let the incident pass as quietly as possible.

On another occasion, we were witnessing a cultural program in an open-air stadium. A little girl, about seven to eight years old, probably a gypsy, came and sat next to me. She started embracing me, touching my clothes and admired the wristwatch I was wearing. As soon as the program finished, the little girl suddenly ran away and got lost in the crowd, and I noticed my wristwatch missing. It was a Swiss watch given to me by my husband as a wedding gift. So I made a little noise and started looking around, in case it had fallen off. This could have happened anywhere but again the Romanian guide took it very seriously. He felt as if the country's image was soiled; they had been trying so hard to present the image of a perfect society.

Anyway, I forgot about it and did not let it spoil my stay. Strangely enough, when we were leaving Bucharest at the end of the festival and had boarded the bus for the station, the leader of the Romanian delegation came over and presented me with a men's Swiss watch (it was probably his, as it was not a new one). I politely refused to accept it but he insisted on putting it on my wrist, urging me to accept it, otherwise his national pride would be hurt.

Later, I had the opportunity of participating in subsequent Youth Festivals which took place in Warsaw, Poland, and Moscow, Russia, in 1955 and 1957. These were held after the exposure of Stalin. Even by then, the situation had not changed much and an artificial demonstration of prosperity and show of well-being of all people, irrespective of class, was thrust upon us, although we could detect that it was a facade. We noticed too much poverty while travelling to Moscow by train through Belarus, to the embarrassment of our die-hard communist colleagues. We also noticed the resentment of people of the "satellite" communist countries like Rumania and Poland toward Soviet domination. When our train stopped at a small station in Poland, some of us stepped down the train and a curious crowd gathered. One of our fellow Indians offered a cigarette to one of the men in the crowd, announcing proudly, "Take it, this a Russian cigarette" but instead of being happy, as our friend had expected, the Polish young man threw the cigarette on the ground and crushed it with his foot, saying he did not want anything Russian. "We can manufacture better ones."

The Fifties Decade

The 1950s was the most interesting and significant decade of the twentieth century, both nationally and internationally. The English as a nation were crazy about the royalty; for them royal events took priority over all others. Within a year of our arrival, King George V died and his funeral procession was paraded at Central London. Londoners came out in huge numbers to watch it. Then Queen Elizabeth's coronation took place. It was a huge event; the nation almost went berserk. People lined up along the route of the coronation parade, spending the previous night on the pavements, in order to secure a strategic spot from where to catch a glimpse of the new queen. For almost a year, every purchase that one made had the coronation seal on it, including toilet paper. My English friends considered us very lucky to be in England at that auspicious time. For days the newspapers had nothing but coronation details. After the coronation frenzy subsided, the colorful sister of the newly enthroned Queen, Margaret's love affairs, and then finally her marriage to a commoner who was also a divorcee, occupied prime space in the newspapers. Even the most serious newspapers such as the *London Times* and the *Manchester Guardian* were not immune to publishing these details of the private life of the royalty. That frivolous aspect of the British press used to amaze us.

Scientific Discoveries

Other events of global significance also mark the 1950s as an important decade. It was in 1952 that the first commercial Jet airline was started. It was called the de Havilland Comet. There was great excitement as it cut down travel time by more than half. Indians and Pakistanis on the BBC staff were provided air travel to India every two years. The employees used to brag about this privilege and we poor struggling students would envy them, as we could only travel by ships, which took 17–20 days to cover the distance between London and Bombay. I remember how the first of the BBC employees travelled to India in a Comet aircraft and how amazed we were all listening to his description of its comfort and the reduced time it took to fly between London and New Delhi. But the Comet developed technical faults after a year and was grounded. But by that time, the technology had further improved and other international companies had also acquired jet aircrafts.

Great and very significant strides were made in the early 1950s in the field of medicine. The penicillin drug was discovered in the early 1950s, a wonder drug for treating tuberculosis which until then was regarded as a "killer" disease. I was also administered penicillin, in powder form—which had a horrible taste—when I was treated for tuberculosis in 1957. But I was found to be allergic to it and, as an alternative, had to take an antibiotic powder called Pass & Ina, which was much more unpleasant to drink mixed with water than a penicillin injection would have been. Another significant medical event was the separating of Siamese twins in 1957. A set of twins attached at the brain was successfully separated by British doctors. It was in the

1950s too that the triple injection comprising diphtheria, whooping cough and tetanus vaccines was successfully administered to babies. My daughter Huma (who is 55 years old now) belonged to the first generation of babies who benefited from this invention.

One of the biggest thrills was when the Soviet Union shot a satellite called "Sputnik" into the outer space on October 4, 1957. This rocked the world. How did the USSR become the first nation to send a satellite into space, leaving behind the scientifically advanced nations of Europe and the USA? These countries could not hide their jealousy and concluded that it could not have been the Soviet mind that had achieved such a scientific feat. It must be the German Jews who had taken refuge in Soviet Union who contributed to it. I remember vividly how the rest of the world was caught by surprise. It indeed was quite an event.

Exposure of the Stalin Regime in Soviet Union

On the political front, Stalin and his dictatorial regime were exposed to the entire world when after Stalin's death Nikita Khrushchev took over as the General Secretary of the Soviet Politburo in 1956. In his inaugural speech in February, 1956, Khrushchev exposed Stalin and laid bare the details of the autocratic, tyrannical rule of the Soviet Union under Stalin leadership. He elaborated how Stalin was elevated almost to the status of a God who blatantly distorted the basic principles of Marxism–Leninism. It was as if a huge balloon had burst. The Iron Curtain was lifted. Communists and the non-communists were equally stunned. Khuruschev's entire speech was published in the English newspaper *Manchester Guardian* on a fateful Sunday morning. Our die-hard communist friends refused to believe it and regarded it as another capitalist conspiracy against the great communist world. The critics of the communist regime were jubilant. For weeks, the only topic of discussion in LSE was Khrushchev's speech and the predicted "fall" of the Soviet Union. LSE, having a special affinity to that regime, was particularly affected by the exposure. The end result was that after several decades, a conservative student was elected president of the LSE Students' Union. It was considered to be such a significant event in Laskis's bastion that the *London Times* gave the editorial space to that event. It transformed the entire political profile of LSE, leaving our Indian communist compatriots hurt and confused. I, being a "reluctant debutante" to the formal fold of the British Communist Party, secretly felt relieved. After joining the party, influenced or rather pressurized by my fellow communist students, I was greatly disappointed by the autocratic working of the party and the hypocrisy of the rich students, who used words like "the downtrodden", "the exploited", etc., without even understanding their meaning. I was required to toe the party line without questioning; otherwise I would be a "traitor." I found the rigidity stifling and the fanaticism of most members similar to religious fanaticism. While I admired the Marxist theory of equality and social justice and its abhorrence of the exploitative nature of capitalism, I was disappointed to experience that the party policies and programs were far from being truly Marxist.

It was also in October 1956, after Stalin's exposure, that Hungary, the first of the "satellite" countries of Eastern Europe, openly revolted against the existing communist regime and the dominance of the Soviet Union. In the same week, Nasser, the prime minister of Egypt, nationalized the Suez Canal, which was under British control. The British Government could not lose such a strategic property and invaded Egypt to reclaim the canal. This aggressive action was widely condemned. There was already a strong movement taking place against the British colonial rule and the British had already lost India only eight years ago. The pressure had finally led to the British Government withdrawing its forces and the canal was restored to its rightful owners, the Egyptian Government. These events caused much excitement in Britain. We watched them with amusement, having secured our own freedom. I remember that the Suez Canal was closed down for some time, and about that time a few of our friends who were returning to India after completing their education had to sail via South Africa, which was a much longer route connecting Asia with Europe.

A youth festival took place in the summer of 1957 in Moscow. The London *Majlis* decided to sponsor me as a delegate. But I had 9-month-old Huma to take care of, whom I could not leave behind. Fortunately, a Sinhalese friend of mine, Kumari De Souza, who later married Lal Jayawardene, a well-known economist from Sri Lanka, offered to move into my flat and take care of Huma. Kumari was very fond of children and would visit us often to be with Huma. I took her offer and went to the Moscow festival. It was another eye-opener.

Despite the efforts of our Russian hosts to impress us with the economic progress of the country, we were hugely disappointed to notice that the life of ordinary citizens was not as rosy as was propagated. For instance, there were many modern buildings but the drainage system did not work in them. The unevenness of development was obvious in other spheres too.

Ten years later, in 1967, I visited Moscow again, and even at that time I found that the availability of consumer goods was no better, nor had the drainage system improved much. This time I went from India as a delegate to a peace conference and was very comfortably lodged in a fancy hotel. I feel a little repetition does no harm as it emphasizes the point. I was told that it was a hotel specially built for the young Czars during the Czar regime; later it was turned into a government-run hotel and used mostly for foreign delegates. But despite the luxuries, we used to feel very claustrophobic, as our movements were so strictly monitored, and one was never allowed to ask a question. We were required to accept everything without questioning. For example, we were to fly from Moscow to Prague on a certain morning. So at dinner the previous evening we were told to collect with our luggage at gate no. 2 to go to the airport. I asked what time was our flight to Prague. Our guide very rudely replied, "I don't know." He could not understand why I should have asked that question. I should have just followed his instructions step by step. I suspected that he himself was only instructed to put us in the bus for the airport at a certain time; he was not told anything beyond that. At the airport, another guide took charge of us. It appeared that the system of strict state control worked because each one was given limited information for the job one was to perform; beyond that the person was not to know anything, and the will to question and learn more was totally killed in ordinary citizens.

I again visited Moscow; I think it was in 1973. That time I had a very interesting experience. I was teaching in University of Delhi then, and took leave to go to Moscow. The University session was still on, and by the time I was to return, the summer holidays would have started. According to the University rules, I had to report back on duty on the opening day after the holidays, otherwise my entire two months' salary would have been deducted. It so happened that I could not get a seat to fly back to Delhi in time. My Russian host told me to continue enjoying their hospitality until they could get me a seat in the plane. They refused to understand my problem. Fortunately, there was an Indian brigadier posted in the Indian Embassy in Moscow, who was known to my brother-in-law. He had informed the brigadier that I was in Moscow and that he may get in touch with me, which he did. I was very anxious to get out of Moscow to rejoin college on time and requested him to use his diplomatic privilege to get me a seat as soon as possible. He told me that he knew an Indian businessman who was so influential in Moscow that he could get me a seat on the required date even if the plane was full and the pilot himself had to get down. I laughed, not knowing that it was almost true. The businessman's technique was to get things done from the highest echelons to the lowest by bribing them with foreign consumer goods. Even such ordinary articles of daily use as plastic bags were a novelty there and most sought after, and this gentleman always carried with him these items whenever he went to meet an official for a favor. I was introduced to him and impressed upon him the urgency of getting back to Delhi. He assured me that he would do his best. Within two days, he informed me that I should meet him at a certain place and that he himself would take me to the airport. There was a 90 percent chance that I would get a seat. While we were on the way, I noticed him carrying a modest-size suitcase. I enquired if he was also travelling. "No," he said, "but this is the magic box, which I hope will do the trick." We arrived at the airport a little late so I rushed through the various procedures, and all along I noticed that he kept doling out plastic bags from the suitcase to the concerned officials. I was finally pushed into the aircraft and found, to my utter surprise, that in fact the plane was delayed since it had been waiting for me to arrive. The occupants of the plane had thought that they were delayed on account of some VIP. Turns out that the VIP was none other than my humble self.

School of Oriental and African Studies

I had joined SOAS for my master's, in 1957. I was determined to get a postgraduate degree to enable me to teach at the university level. I could not do a PhD from the University of London as fieldwork was an essential requirement for it. I had chosen to work on Indian Muslims, which meant that I would have had to come back to India, collect field data, and then return to London to write the thesis. I did not have the financial means to do that, so I settled with the MA.

I had fortunately met many people who helped and supported me throughout my stay in London. My supervisor, Dr. F.G. Bailey, a well-known social anthropologist and an expert on India, was very helpful, as was the Head of the Department at the SOAS, Professor Von Furer Haimendorf. Their support made it possible for me to manage a home, a child, and a job. I did take twice as long as was expected to complete my master's, but finally I did. Hayat was still struggling finishing his BA (Hons.) in History from the Birkbeck College. I was very keen to return to India but we had to wait until Hayat completed his course; he could not go back without having acquired a degree. We also had to work and save some money for the first few months in India, before we would find jobs.

After Hayat finally passed his BA (Hons.) exam, he also qualified for supply teaching and we decided to give ourselves at least six months to save some money and then return to India. Around that time, we received the bad news that his mother was suffering from cancer. In the early 1960s, cancer was incurable and I knew that she would very much like to see her son before she died. We also started getting letters from home urging us to return. I persuaded Hayat to go back as soon as we could get tickets. So, with the meager savings that we had managed to collect, we returned home in March 1961, after being away for over nine years. Those nine years were crucial in my life as I had practically grown up in England.

9

Return to India

Our family's perception of us being "England-returned" was very different at that time. Not many Indians went to England and those did belonged to the upper crust of Indian society. A middle-class person going to England for higher studies, and a woman at that, was a rarity. My parents had imagined that I would have become a "memsahib" with short hair, smoking cigarettes and speaking only in English. They had thought that my taste in food would have changed too. They had also expected us to have become prosperous. They had no idea how financially weak we actually were. My brother Khalid and sister Sehba were sent to Bombay to receive us. My uncle Jan Nisar Akhtar (the poet–lyricist Javed Akhtar's father) hosted us in Bombay. I did not recognize my siblings at Bombay Port. Sehba and Khalid had both grown up in the 10 years of my absence from India and I just passed by them, then Khalid recognized us. He called out to me, "Bajiya, I am Khalid" (as an older sister I was called Bajiya). It was such a wonderful surprise. I was so excited to be back and very touched that my sister and brother came all the way from Lucknow to receive us. We stayed in Bombay for a couple of days and then traveled to Lucknow, where not only my entire family but also near relatives were at the platform to receive us with garlands. It was quite a homecoming. We embraced each other and shed tears of joy. Huma loved the floral reception. She had so many garlands around her neck that we could hardly see her face; she loved them and did not want to part with them. My parents were absolutely delighted to see their first grandchild (Huma was five years old) and to find their daughter looking like a solid Indian woman, with a *jooda*,[1] clad in a sari,

[1] Hair tied in a bun.

not wearing high heels and no makeup except kajal[2] in her eyes. Our train had arrived early in the morning so we were home for breakfast. It was so nice to be served breakfast instead of having to make it ourselves. But I was surprised to find that for us; special bread and butter were brought, along with knives and forks, to keep with our assumed Westernized habits. I was looking forward to hot parathas or roghni rotis[3] with *aloo ki sabzi*[4] or omelets, which used to be the usual breakfast in our home those days. But instead there was bread which had been toasted on a hot skillet. So I took out the electric toaster that I had brought from London, a novelty in those days. My parents were intrigued but delighted to find that a little boxlike thing could toast a piece of bread so nicely. Everyone was particularly thrilled when the toasts popped out automatically.

We were instructed by Hayat's father to go to his village in a car. The usual mode of transport was by bus, but the England-returned son should go to his native village in style. Since my parents did not own a car, we hired a taxi. *Dadi*, as I called my mother-in-law, was very sick, in advanced stage of cancer, and was overjoyed to see her son and granddaughter.

We soon started looking for a job. We both wanted a job in the university, preferably in Lucknow or Delhi. But to our utter disappointment we found that either there were no vacancies or whenever a vacancy occurred the university appointed its own students. The shine of a foreign degree had rubbed off by then and one needed a godfather to get a job. We had none. I had not studied in an Indian university, and had just dropped on the academic scene out of nowhere.

We were frustrated, the small amount of money that we had brought was running out. Hayat's mother's condition was getting worse and finally she succumbed to the dreadful disease.

Delhi of the 1960s

Hayat and I we finally got the UGC fellowships; I got one in the Delhi School of Economics (D-School) and registered myself for a PhD program under the supervision of Professor M.N. Srinivas. Hayat again decided to change his subject and became fascinated by the Chinese

[2] Kohl.

[3] Kind of moist bread.

[4] Potatoes cooked in Indian style.

1. My Parents.

[All photos and letters are from author's personal collection, unless specified.]

2. Me, as a 10 year old.

3. With Prime Minister, Mrs Indira Gandhi.

4. Me with my cousin, the poet-lyricist Javed Akhtar, and my sister, Seemin.

5. Myself, presenting an award to a student at the University of Kurukshetra.

6. Myself, delivering the keynote address at a women's studies conference in Lucknow.

7. Myself, discussing women's issues at a seminar in New Delhi.

8. Me and my family in San Diego.

9. I, with my family and Dr Romila Thapar, at the launch of my husband's book of poetry in New Delhi.

10. Me and my husband at our residence in New Delhi.

11. Me in my 30s.

language. He joined the School of International Studies at Sapru House, which was newly established under Professor V.P. Dutt's chairmanship. So finally between us we were able to get an income which was just about enough to survive moderately. We were happy to have found work in Delhi as we liked the city, which was beautiful in the 1960s. I remember it as a city of gardens. The Delhi School of Economics was blooming with roses. The city was not so crowded; it was clean and had wide roads. Delhi had a distinct character of its own with its historical buildings and the newly constructed Lutyens' Delhi. In the 1960s, the city had just begun to expand—a few houses were coming up in Defence Colony and Lajpat Nagar in South Delhi. The city ended at Ashram. Jamia Millia Islamia was regarded as outside the city limits; no one went beyond Ashram at night; those who came from outside Delhi would spend the night in the main city and would avoid going to Jamia at night. It was considered to be so unsafe beyond Ashram. When the Zakir Hussain Co-operative Housing Society was allotted land close to Jamia, we were very happy that it was in a quiet peaceful place. But within a couple of years when the colony started building, the area became crowded, and now it is one of the busiest areas of South Delhi. New Friends Colony came up in the 1970s and, later, Ishwar Nagar in the 1980s. At that time Sarita Vihar, now a huge DDA colony, did not even exist. In the last 40 years or so, Delhi has become so crowded and has lost its charm. I remember how there used to be an arrow on the Mathura Road, just opposite Nizamuddin West, in South Delhi, pointing toward the city saying "To the city of Delhi" and the road used to be so empty with hardly any traffic. Schoolchildren, including our daughter Huma, would cross the road after getting down from the school bus, unescorted. One could not imagine in one's wildest dreams in the early 1970s that Delhi would become like this.

University of Delhi was situated in North Delhi, so we had decided to find a place to live near the University. Model Town, a new residential area had come up in the vicinity. Hayat came to Delhi to look for the accommodation while I stayed behind in Lucknow with Huma.

To our astonishment, we found it difficult to rent a place on account of being Muslims. We had faced a similar situation in London too, where we used to be rejected on account of being Indians. We were very disheartened as we did not expect such prejudices to exist in free India. After all, Muslims had made a considerable contribution to the freedom movement, including my own uncle Ansar. I was brought up in Lucknow where we had never felt discriminated as

Muslims. Even during the turbulent days of the 1947 Hindu–Muslim riots, Lucknow had remained unaffected and the two communities had lived peacefully as before. However, after several rejections, we finally found a small two-room flat in Model Town, and Huma and I came to Delhi. We found that although the landlord, who was a lecturer in University of Delhi, had rented the place to us, it was on the condition that we would not cook or eat meat on the premises. It was a difficult condition for us to maintain but we were so desperate that we accepted it, and hoped to look for another place soon, where we may have more freedom to live as we liked. But we soon became tired of this imposed vegetarianism and started cheating our landlord by bringing cooked meat from Old Delhi. We impressed upon Huma not to tell the landlord or his family that we had been eating meat. One day our landlord was with us and Huma whispered to me, in his hearing, "Mummy, I will not tell him that we had kebabs for lunch." He overheard but smiled and said that as long as we did not cook meat in the flat he did not mind if we brought it from outside. What a relief it was! In fact, by that time our landlord and his family had become quite fond of us and had accepted us as decent persons despite being Muslims. Many prejudices are nurtured due to lack of contact between different communities—obviously they had not interacted with Muslims and had some stereotyped notions about the community. When he had an opportunity to interact with us closely he found us to be normal Indians and became friendly.

After moving in we went the same day to the Panchkuian Market, a furniture mart in Delhi, and ordered some rudimentary furniture and other essentials for starting a home. I was very happy to have our own place, though it was small.

We continued to stay there until we found a bigger and better place in the same area. The monthly rent of that flat was only ₹125; such were the rents in the late 1960s in Delhi. The cost of living was such that we managed comfortably with our combined income of ₹800 a month, which included the house rent and Huma's school fees in an English-medium school as well as the cook's salary (a woman we had brought from Lucknow).

Delhi School of Economics (D-School)

I joined the D-School that was regarded as one of the prestigious colleges in University of Delhi. Sociology had been introduced there as a new subject and the Department of Sociology, under the chairpersonship of Professor M.N. Srinivas was in a separate building in the same compound. The D-School had a very rich academic environment—at that time Professor V.K.R.V. Rao had just retired as the Head, and Professor Ganguly had taken over. It was in 1962 and 1963, respectively, that Professor Jagdish Bhagwati and Professor Amartya Sen were appointed. The fact that both these young economists were in their early 30s and were given the position of full professors had made headlines, as until then the status of a professor was generally given to seniors after a number of years of teaching experience and after climbing the ladder of lectureship and readership. Professor Sen and Professor Bhagwati were appointed directly to the post of professors, which spoke well of their competence as economists as well as the change in the mindset of both academics and administrators. There was a very rich academic environment at D-School and a great deal of free mixing between students and teachers, which was highly appreciated by the youngsters and widely commented upon. I remember Amartya Sen sitting on a bench and freely chatting away with students almost as an equal, unusual in those days on campuses.

That free environment did not exist in the sociology department. Dr M.S.A. Rao, Dr Andre Beteille A. and Dr Arvind Shah were on the staff. Andre used to be friendly with us students and we felt more at home with him. At that time, sociology was not offered at the undergraduate level in any of the DU colleges. The subject itself was in a seminal stage, mostly confined to village studies and heavily loaded with caste studies. Indian sociological theory was in its infancy and the observation–participation methodology was hotly debated. The Department of Anthropology was a separate department housed in the main building of the University that taught courses on physical anthropology. This arrangement was different from what I had known at the University of London where LSE had separate courses and awarded separate degrees under the title of Sociology and Social Anthropology. I had chosen social anthropology as my main subject in LSE and had sociology as a secondary subject, according to the regulations.

Besides myself and Karuna Chanana, I do not remember any other female student. Imtiaz Ahmad and I were the two Muslims and both of us were reminded of this at the slightest instances. Professor Srinivas had taken both of us under his wing as a supervisor and we were advised to choose topics relating to the Muslim community. We followed the advice, also because there was hardly any sociological study done on Muslims except one on Muslim caste by Ghaus Ansari, who was living abroad. Muslims were regarded as a homogeneous community with an entirely different culture of their own and only other Muslims were considered suitable to study them. I decided to work on "Muslim Social Institutions" and chose a village near Lucknow for my fieldwork. Professor Srinivas never took any interest in our work and hardly supervised us. Both Imtiaz and I ended up without a PhD degree. In my case I had some interruptions on account of personal problems including a divorce and remarriage to a Christian. Both these acts of "sacrilege" were looked down upon by my professors. Professor Srinivas refused to recommend me for an extension and I gave up in disgust.

After joining our courses, our next step was to get Huma admitted into a good English-medium school. We were advised that the closest one to Model Town would be Presentation Convent, which was situated just opposite the Red Fort, and which had a school bus that came to Model Town. We had earlier tried a few other places but unsuccessfully, as their waiting lists were extensive and often a candidate had to wait for a couple of years to get admission. We, not having been in the country, were not on any waiting list. We met the same fate at Presentation Convent initially but luckily, I had carried Huma's birth certificate. It was a novelty at that time, as births were not regularly registered and most parents concealed their children's real age. Somehow, the moment the Sister in Presentation Convent saw a proper birth certificate from the county of Marylebone, London, she got so excited that she picked it up and showed to everyone in the room saying, "See, this is what a proper birth certificate looks like in my country England." I suppose she felt nostalgic, and Huma also shed her shyness in the company of a white nun—she had until then interacted mostly with whites—and talked smartly with the principal. The magic worked and Huma was immediately admitted to Presentation Convent in Upper KG, as she was just five years old. It was a huge relief for us. She soon settled down in the school. Fortunately, she had a great deal of curiosity. In India, everything was new to her; she was hugely pampered by my parents and amused everyone with her English accent. We had spoken to her in Urdu while in London, so she understood the language but did not speak it there. But soon after coming to India she stopped speaking English and talked mostly in broken Urdu. Everyone was surprised and would remark about it. But I encouraged her to speak Urdu as I knew she would learn English anyway when she would go to an English-medium school. It was a great pleasure for us to watch her growing to be a very intelligent and perceptive child and to see her adjust to a different environment quickly.

My father had not travelled abroad and was very curious to know about life in England. He would ask me many questions about the style of life there, about food, etc. Curiously enough, he never asked me whether I had tasted products made from pig meat. I think he might have been afraid that I may answer in the affirmative, and that would not have been acceptable to him. Eating pig is abhorrent to Muslims. But one day Huma made a blunder. My father and she were talking about having a party for her friends, and my father asked her what she would serve to her friends. She blurted out "Ham sandwiches and beer." I almost froze and quickly diverted the topic before *abbujaan* understood what she was saying.

I remember being happy during the initial period in Delhi. We had a small flat, with minimum furniture, but it was home and for the first time we had a place with a separate bedroom. The bedroom in our first Model Town flat was small, with space only for two beds and a low small bed for Huma, which we would push under one of our beds during the day to create a space to move around. I liked being at D-School, which was newly established and had already built a good reputation. The city of Delhi was not crowded and had the Ridge and many parks; there was a lot of greenery around. D-School itself had a beautiful garden with roses blooming. I loved the environment and made a number of friends.

My uncle, Ansar Harvani, once took me to meet Humayun Kabir, the then Union Minister of Education; we were treated like showpieces. Our relatives took pride in having "England-returned" relatives and even our landlord would tell his friends that his tenants were "England-returned." It is amazing how the standard of living and the availability of consumer goods in India has improved in the last half-century, at least for the middle class, despite its pockets of poverty. Imports were very limited in my time, so there was a craving for imported goods. We had brought a few household items like a fridge, and small items of everyday use like an automatic toaster and a pressure cooker. Even these things were outside the reach of middle-class families. I remember that one day our pressure cooker made a noise and I heard our landlord's sister comment, "Oh, so even your tenants have a pressure cooker." To that the landlord replied, "They even have a refrigerator, and all these things are imported too."

But despite these silver linings, our professional and personal life was not satisfactory. Hayat found Chinese very difficult to cope with, and I found Professor Srinivas very communal in his attitude toward me, and unhelpful as a supervisor. I remember every time I went to see him, he would make me uncomfortable by his remarks about my being a Muslim, a woman and belonging to UP, the state of *bhaiyyas*.[5] All these attributes had negative connotations for him. However, despite Professor Srinivas's negative attitude, I found a village for my fieldwork, not far from Lucknow, a Muslim-dominated village both numerically and economically. My father knew the dominant landholding family there, who exercised considerable power in that village. So I settled there with Huma and gave it the pseudonym of Kasauli. I spent six months in the village collecting data for my thesis. It was easier to create a rapport with the villagers due to my proximity with the dominant landholding family; my hosts made my stay there comfortable.

Fieldwork Experiences

I started my fieldwork in Kasauli in 1962, more than half a century ago. Anthropological fieldwork is technically called the observation–participation method, which entails living with the subjects of the study and observing and participating as far as possible in their daily activities. This method does not depend merely on statistical calculations for analytical purposes. Observation–participation has its own limitations, mainly the danger of subjectivity in perceiving situations. Above all, it requires establishing a rapport with and gaining the confidence of the subjects of the study. It was a novel experience for the village to see a young woman, dressed in a jacket (it was winter time), go round the village without a veil and talk to men uninhibitedly. The villagers were full of suspicion and very curious about my identity and purpose. Politically the situation was not very congenial either for an outsider to gain the confidence of the village folks. The Indo-China war had just ended and while it was on, ordinary citizens were given a call to financially support it by donating money and also the family gold. So first the rumor went around that I was a man disguised as a woman so that I could get access to the interiors of their houses. But the fact that I lived in the house of the landlord puzzled them. If I was actually a man, how could I live in the "sarkar's" house along with his wife and young daughters? When the landlord heard the rumors, he called the panchayat[6] members and dispelled their doubts about my

[5] Derogatory term is used to describe the inhabitants of the State of Uttar Pradesh.

[6] Village council consisting of five members.

sexual identity. He told them that I was the daughter of his friend and was writing a book about the good work the village was doing. This removed the first hurdle and I was allowed to enter their homes and talk to their women.

I had to record the villagers' conversations and impressions and write them down, often in their presence. One of the enquiries related to their financial situation. This led to further suspicion and considerable hostility toward me. They decided that I was a government secret agent, sent to rob them of their gold and financial assets. My hosts again came to my rescue and pacified their fears, but some suspicion lingered on throughout my stay there. This led to some rather comic situations too. First thing I noticed was that the village folks were not as innocent, simple and unintelligent as they might appear to an educated city dweller. Lack of education and even illiteracy does not guarantee stupidity. I found men and women who were very perceptive and sharp in assessing situations and in judging me in particular. However, despite many misgivings on their part regarding my identity and purpose, the fact that I was married and had a child went a long way in dispelling some of their suspicions.

One of the questions I used to ask was about the number of cattle a family owned, as an indication of their financial situation. The moment I would emerge from my residence, a number of idle young men would follow me out of sheer curiosity and the entire village would come to know that I was out visiting homes. One clever woman had a cow which she quickly locked in the single room she had. When I asked her about owning any cattle, she point-blank said, "None." She described her family as being very poor—there was a general impression that if I was a government servant I could also get some government benefits for the very poor. While she was denying owning any cattle, the poor cow started bellowing from inside the room and banging the door!

I also used to notice certain assets, like sewing machines or small agricultural implements, being hidden away before I visited a certain home—all in order to impress upon me the level of their poverty, in the hopes of getting some financial support from the government on my recommendation. I found this aspect of my fieldwork rather heartbreaking, since I had no power to reduce their plight; I could only disappoint them. I benefited from them but could not give them anything in return.

On another occasion, I even led to fights between sisters-in-law and a great deal of hurt to some daughters-in-law of a household.

Joint families were the norm so wives and children of brothers lived together in the same household. Among other ways of assessing a household's financial status and to gauge the extent of dowry given, I would ask each *bahu*[7] what she had brought as dowry. This caused a lot of heartburn and competition among the sisters-in-law. The ones who had brought more dowry looked upon those who had brought less and the latter felt hurt and inferior. I had not expected this kind of reaction and felt very bad for causing such a friction.

One time, to assess the impact of family-planning, I asked an old man how many children he had. He said "two" at which the usual hangers-on who used to follow me laughed and said that the old man was lying. He had five children, three daughters and two sons. The old man defended himself by informing me that he did not count the three married daughters as his anymore, since they now belonged to their husband's household. It made perfect sense to him but I could have recorded wrong information, had it not been corrected by the crowd.

After completing the fieldwork, I started analyzing the data. I found that Professor Srinivas took no interest in my work; in fact, he never had time to even look at my thesis. Five years, the maximum requirement for a PhD thesis, passed and I never received a PhD from the University of Delhi. Professor Srinivas would not recommend an extension for me. Imtiaz Ahmed met the same fate. Fortunately, both of us received some recognition for our research work from other quarters. The ICSSR even gave me a post-doctoral fellowship called "Housewife's Fellowship," recognizing the quality of my research. Mr. J.P. Naik had established this fellowship at ICSSR for qualified professional women who wished to return to work after a gap. Such were the communal prejudices operating at the university level in India at that time.

Sociology as a full-fledged discipline was introduced in University of Delhi's colleges very late, in the 1960s. This was around the time I was looking for a job. Five University colleges introduced sociology at the Honours level, so five sociology positions were created. I applied for all of them and was rejected by a veto from the Head of the Department, namely, Professor Srinivas, who at that time had the power to veto the selection committee's decision. Despite an Honours degree from the LSE, which at that time was regarded as one

[7] Daughter-in-law.

among the top social science institutions in the world and a Master's from the SOAS, University of London, for which I had written a full-fledged thesis under the supervision of Professor F.G. Bailey, a very well-known social anthropologist whose work on India was highly valued; having almost completed my PhD thesis and even with a published paper in the *Economic and Political Weekly*, India's prestigious academic journal, I was rejected in favor of second-class MAs from Department of Sociology, University of Delhi, just because they were Professor Srinivas' students. It was then that I realized that to get a position in a university, you needed a godfather. Professor Srinivas, as the chair of the Sociology Department, always had the last word in appointments and he only appointed his own students.

It so happened that during my period of job-seeking, Jesus and Mary College (JMC) had three vacancies. I appeared for interviews every time and had been rejected in favor of Professor Srinivas' students. The principal of JMC felt that it was a case of prejudice exercised by the Head of the Sociology Department and finally lodged a complaint with the Vice Chancellor. The Vice Chancellor was acquainted with me as we had been on the same panel broadcasting from AIR a couple of times. He advised the JMC principal to take me on an ad hoc basis. I was given five ad hoc appointments as Professor Srinivas and then Professor Shah, who had taken over the Chair from him, would not give a nod to my permanent appointment. Fortunately, later a vice chancellor's nominee was included on the appointment committee, and I was finally given a permanent position in JMC. I owe my professional survival to that determined Principal Sister Aquianace, who stood against injustice and finally won the battle.

After giving up at D-School, I got divorced and remarried and, as if it was not bad enough, I also married outside my community. These factors added to me being undesirable and not being fit for an "honorable" position as a lecturer, and contributed to my subsequent rejections.

Meanwhile, my personal life was under great stress. In London, Hayat and I were both students and there were no traditional role expectations, such as the husband being the bread earner and wife being the homemaker and mother. I was more sociable and had a wide circle of friends, both male and female. Hayat did not object to my friendship with my male colleagues, who respected me and in all those 10 years of our stay, none of our male friends ever tried to take advantage of me physically. If anything, they admired me and supported me in my struggle. Hayat was himself a decent person; he was not evil and was not over possessive as a husband. We had common friends, who would often drop in for an Indian meal and after Huma was born, would come on weekends and play with Huma. So life had somehow moved on in London. My focus had been on increasing my educational qualifications. I was so heavily preoccupied with studies, working for money and rearing Huma that I did not let the incompatibility between my husband and I get the better of me. We used to have fights, as I kept growing in learning and experiences while Hayat almost remain static. I was getting more and more frustrated with him, while he was frustrated because of his own inability to cope with life there and his failure in meeting his educational aspirations. He was fond of Huma and helped in rearing her. But I could notice that his temper, for which he was known, was going from bad to worse. During one of our arguments, he once slapped me. I could not take that humiliation and walked out with Huma who was just a few months old. I went to a friend who, although sympathetic to me and provided a shelter, advised me to rethink my action. Hayat came over and impressed upon me and the friend that he loved me and could not live without me and Huma. I yielded then, having no better option, but on one condition, that if he ever raised his hand on me again I would leave him forever.

I had mentioned earlier, how, on our return to India, the contrast between our personalities was more noticeable and people would openly comment on it. Hayat was made more and more aware of his inability to play the traditional role of a dominating husband. We were referred to as an "ill-suited couple" and he as a "henpecked" husband. By then we had been married for 12 years, had a five-year-old daughter, and were still living hand-to-mouth. We had no savings, no investments and saw no prospects of improving our situation either. In India, people like to interfere in others' personal lives, so friends and relatives' constant comments on our situation added to our already strained relationship. The unfortunate result of this was that Hayat started getting jealous about me and would question me about my interactions with any man I came in contact with. This was a new development and I found it very distressing. He had not shown any distrust in me earlier, and this sudden change of behavior became very difficult for me to handle. His suspicions grew and one day, during an argument when he accused me of having an affair with a common friend, he became aggressive and beat me up and locked me in the bedroom. We had a maid who took care of Huma; she gave the child dinner and put her to sleep in the living room. He slept in the living room as well while I was locked in the bedroom. In the morning, I started banging on the door and told him that if he did not let me out I would shout for help. Before this drama started, the maid had sent Huma to school. To this day, I do not know whether Huma remembers this incident or not but I feel extremely distressed when I think of what negative impact it may have had on that innocent child. However, Hayat finally opened the door and shouted at me to get out, which I did, holding my bloodstained dupatta. I went to an old close friend who lived in a flat in Nizamuddin West. When my friend saw me in that distressful condition, his comment was, "Zarina, why did you wait so long for this to happen?" Apparently, my friends were of the opinion that I should have separated from Hayat much earlier. But my middle-class background regarded divorce as most distasteful, and despite being unhappy, I had stayed in the marriage. So they made me comfortable and I went to Huma's school to take her back with me. I still remember how heartbreaking it was when I saw Huma entering the principal's room with a very worried expression. She knew that I had been beaten up. But I had worn dark glasses to hide the wounds. The moment Huma noticed that my face did not show any signs of a beating, a smile of relief spread on her face. That smile is still registered on my mind.

Living Alone with Huma

I immediately looked for a place for Huma and myself in Nizamuddin and found a tiny one-room kitchen with a makeshift bathroom. I could just about afford that, and moved in as it was not considered decent to live in a flat with two men (my friends) without their wives. Hayat went to Lucknow the same day to inform my parents that I had "walked out on him" as I needed freedom to flirt around. Fortunately, my parents did not buy it and told him that if their daughter had walked out after 12 years of marriage, there must be a good reason for it. My father then visited me in Delhi and provided much-needed moral support. It was unusually understanding on my parents' part. Usually, Indian parents insist on daughters staying on in the marriage no matter how difficult it may have become. My parents' support was very crucial for me in not developing feelings of guilt. Mine was the first separation in the entire extended family and I did not know any friend, except one in England, who had had a divorce. As late as in the early 1960s, divorce was uncommon in India and was severely looked down upon. Moreover, it was always the woman who was blamed for the break-up. Even after living for a while in Nizamuddin and making friends with the neighbors who liked me too, I still had to hear comments like, "You know our neighbor, Mrs Bhatty, she is such a nice person, but she is divorced." The stigma of being a divorcee has stuck to me forever. Thank God the attitude toward divorce is changing and it is not looked upon with much disapproval anymore.

10

Destiny Plays a Hand

I am not overtly religious but I cannot deny the role of destiny in life. It certainly played an important part in determining certain important events. The first good thing that happened soon after I separated from Hayat was that Professor Srinivas finally yielded and appointed me as a lecturer in Delhi College (now known as the Zakir Husain Delhi College). This gave me a little more money than I had been getting as a fellow. It was also a job that I had been aspiring for. I was delighted as I loved teaching, not knowing that it was going to be only a short-term delight. I arranged my teaching schedule in such a way that I taught in the morning sessions and was able to return home just before Huma came back from school. Muslims allow remarriage of divorced women. In fact, there are Koranic instructions that a young widow or a divorced woman should be remarried soon after the *iddat*. So my father, being a God-fearing Muslim, felt it to be his duty to encourage me to get married as soon as I found a suitable person. But I was in no mood to even consider remarriage. Although, as I started living alone, I found that men, including my friends from the University, considered me an easy prey to their lecherous intentions. I found I was suddenly much in demand. At the same time, I also realized that living as what was called "unattached" was not going to be easy. I was only in my 20s and had a daughter, who over time would also grow up into what appeared to be a beautiful woman. So, I not only had to protect myself from these lecherous advances of men but also Huma. This was what my father kept impressing upon me, to persuade me to seriously think about remarrying.

While I was still living with Hayat, our relationship had worsened. One evening, the two of us were walking with Huma in

Connaught Place. We spotted an old friend who was at LSE during my time there. He had been married and sent by his company to LSE to do a one-year course in personnel management. He used to visit us very often in London. We lost touch with him later and then it was after several years that suddenly we came face to face. We were delighted to meet him as there was so much to catch up on like what had happened in our lives and in the lives of our other Indian friends in England. He kept looking at his watch and said that he was catching an early morning flight back to Ranchi where he was posted and had been invited for a dinner as well that evening. But we wanted to spend some time together. So, he insisted that we go with him for dinner to his friend's place. He explained that his friend was a bachelor—an informal friendly person—and had an excellent cook; his friend would not mind having extra persons. He managed to persuade us and we went with him to this friend's house. The man had the most unusual Arabic name, Idrakul Zaman. He was an economist and worked at a research institute in Delhi. Our friend and he had studied together in Allahabad University. Idrak lived in Jangpura which is adjacent to Nizamuddin where my friend Zia lived. We arrived at his very small but functional flat unannounced, but found Idrak very welcoming and cool about the three of us descending on him this way. I remember having a somewhat pleasant evening. He took particular interest in Huma and I could notice that he was very fond of children. He told us that he took a lot of interest in his younger brothers' children. Although he was the eldest of three brothers, he remained a bachelor. I remember remarking, "So you are a confirmed bachelor," to which he replied only with a charming smile. Idrak was wearing a Lucknowi *kurta pyjama,*[1] a typical UP Muslim dress. His Muslim servant, Anwar, presented a pretty decent Mughlai dinner. While parting and thanking him for his hospitality, he suggested that we exchange telephone numbers as we may like to keep in touch because we had similar academic interests. We did not have a telephone at that time but I reluctantly took down his number.

Soon after that meeting, I found myself bumping into him at various places. Now that we recognized each other and had similar interests, particularly in music and poetry, we often found each other in concerts and mushairas. Hayat was not particularly interested in such events so I used to go alone or with friends.

[1] Set comprising a long shirt and pant that are worn daily in India.

I had a female friend, Zahida, who was teaching at Miranda House—a women's college in Delhi—and was keen to meet a suitable young man. I thought Idrak and Zahida may click and arranged a dinner at my place to bring them together and invited a couple of other friends too. It turned out to be a nice party. Zahida was a poet and recited some of her works. Idrak enjoyed the poetry sessions but did not show any interest in Zahida, although Zahida looked very pretty and sophisticated. I concluded that Idrak was a confirmed bachelor after all. Soon after that, Hayat and I separated and I came to live in Nizamuddin West. One evening, I had gone to shop in the Nizamuddin West market and spotted Idrak strolling there with his dog. I had no idea that his residence was next to Nizamuddin West and he also used that market. Earlier, when I had gone to his flat in Jangpura, I had gone in a car with a friend. It was nighttime and did not notice the proximity of Jangpura to Nizamuddin West. He explained that he lived next door and asked what was I doing there and how were Hayat Saheb and Huma? I had to tell him that I had separated from my husband and was living in Nizamuddin West. "What about Huma?" he immediately asked with some concern. I told him that she was with me. He sounded very protective and told me that if at any time I needed any help, his servant Anwar did not have much to do, so I should not hesitate and ask for help. He walked me to my place. I appreciated his courtesy but I think he also wanted to identify my place of residence. Not long after that chance meeting, an opportunity came when I needed his help. One day, the principal of my college called a staff meeting in the evening. I normally used to return home around 2 p.m. to pick up Huma from the school bus. I requested the principal to excuse me from the meeting and told him the reason. He was most non-cooperative and insisted that I should attend. I was in a fix. I had just joined and did not want to displease the principal. So I thought of Idrak and called him and requested him to send his servant Anwar to the bus stop to pick up Huma and keep her until I returned. He assured me that I need not worry and that he would take care of her. He himself came from his office and took Huma for lunch to a nice restaurant. He kept her amused until I returned. When I went to collect Huma from his place, I found her very happy and excited. She told me what a nice lunch she had with Bhatty uncle, who had also got her an ice cream and bought Ludo for her. I was very touched by his kind gesture and thanked him profusely. He graciously accepted my thanks and added that it was a pleasure to have Huma around and that maybe we should keep in touch. This was the beginning of a deep friendship which finally ended up in our getting married almost a year after.

A couple of instances made me realize that Huma, more than me, needed a man around the house. Idrak, as he was living alone, would often drop in on his way back from office and we would have tea together. Huma always enjoyed his company. One day, I dropped our towel on the parapet and did not know how to pick it up. It so happened that Idrak came over that evening. Huma told him that our towel had dropped on the parapet and we could not jump down to pick it up. Idrak, being a young man, immediately jumped down and picked it up to Huma's delight. A couple of days later, I noticed that she had deliberately dropped the towel again and declared that it didn't matter because when Bhatty uncle came, he would pick it up for us.

Huma used to go to meet her father at a mutual friend's place who lived nearby, on a certain fixed day and time. Once, Hayat sent for her unannounced. Huma was not at home at that time as she had gone out to play. I looked for her but could not find her. I got agitated because her father would have made a fuss. I feared that he would accuse me of neglect because I did not know where my daughter was. However, after a while, I found her on our street. I grabbed her hand to bring her inside but she would not let me hold her hand which was bunched into a fist. So, I angrily asked her what she was hiding. She opened her fist to reveal small pieces of paper. These were invitations to our neighbors to come to our place for a fete. I asked her why she was inviting people over without telling me. With tears in her eyes, she said that since no one visited us, she thought this way friends and neighbors would come to our house. How terrible I felt! Ours was not a complete household, so even neighbors avoided us and looked upon us with suspicion. A young woman living alone with a small daughter was so unusual. It then occurred to me that Huma acutely felt the need for a father. Huma also wanted a sibling. She would often ask me when she was going to have a baby sister and just to pacify her I would say, "After your next birthday." After I had separated from her father, she again asked the same question on her next birthday. This time, I explained to her that since I did not have a husband, I could not give her a baby sister. And she blurted out, "Let's tell everyone that Bhatty uncle is your husband and then you can give me a baby sister."

My father, on the other hand, was pressurizing me to look for a suitable person to marry because I had begun to feel insecure as a young woman with a daughter living alone. It was a very unusual situation in those days. As I mentioned earlier, my male colleagues had started bothering me. One of my acquaintances from the University started coming over often, late at night, and would give the excuse that he was in the neighborhood and so decided to look me up. Another would call me and ask me to go out for lunch, yet another would drop in after classes to tell me that he had decided to look me up and have a cup of tea with me as I was alone and maybe needed some company. I shooed them off and told them that I was perfectly all right and did not need their sympathy or support. But such visits were becoming a nuisance. It was also very disheartening to feel that these were the men with whom I had interacted at the University campus as colleagues and as soon as I separated from my husband, they started looking at me as a woman "with no character." Men, in those days, thought that a young divorcee living alone could be an easy prey to their licentious behavior. In fact, a professor whom I had known quite well, also tried to befriend me during the days of my separation. I met the same man again a couple of years after I was married to Idrak and he made quite a shocking statement. He said, "Zarina, I met your husband a couple of days ago. He looked quite young, very handsome, and spoke so well at a seminar. Really, a very erudite, pleasant young man, and did you say he was a bachelor when he married you?" All this was said with such astonishment as if he found it unbelievable that a person of Idrak's description could marry a divorced woman with a child from her earlier marriage. As if I had nothing to offer to a man, no looks, no education, except being "soiled" by a divorce! I was good enough for this professor to flirt with but of course not good enough to be married to an educated, good-looking person, and who was a bachelor as well. Such were the attitudes that I was confronted with in those days.

It so happened that Idrak was also under pressure to get married and set up a home. His two younger brothers were married with children. His parents were getting older. They owned and lived on a farm near Nagpur in Maharashtra. His father was too old to manage the farm and the parents needed to move out of there and live with one of their sons. The two married sons could not offer to let the old parents stay with them as their wives did not get along with the mother-in-law. Idrak, being the eldest son, felt responsible for providing a home for his parents. He had just then started thinking that he should get married. He was 39 years old, handsome, intelligent, well-placed professionally, and was regarded as a very eligible young man in the Christian community. He had sown his "wild oats" long enough; he was fond of children and wanted to have his own family. That's when I came along, a 29-year-old educated, mature woman, having proved my ability to bear children. Idrak composed poetry in Urdu and was impressed by my chaste Lucknowi Urdu and my interest in Urdu poetry. My uncle, Majaz, and uncle-in-law, Jan Nisar Akhtar, were well-known Urdu poets. I admired Idrak for his ability to compose Urdu poetry. In fact, this ability and appreciation of his poetry has been one of the binding factors between us. I was an LSE graduate which impressed not only him but his economist father too. Over almost a year, we had known and grown fond of each other. About that time, Idrak received an offer of consultancy with ECAFE—now known as ESCAP—a UN agency with its regional office in Bangkok. He had not only grown fond of us but had also become very protective of Huma and me. At that stage, I did not know that he was a Christian by faith.

I considered myself more of an Indian than a Muslim. I did not practice Islam and was critical of the Islamic position of women. In fact, I had no definite views on religion. I grew up in an Indian Muslim family which was more of a social construct than a purely religious one. Religion had not been the overriding force in my life and being an idealist, I regarded all people as either good or bad and did not attribute any special virtues in being overtly religious. If anything, I had a kind of suspicion of very religious persons. I had witnessed the lecherous behavior of mullahs and bearded Muslim men toward low-caste women and even young girls.

I must concede that my perception of Indian Christians was similar to that of an average Indian. The stereotype of an Indian Christian is that they are highly Westernized, speak mainly English, have Western names, wear Western clothes, are not very family-oriented, drink, smoke and so on. I had no interaction with any Indian Christian in India except one old lady. She was a widow who used to live with her married son down the lane from my parents' place. She often visited uncle Siraj and mostly interacted with him rather than the women of the household. She mostly spoke English or in broken Hindi and wore Western dresses too. She was very unkind to her daughter-in-law and wanted her son—her only child—to leave her house. When the son whom she called Harry but he introduced himself to people as Hari, refused to move out, she took him to court to have her house vacated.

It was against traditional Indian culture to behave in such a hostile manner toward your son in the land of "son" worship. So my image of Christians formed on this very limited exposure was not a positive one. I now realize that she was a very unusual Christian woman and, if anything, did a disservice to the community. She was certainly not representative of Indian Christians. But that is how stereotypes are formed, in extreme cases leading to religious fundamentalism.

Despite not having a very positive image of Indian Christians, I still believed that a community should not be tarnished by the deeds of certain persons. There are good and bad human beings in every community. My experience with Idrak had been a very positive one. He appeared to be very gentle, fond of children—which was very important for me—had an air of wisdom about him, and was academically oriented, a factor which I admired. Above all, my being divorced and having a child from my first husband did not matter to him at all. On the contrary, he considered it courageous on my part to have taken a divorce and get out of a bad marriage at a time when divorce was socially disapproved.

So circumstances were created for us to marry. Call it destiny or God's will, both Idrak and I started thinking of formalizing our relationship. Fortunately, I had not become bitter after my divorce and still believed that I could have a successful marriage, provided I found a compatible partner. I was not in a hurry but circumstances led me to take a decision earlier than I had imagined.

Although Idrak had not formally proposed to me in the conventional manner, we had assumed that we would eventually marry each other. I was not formally divorced until then. As a Muslim woman, it was very difficult for me to seek divorce, unlike a Muslim man who could divorce at will by saying "I divorce you" three times even without a witness. For a Muslim woman, it was very difficult to demand divorce (it continues to be so as the archaic, most gender-discriminative Muslim Personal Law is still operative in India), without the husband's consent. Hayat was angry with me and took my request for a divorce as personally humiliating. He had started a campaign to discredit me. So after he considered that he had destroyed me morally and no one would dare marry me, one day he called a common friend and gave him a piece of paper on which he had written three times as per the requirement of the Muslim Personal Law, "I divorce my wife Zarina by Khula." He said he was divorcing me knowing fully well that no one would now marry me. But the unbelievable had happened; I had, in fact, procured a divorce. For those who may not be familiar with the Muslim Personal Law, divorce by Khula means that divorce is granted at the request of the grieving wife and in such a case, the husband is neither legally bound to pay the *mehr*[2] nor the maintenance. It is only if a husband initiates a divorce that he is bound to pay the agreed *mehr*. The amount of *mehr* varies according to the economic status of the husband's family. Some clever families insist on fixing the amount of *mehr* the same as the *mehr* of Prophet Mohammad which used to be just a few rupees. I have been told that among the poor and even among the more clever upper- or middle-class families, the husband requests the wife to forgive the *mehr* on the wedding night itself. The poor bride has no choice but to do so.

Until then, I had taken Idrak to be a Muslim. There was no indication that he was not. His name was Arabic—Idrak ul Zaman—his mother's name was Feroza, his brothers were Feroze and Farhat. All these are Urdu/Muslim names. A few relatives that he introduced me to also had similar names like Bhai Muneer, Najummnnisa, Talat and Sarfaz. Idrak usually wore Lucknowi *chikan kurtas*,[3] ate Mughlai food cooked by a Muslim cook, composed poetry in Urdu, and his younger brothers called him *qibla*, a very respectable Urdu word for older persons. I never saw any Christian literature in his home; to my knowledge he never went to church. How on earth was I going to know that he was not a Muslim? When he disclosed his Christian background in a casual manner, I did not give much thought to it and assumed that he was a Christian in the same way as I was a Muslim, unconventional and non-practicing. His two brothers also had interreligious and unconventional marriages. Farhat was married to a Rajasthani Hindu girl and Feroze to a twice-removed Anglo Indian girl—Margarette—who claimed to be an atheist and was an active rationalist.

So, once the technical hurdle in my getting remarried was removed and we finally talked about formalizing our relationship, we naturally also talked about the form of marriage. Without any hesitation, I said that we should have a civil marriage as we belonged to different religious communities. To my surprise, Idrak disagreed with me. He argued that to him, marriage was a sacred act and should be blessed

[2] An agreed amount, in cash or kind, that a husband promises (it is regarded as a divine promise) to pay the wife before consummation of marriage. In practice, it is just a formality and in most cases never paid.

[3] Chikan embroidery on a cotton kurta.

by a divine force. Therefore, he could not have a civil marriage and would like to have a church marriage. He explained that although he did not go to church regularly and did not wear Christianity on his sleeve as it were, at heart, he was a believer and had strong faith in his religion. He further elaborated that his liberal and unbiased attitude toward people—irrespective of caste, class and creed—emanated from his faith in Christianity. Christianity, to him, was the most humane religion that preached unqualified love for all people. I could not disagree with such a philosophy but still several questions bothered me. I went through a period of doubt and needed time to sort myself out.

My father had met Idrak at my place in Delhi and had liked him too. As he had been pressurizing me to seriously think of remarrying, I decided to share with him my concerns about marrying Idrak. He regarded Idrak as a good match for me but was, like me, surprised to know that Idrak was not a Muslim. His first reaction was that it did not matter as long as he agreed to have a *nikah* but in case I was thinking of a civil marriage, that would be unacceptable to him as he believed that a marriage should have divine sanction and a civil marriage would, for him, be like living in sin. I explained to him that Idrak was of a similar view and would like our marriage to be solemnized according to the Christian faith. He saw no problem in this because Christianity—like Islam—was also a religion of the book. I was also concerned about Hayat's reaction to my marrying a Christian. He might object to his daughter growing up in a Christian home. *Abbujaan* did not think so as Hayat claimed to be an atheist anyway and had information that Hayat was planning to get married to a Hindu girl. In fact, I knew that he had a girlfriend and had been in a relationship with her even since we were together. Therefore, *abbujaan* did not think that Hayat would be bothered and advised me to go ahead and marry Idrak according to the Christian faith.

I thanked my father for helping me to get over my dilemma and we agreed to have a Christian wedding. But Idrak was not a member of any church in Delhi or elsewhere. So, until he formally became a member, no church would marry us. Idrak's paternal uncle was a priest and had a certificate to marry couples, so Idrak decided to request him to marry us. We went to Yerala, a village near Nagpur, where his father had a farm and we had a simple wedding under a tree on the farm. Idrak's brothers came with their families and Shankar, a very close friend of Idrak, came from Bombay. My brother Khalid came to represent my father. I had sent Huma to my parents in Lucknow. She had winter holidays then and I was not sure what her reaction would have been to her mother getting married as remarriages were not so common at that time. Besides us, both our families were very happy, especially Idrak's family, which had been pressurizing him to get married and have a home of his own for some time. Idrak's father had invited a few of his friends from Nagpur, so altogether we were about 30 persons. Baba, their cook, had also invited his friends from the village, so they also formed a part of the "distinguished" guests. There was a huge tree in the bungalow compound and a sort-of stage was erected under the tree. A floral cross was drawn on a white sheet that worked as the pulpit and Idrak's uncle officiated the ceremony. The villagers sprung a delightful surprise by making some music from the various pots and pans that they had carried with them. That was the most delightful part of our wedding ceremony that I still cherish.

We returned to Delhi and found a two-bedroom flat in Nizamuddin West. We set up a home, sort of, because neither of us had any savings to buy proper furniture. The proper setting up of a home was postponed as Idrak was going to Bangkok on a UN assignment where he would get a high salary that we could use to purchase what we needed. In fact, he did not even have money to buy me a wedding ring despite a four-figure salary which, at that time, was regarded as being on the high side because he was an extremely generous person and never cared to save. So, he had to request his office to give him some advance to buy me a ring. But as luck would have it, he was pickpocketed and lost his entire salary. Finally, his parents bought the wedding ring and the wedding sari for me. His generosity was the hallmark of his personality; he had a strong tendency to give benefit of doubt to the other person, an admirable characteristic but in practical terms a difficult trait to live with.

I would like to relate an interesting story of his large-heartedness. Once a shoeshine boy, who must have been 10 or 12 years of age, came to his office crying that his shoeshine equipment had been confiscated by the police and he had lost his source of livelihood. He requested for some money to buy a shoe polish and brush. He was taken to Idrak who had the reputation of being generous. Idrak lived up to his reputation and gave him the required sum of money. From then onwards, the boy made it a habit to come and ask for money on some pretext or the other. One day, he came crying and said that he had lost his mother and needed money for her last rites; sure enough,

Idrak gave him some. But then, the mother died a couple of times more! Every time the boy would convince Idrak that he had lied the previous time but this time it was true. My husband would believe him each time. Finally, even his colleagues found the boy to be a nuisance as he would turn up at the office every now and then. So Idrak's PA[4] called me and said, "Madam, talk to sahib to stop the boy from bothering him and lying to him. How can a person die more than once?" I spoke to Idrak and he accepted that the boy had been lying, but if it was true the following time and the mother had actually died, then he did need the money.

As I had mentioned earlier, Professor M.N. Srinivas finally conceded and I was appointed as Lecturer in the Delhi College. This college was originally established for Muslim youth and continues to be predominantly Muslim. That was the only place Professor Srinivas considered fit for a Muslim candidate. Before me, another Muslim student of his and my batch mate, Imtiaz Ahmed, was given that post. It was after Imtiaz left that I was considered suitable to teach in a Muslim-dominated college. Such was the level of communalism among some of the reputed scholars in India. The irony was that Professor M.N. Srinivas was later appointed at the Minorities Commission set up for the protection of minorities. However, I enjoyed being a lecturer. My ambition to teach at a university was fulfilled and on a personal level, I had married the man of my choice whom I admired and loved. I believed that my troubles and struggles were over. But who has seen the future?

The danger bells rang when on my return to college after marrying Idrak, I met the principal, Mr Beg—known to be an enlightened Muslim—and told him that I had remarried and my surname had changed from Ahmed to Bhatty, which needed to be entered in my official records (I was not a feminist in those days and it was customary to adopt the husband's surname). I noticed that Mr Beg's attitude was not cordial. He did not congratulate me. Instead, he said that since my life had changed now as I had married a non-Muslim, I may not like to continue teaching there. I was totally taken aback by his remark and his knowledge about me having married a Christian. I tried to assure him that this had nothing to do with my professional life and I had no intention of quitting my job, which I was enjoying. Also, my husband—himself being an academic—had

[4] Personal assistant.

no objection to my continuing in the college. Mr Beg tersely replied, "Well, we will see" and left it at that. I did not get any sacking orders. Idrak left for Bangkok after two months of our getting married and I continued teaching. We had decided that I would join him for the summer holidays and return to Delhi after the holidays were over. Idrak's appointment in Bangkok was only for a year, so there was no need for me to quit my job. There were no good English-medium schools in Bangkok at that time, so we decided to put Huma in All Saints' School in Nainital where Feroze's wife was teaching. I was all set. I moved into the flat that Idrak had taken for us in Nizamuddin West before leaving for Bangkok. My brother Khalid and my brother-in-law Feroze, both were working in Delhi and moved into that flat. I was eagerly waiting for the summer holidays to start when I would join Idrak in Bangkok. In those days, University of Delhi's colleges closed on May 1 for the long holidays, so Idrak had booked for me to fly to Bangkok on an early morning flight on May 1 itself. On April 30, at 6 in the evening, I got a letter from Mr Beg informing me that my services had been terminated. He did not have to give any reason for the termination because though I was appointed on a permanent post, the first year was regarded as a probationary year. It came as a shock to me because I was a popular teacher, my students adored me, and my relationship with the staff was very cordial. Obviously, my crime was that I had married a non-Muslim. I was flying to Bangkok in a few hours after receiving the termination notice; there were neither any email facilities then, nor were telephones common. I had no telephone and so did Idrak at his residence in Bangkok. It would have been nighttime in Bangkok, so I could not call him in office either. There was no way to consult him. I was angry and disappointed but what could I have done? There was no feminist movement to appeal to either, so I accepted my fate and flew away to my husband. To this day, when I think of that precious moment when I arrived at the Bangkok Airport and saw Idrak waiting so eagerly to receive me—looking young and handsome, wearing a new suit and fancy shoes—I feel no regret in not delaying our reunion. He approved of my decision to just accept and forget about it. But nevertheless, it was a setback for me.

I enjoyed my stay in Bangkok immensely. For once in my life, I had money to spend; Idrak took me to a huge Thai store and told me to buy whatever I fancied without looking at the price tag. I was so touched by his generosity and desire to make me feel happy. I liked socializing and there were plenty of occasions to do so with the prosperous, leisurely UN wives, who had organized themselves into an association which held parties and programs regularly. I met an old friend of mine, Krishna, from the London days whose husband was also posted in Bangkok and we did a lot of things together. On the whole, I had a dream time there. What an extended honeymoon it was! I also conceived my second child Kiran there, which delighted Idrak to no end and returned to Delhi as a happy, expecting couple, loaded with gifts for friends and relatives and, of course, for Huma.

Setting up Home with the In-laws

Idrak had talked to me about bringing his parents to live with us as they were too old to run the farm. I did not object to his plan as my widowed grandmother used to live with us and was a great help to my mother in running the household. Idrak had also assured me that since his mother loved him very much, she would extend that love to me too. It was decided that the parents would sell the farm and move to Delhi. Idrak's parents, in their own way, were devout Christians. His father had retired as the General Secretary of the National Christian Council of India and had also represented the Indian Christians at the Constituent Assembly of India. He had founded a welfare organization called the Christian Association for Social Action (CASA) and had actively participated—along with Idrak—in the rehabilitation of refugees after the horrible post-independence Hindu–Muslim riots. Papa was regarded as a broad-minded, distinguished member of the Indian Christian community. He was also responsible for uniting the various sectoral churches of India into unified churches called the Church of North India and the Church of South India. He did not approve of the exclusiveness of the Indian Christian community and had voted against reservation for Christians. All this impressed me greatly and I felt assured that I had married into a liberal, broad-minded family.

Idrak had not told me that his mother had adopted Pentecostalism, a Christian sect of very extreme views who were very exclusive. Although papa was often embarrassed by his wife's extreme religious behavior, he did not interfere. When they were looking for a buyer for their farm, one of mamma's Pentecostal brothers offered to buy it to run a home for abandoned children. The idea appealed to the family and it was sold to him for a pittance and both parents moved in with us. They found it rather stifling to live in a small flat after having lived on a spacious 80-acre farm. They brought their old and very faithful servant, Yusuf, with them. Everyone called him Baba. He was the most wonderful human being I have known besides being a good cook. He was a great help and support to me.

My mother-in-law was a very strong and bitter person. She did not like her husband and had depended a great deal on Idrak, who had remained a bachelor until the age of 39 and was the apple of her eye. Although, initially she did not object to Idrak marrying me, probably hoping that I will turn into a fanatical Christian like her, when she found that I continued to associate with my family and friends as before, she resented it and expressed her resentment in no uncertain ways. In fact, she almost hated me and could not stand the sight of me. She became extremely jealous of Idrak's affection for me and Huma. Seeing her attitude toward me and my child, I decided to let Huma continue in the boarding school in Nainital. We did not want Huma to be exposed to my mother-in-law's hostile behavior. We were living on only Idrak's salary—since I had lost my job—and could hardly afford to keep her in an expensive hostel but Idrak, after assessing the situation and in his commitment to protect Huma, willingly agreed to my decision.

However, I was as shocked at my mother-in-law's behavior toward me and my child as was Idrak. We did not know how to handle her. Here, I was looking forward to a happy, compatible marriage which was suddenly turning into a nightmare. Idrak loved his mother immensely and was committed to taking care of her and his father. She was not keeping good health and just then it was discovered that papa was suffering from cancer. So, I had two sick and hostile in-laws on my hands. Papa's behavior was that of indifference; he sort of passively accepted me but was kind to Huma which was a relief. I found myself surrounded by a hostile and unexpected environment in my own home. I was used to having my own home and running it as I liked for 12 years of my first marriage but now I was constrained at every step by my mother-in-law's whims and fancies. There were some genuine cultural differences in our lifestyles—I understood that—but despite that, I found it very disturbing to accept her frequent outbursts of disapproval and constant loud emotionally charged expressions of her faith. Her prayers consisted of strange jabbering, loudly uttered, which she called "talking in tongues" when she was believed to have been overtaken by the Spirit of Christ. She was constantly visited by her Brothers in Faith, who would pray with her in a similar fashion and extract money from her. Idrak was spared of all this strange behavior as he was in office most of the day but I was at home all the time, having lost my job and being pregnant with Nikki. She disliked my Muslim friends and relatives and did not welcome them. I also found that Idrak did not disapprove of her and regarded her strange form of religion as her individual right to practice what she liked.

Till then, I was ignorant of the various Christian sects and the differences between them. I was impressed by Christianity and its concepts of love, forgiveness, and compassion for human beings had appealed to me greatly. I was particularly impressed by Christ being the most loving and forgiving spiritual entity, as opposed to our Allah, who was projected to us since our childhood as stern and unforgiving and severely punished erring human beings. We, as children, were taught to fear Hell which was full of burning fires and demons and Allah would send us to Hell if we faltered. So, I distanced myself from the version of Islam that had been taught and felt comforted by the way Christ was projected to me. I regarded Christian teachings as most humane and peace-loving. Idrak had also always emphasized these basic tenets of Christianity and himself showed these Christian qualities in his behavior. He was very loving toward everyone, very generous, compassionate, self-effacing, and always gave benefit of doubt to others. He was very good to my parents and siblings and to my friends, without making them feel that they were any different from him and certainly in no way inferior. But I found that these qualities hardly showed in mamma's behavior except in her professing her religion by shouting "Praise the Lord" several times in a day and keeping Bible close to her. To some extent, I understood her resentment against me because I had all the possible disadvantages as a daughter-in-law that she could think of. I was divorced (she herself had lived with a husband whom she had disliked from the very first night that she met him—as admitted to one of her daughters-in-law—without divorcing him), I had a child from another husband and, above all, I had grown up in a Muslim family who, according to her, were spiritually inferior. I could not help but notice the contradictions in her. I also began experiencing such contradictions in Idrak's other relatives too, most of whom (not all) lived fairly secluded lives, restricting their interactions within the community itself. It is observed worldwide that smaller a community living in a culturally and socially different dominant society, the more it develops the tendency to stick together. I had an idealistic view of Christians whom I considered more loving, compassionate, and broad-minded, but to my dismay, I found that my perceptions were more coated by idealism than reality. Besides, somehow I had not given any thought to the cultural differences which would be exhibited in our day-to-day life and in culturally different perceptions of situations. After all, I was marrying not only into another religious community but also outside my region. I had not had any contact with Punjabis until I met Idrak, whose habits and lifestyle, including the language he spoke, was more like a Lucknowi Muslim than a Punjabi. His food habits were so unlike the Punjabis. He did not eat yoghurt and did not like dishes such as *rajma*[5] or *chhole*[6]. Idrak's mother was more Punjabi in her taste and so were some of his relatives. I still remember an instance when Idrak's Punjabi brother-in-law visited us. It was tea time so I offered him tea and some biscuits. I had taken pains to arrange the biscuits rather aesthetically to make them look attractive. Our brother–in-law did not touch the biscuits so I urged him to take a few. He angrily replied, "Stop urging me to take a few, you have brought such few biscuits and asking me to take some." He totally ignored the way the biscuits were arranged; he'd expected them to be overflowing the plate. Another time, soon after we were married, my mother-in-law invited her cousin for lunch. She was an elderly person like mamma, so keeping that in mind, I decided not to serve heavy greasy food. Our *khansaman*[7] used to make a very special bread called *sheermal*,[8] so I decided to serve that along with chicken curry, *shami kebab*[9] and a mixed vegetable. Since the *sheermal* was fried, I decided to serve plain rice, thinking that biryani[10] and *sheermal* would have been too heavy for the two elderly ladies. But my mother-in-law took it amiss. She complained to Idrak that I had humiliated her cousin by serving "plain" rice. I did not know then that Punjabis do not relish plain rice. Instances like these kept happening but I was able to handle them as I understood that some cultural differences were inevitable. What did make me a little sad was that the expectations were only from me to adjust, no consideration was given to my background. That reflected the strong patriarchal thinking to

[5] Red kidney beans.
[6] Chick peas.
[7] Male Cook.
[8] Saffron flavored traditional flatbread.
[9] One of the varieties of kebabs.
[10] Asian dish made from rice with meat.

which even Indian Christians were subjected to. After knowing the two Indian communities—Muslims and Christians—from inside, which I regard as an unusual privilege, I have come to the conclusion that scratch the skin and all Indians are the same. Religion is only a coating. There are exceptions as there are always genuinely spiritual persons everywhere but on an average, human beings, without knowing and understanding the religious texts, use it as a shield for their human frailties.

My domestic life was dominated by my mother-in-law's whims and fancies, her constant disapproval of me, her emotional outbursts, and the bitterness that she carried. I often wondered what was the cause of her bitterness. I did notice, very rarely, glimpses of a witty and affectionate person in her, especially when she was with her sons. I appreciated her as a mother. She had brought up three wonderful sons who had a deep sense of commitment and were men of integrity. They doted on her and her husband was quite fond of her too. I was at a loss to understand her dissatisfaction with life. I was also intrigued at the fact that mamma's other two sisters, the older and the younger, were medical doctors but mamma had been married only after intermediate. It was only a few years ago, during my visit to Lahore where I stayed with Talat, a cousin of Idrak, that I found out the reason for her almost shattered personality. Talat, Idrak's cousin in Lahore, told me that my mother-in-law had a love affair with Talat's uncle. They were madly in love with each other; he was a fine young man but did not have a regular job and my mother-in-laws' parents did not approve of him. So, to cut the love affair short, they hurriedly married her off to a man she did not even know and from the very first day developed a dislike to. Mamma's feelings for her lover were very strong and were reciprocated to such an extent by her lover that he never married. Mamma herself could not reconcile to her marriage, but as was the custom in those days, she did live out her married life with papa. Had Idrak told me this sad story, I may have found it easier to bear with her. But either Idrak did not know or chose not to tell me.

However, I started accepting these unexpectedly unhappy aspects of my personal life as well and as long as I had the support of my husband, I was able to cope with the unpleasantness created by his mother. I realized that it was even harder for Idrak as he tried his best to please both of us. Then, Kiran's arrival brought a lot of cheer in the family. Kiran was a beautiful child with a very sweet face. She was a delightfully charming baby. Although my mother-in-law and even Idrak had looked forward to having a son, to me Kiran signified the flowering of our love. Once Kiran was born, they accepted her wholeheartedly. In fact, they doted on her. Even the old servant Yusuf was delighted and took care of her most lovingly. So, Kiran received a great deal of love from the family.

"Son Worship" in India

To my surprise, even the Indian Christians like other Indians, particularly Indian Muslims, valued fair complexion. I was also surprised to learn that "son worship" among Indian Christians was as acute as among other Indian communities. I had expected that Christians, being more educated and not having any prejudice toward women working outside the home, would be more broad-minded but this characteristic of being Indian did not escape the Christian community either.

When I was expecting my third child, I already had two daughters, one each from my two husbands. One day, my mother-in-law said to Kiran who was then an innocent two-year-old, "Tell your mother that if she produces another daughter, she should leave her in the hospital and not bring her home." I was quite shocked by her remark as I had thought that preference for sons was a peculiarity of Hindus and Muslims only. As luck would have it, my mother-in-law died two weeks before my third daughter, Nikki was born, who was not as fair as Kiran but has now grown up into a stunningly beautiful woman. Fortunately, my husband and his immediate relatives welcomed her as they would have welcomed a son. In fact, Idrak's younger brother had three sons and was yearning for a daughter. They tried for the fourth time and luckily he had a daughter whom he pampered a lot.

It is amazing to see how much a male is valued against a female in our society and despite an increase in female education and women's liberation movements, not much change has taken place. The incidence of growing female feticide is a witness to this extreme form of gender discrimination. As late as 1968, when my third daughter was born in a hospital in Delhi, I experienced this discrimination. There were no ultrasound devices available at that time, so the sex of the fetus was not known beforehand. The moment my baby was born, I enquired about its sex. I noticed a complete hush in the delivery room and my repeated queries were received with silence. Finally, when I was taken to the ward, the doctor came to my side, affectionately pressed my hand and said in a low voice (as if she was about to deliver a death sentence) that I had given birth to a daughter. I was furious at her attitude. Pushing her hand away, I asked, "Have I not given birth to a human child? You are behaving as if I have produced a monster." She was embarrassed and replied that mothers generally break down at the birth of a girl, some even refuse to take the baby home, so she had to be cautious. I had to convince her that my baby girl was as important to us as a boy and at the same time thanking God that my mother-in-law was not alive. On my return home from hospital, my neighbors did not congratulate me. Some even tried to avoid me if by chance we met on the road. When I would encounter them and tell them that I had a baby girl, they would say, "I'm sorry Mrs Bhatty, to hear that you had another daughter."

However, I realized that I had to accept my husband's feelings for his parents. They were old, infirm, and needed to be looked after, so I accepted the situation and tried my best. There were silver linings in that situation too. Idrak, being an academic, often discussed research projects of his office with me and informed me of seminars relevant to my interests, which I sometimes attended. This enabled me to keep my mind alert. It was not feasible for me to get back to a full-time job but I managed to get back to broadcasting. I managed to get a foot into the AIR easily on account of my experience with BBC, London. In addition to broadcasting talks and participating in panel discussions on social issues, I would also conceptualize and script design, write and produce short programs on current issues, especially those dealing with women's problems. Such occasional opportunities to get out of the house and interact with like-minded people provided a welcome relief for me from domestic chores.

Kiran was growing up as the most delightful child, loved by all. Huma had been demanding a baby sister so she was delighted when Kiran arrived. Huma, being in hostel in Nainital, would have only a week's holiday in summer and 10 weeks holiday in winter, when she would be home. However, during winter holidays, Huma's father—Hayat—would take her to his village for a month. Idrak and I had decided that she should keep in touch with her father, although he did not contribute anything financially toward her upkeep or education. Idrak happily took care of her in every way. Since under those circumstances Huma had very little time to be with Kiran, we decided to shift her to La Martiniere in Lucknow. My parents and siblings lived in Lucknow, so Huma was able to enjoy their love and affection. They visited her every week as her local guardian. I also visited Lucknow at least twice a year or more, so Huma was able to see Kiran more often than was possible when she was in Nainital. This helped in forging a stronger bond between them.

My mother-in-law continued to dislike me and could not bear Huma's presence when she came home from hostel. During one such visit, mamma said many unkind things about us and threatened to move out and live with a Christian neighbor. Idrak, though he felt extremely unhappy, did not stop her, saying that he had a commitment to Huma and would not distance himself from her. Feroze, my youngest brother-in-law, and his family were living with us in our flat in the *barsati*[11] upstairs, so finally it was decided that they would take a flat nearby and both my in-laws would move with them. Feroze's wife, Margarette, belonged to a Christian family. She was mamma's favorite, although Margarette had turned into a Rationalist and did not practice Christianity or bring up her children as Christians. Papa's health was falling and after a few months of moving, he succumbed to cancer.

Every evening after returning from office, Idrak would take me and Kiran to visit mamma, come rain or storm. There, mamma would play with Kiran and talk to her son, ignoring me totally. I would serve her whatever dinner would be there and return to our flat in Nizamuddin. Every Sunday, she would come to us. I used to dread Sundays. By then, we were already married for three years. After Papa's death, Idrak became more protective of his mother which was natural on his part. She came to live with us again. She was getting older and not keeping well, and passed away after moving back with us. This ended one difficult phase of my personal life. Looking back, I now feel that mamma herself was a victim of our gender discriminatory culture where a woman can not even choose her life partner.

However, after both parents were gone, Idrak assumed the responsibility of being the eldest in the family which included, among other things, defending his faith. He started going to church regularly. Kiran was baptized during mamma's lifetime and even Nikki, who was born after mamma had passed away, was baptized in the Methodist Church. I found that Idrak now desired to establish more overtly that ours, or rather his, (he had started acting like more of a patriarch) was a Christian household. He turned into a more conscious Christian and liked me to accompany him to church. Our two little daughters were sent to Sunday School. He also hinted that I might like to

[11] A small rooftop room on the terrace with a veranda outside.

baptize Huma but I did not want to do so for two reasons. First, for the fear of losing her as her father would have definitely objected and would have asked for her custody. Second, I was not convinced that such formalities were all that important. Fortunately, Idrak neither changed his attitude toward Huma nor forced me to be a conventional Christian. But this change in him came as a surprise to me and was often a source of friction between us. But we all enjoyed celebrating Christmas with gusto and included the children of the neighborhood too in our festivities.

Mussoorie

During the first three years of our married life, while my in-laws were living with us, we did not holiday anywhere. Their unfriendly attitude toward me, their illness and then their passing away had put us under a great deal of stress. After mamma passed away—two years after papa's death—a good friend of ours, Ram Singh, suggested that we must take a break and go somewhere for a holiday. I was not much inclined to travel with two small children as Kiran was just about 3 years old and Nikki was only six months old. Also, carrying them with bottles and nappies would not have been much fun. But Ram Singh suggested that we go to Mussoorie for the summer and he would hire a cottage for us. Ram Singh's wife was an American and lived in Mussoorie where their three boys went to the American Woodstock School. Woodstock is situated in an area called Landour near Mussoorie. It is beautifully wooded and secluded from the main town. Landour has a cantonment which has prohibited any commercialization. As a result of this, the area has remained woody and lush green, unaffected by the fast-growing population of tourists. So in the summer of 1969, we hired a cute little cottage called "Uncle Tom's Cabin." We took our dog, Pappu, and our cook, Baba, along as well. We also invited our friend, Vaidyanathan, and his wife and two daughters who were close to Huma's age, to go with us. Idrak was familiar with Mussoorie as he used go there in his childhood with his parents. In those days, hardly anyone took cars or motorcycles there as everyone walked. I remember walking up to our cottage carrying 6-month-old Nikki in my arms from the bus stop. Nowadays, no one wants to walk. Most Mussoorie residents have some vehicle. The tourists also go up in their big cars. But thanks to the cantonment policy of restricting commercialization and even building of residential houses because of which Landour has remained almost as peaceful as it was in 1967, when I went to Mussoorie for the first time.

That summer, we had a wonderful time and I liked Mussoorie so much that we started hiring a place there every summer for the next few years. The American and English missionaries resided almost exclusively in Landour. Various missions owned property there. The Woodstock School—which is now over a hundred and fifty years old—was established for the children of foreign missionaries. The school follows the American and British system of education to facilitate the children to move to their home country for college education. In those days, the school admitted very few Indian students, mostly those from the princely class. Every summer, a few cottages were made available for rent as the foreign missionary families would go on furlough to their respective countries. We would take advantage of that situation and with the help of Ram Singh, who identified for us the cottages which would be available for renting, we would book one in advance. So, we lived in about half a dozen different cottages in Mussoorie before we managed to buy one. After India's independence, missionary activity reduced considerably, so the mission-owned property in Landour became redundant and a number of houses were put up for sale.

We put in an acquisition to buy one. The prices of properties were then nowhere as high as they have become now, so we reckoned that we could afford a small cottage. We did not have a choice as to which cottage we wanted as preference, understandably, was given to Indians working for Christian organizations. However, the Presbyterian Mission decided to sell one of their cottages to us, named "Woodside," a largish property that had a fabulous view of the entire valley below. We grabbed the place. As luck would have it, just prior to the allotment of "Woodside", my husband got a UN assignment which provided the money to purchase and renovate it. It is a 200-years-old house, solidly built. It was built by a Reverend Woodside. "Woodside" is situated just above Woodstock School, surrounded by silver oak and pine trees, away from the now heavily crowded roads on both sides. Its distance from the roads attracted us as it provided privacy and a noise-free environment. We had no other place of our own in Delhi or elsewhere, as Idrak's father had sold his 80-acre farm near Nagpur. Both my in-laws were devout Christians and believed that God will provide for their sons.

We were young when we bought "Woodside"—nearly 40 years ago—but now in our old age, we find it difficult to negotiate the path.

We have found an answer and we climb down both ways from the road which is less strenuous than climbing up. Our daughters and grandchildren love it too and find it a good exercise to climb up. We retired there. We almost completely renovated it and it is now one of the most beautiful eight-bedroom houses in Landour. We feel very privileged to have it and enjoy our old age here. I still live here on my own. The grandchildren enjoy having holidays at "Woodside." We have kept it an "open" house and our friends and relatives keep visiting us. Our daughter Huma as well as our nephew and a friend's son even spent their honeymoon at "Woodside," as it is very private and has the most fabulous view of the entire valley of Dehradun.

My Association with the YWCA

After my in-laws died, I had a little more time at my disposal. So, I joined the Young Women's Christian Association (YWCA) of India. Actually, I was drawn into it by chance. Miss Ivy Khan was the General Secretary of the national YWCA at that time. She was a very intelligent and competent person, totally devoted to the "Y." I still remember seeing her for the first time. Idrak and I had gone to the YWCA guest house which was in the same compound as her office. I was pregnant with Kiran at that time. Ivy came out of her office wearing a red sari, looking very smart and efficient, saw us and said in her broken Hindi (she was a Bengali) "Idrak, good to see you, I hear you have got married (he had remained a bachelor for so long that the news of his succumbing to marriage had spread) and *baap re*[12] what a *sundar*[13] wife you have got." Then she turned to me and said, "When this (gesturing toward my swollen tummy) is over, come and see me." I did as she had asked and when Kiran was a few months old, I started going to the "Y" for a couple of hours, two or three days a week. Ivy always had something to do for me. I enjoyed my association with the "Y" and particularly liked interacting with Ivy. I owe a lot to her. She taught me a great deal about the women's movement, not only in India but internationally, and about volunteerism. I even learnt how to dress gracefully. She had very good taste in clothes and ran the "Y" with much grace and sophistication. It was my first experience with a voluntary organization and I learnt much because of this association.

---

[12] Oh father! An expression of astonishment.

[13] Beautiful.

It provided an opportunity to me to get out of the house and use my education for something productive.

Once when a YWCA National Conference was going to be held, Ivy entrusted me with the task of preparing the workbook for the conference. This gave me an opportunity to learn all about the "Y" movement and the issues that the organization was dealing with world over and India, in particular. I enormously enjoyed my work. It was unpaid but challenging. Ivy, who had an eye for spotting talent, had me nominated to the National Executive and when elections took place at the National Conference held in Nagpur—I think in 1967—I was elected to the National Executive. I occupied various positions in the "Y" during my long association with it for over 35 years, including the presidentship of the Delhi YWCA. Ivy was a good administrator, very broad-minded, and secular. She made many changes during her tenure, which lasted almost a quarter of a century. She opened the "Y" to non-Christians and tried to bring it out of its very closed, almost claustrophobic, existence. She realized that in order to be a force for social change, the "Y" must be a part of the wider Indian society, without of course, losing its base in Christian faith. She believed it was important and possible to address Indian women's issues even within the confines of Christian ideology. Therefore, it should not be limited to Christian women only. She faced a great deal of opposition, especially from the more orthodox sections of the Christian community who feared that by opening its doors to non-Christians, the "Y" would lose its Christian character. Ivy tried to counter such fears. Earlier, one had to be a baptized Christian and sign a declaration accepting Christ being the leading light of the movement and produce a Baptismal Certificate to prove their Christian identity. Ivy did away with this condition and had it established that even a non-baptized person could be nominated if she accepted the basis of the movement in Christianity. Thus, a few non-baptized members were accepted in the National Executive Committee which made "Y" richer in expertise and experiences. Some of these nominated members made very useful contributions to the movement. Ivy had won this right after a long battle with the orthodox Christian section. The YWCA was, and to a large extent, continues to be dominated by Kerala Christians who are not only much larger in numbers but also richer and culturally more conservative. However, she did not succeed in getting the non-Christian nominated members any voting rights to be a member of any decision-making body in the "Y."

During my association with the YWCA, I had the opportunity of meeting women from different parts of India. The "Y" has 85 local associations in India. Each one is independent and deals with local issues. I often travelled and attended the meetings of local associations. These occasions enriched my range of experiences enormously and led to a greater understanding of human behavior across religious beliefs. I was struck by the tenacity of Indian culture which had impacted all Indian communities across regions and religions. I was surprised to find that among Kerala Christians, the rate of dowry was highest and even the church, instead of discouraging this heinous practice, accepted 1 per cent of the dowry. Christian women, despite being educated, played a subservient role within the family. The Indian Christian Personal Law continues to be gender discriminatory. Although Indian Christians do not practice caste system like the Hindus, they too avoid physical contact with untouchables who have not converted into Christianity. Caste consciousness and status awareness is very strong among them. The lower class Christians, believed to have converted from lower Hindu castes, are referred to derogatorily as typical native Christians (TNCs).

I once had the privilege of actually interacting with Prime Minister Indira Gandhi, when I, as President of Delhi YWCA, escorted her to the "Y" Annual Flower Show. She used to visit the flower show—the best in town—every year. But the year I was the president, I was informed that the prime minister regretted that due to a busy schedule that day, she was unable to grace the show. I was naturally very disappointed. Then, around lunchtime, I suddenly heard an announcement, "Please, Mrs Bhatty, come to the main gate immediately as the PM has arrived." I rushed to the gate and found a beaming Indira Gandhi saying that she just could not resist coming as she loved flowers, so she decided to use her lunch break. In my excitement, I managed to mumble whatever I considered an appropriate response to her graciousness. But, she immediately put me at ease in her usual style. Indira Gandhi had this amazing capacity to change roles instantly. There was the Prime Minister of our vast and complex country walking with a humble volunteer, totally relaxed and chatting away like an aunt next door. She told me that flowers were like children, they had to be nurtured lovingly and that she was trying to instill the love of nature in her grandchildren too. To that I mumbled, "Madam…." She interjected and said, "Don't address me as Madam; Mrs Gandhi is good enough." I resumed, "Maybe Priyanka and Rahul would have enjoyed accompanying you." "Oh yes, they wanted to come," she said, "but I had to discipline them. You see, they had been missing their tuition for the last three days on some pretext or the other, so I had to be strict and told them that they have to have their lessons today. The tutor will not be sent back again."

She visited each and every stall and exchanged a few sentences with each stall holder. A security person must have followed her but so unobtrusively that I did not notice him. Next morning, I read in the papers that Mrs Gandhi went straight to a cabinet meeting from the flower show, where she made important decisions, some not very popular though.

Another example of Mrs Indira Gandhi's down-to-earth personality was that she liked to dress up and had a fabulous collection of saris. It so happened that in those days, a particular weave of Bangladeshi saris called Jamdani were very sought after in India. Jamdani saris were not easily available in India and were very expensive due to heavy duty on their import. Idrak happened to go to Dhaka on a six-month UN assignment. I did not accompany him as our children were still in school and their studies would have been interrupted. But for me and for my close relatives and friends, it was a golden opportunity to acquire Jamdani sarees. So whenever he came to India—which he did every other month—he brought these saris. Fortunately, he had a good taste too. Around that time, my colleague at JMC, Vatsala, was getting married. Huma and Kiran had just started wearing saris on important occasions, so they also wore Jamdanis at Vatsala's wedding. Vatsala was closely related to Mrs Gandhi and Mrs Gandhi had come to the wedding with both her daughters-in-law. She participated enthusiastically in the wedding and in its rituals, including singing Kashmiri folk songs along with other relatives. Both Huma and I were showing off our Jamdanis. It so happened that Sonia Gandhi was also wearing a Jamdani exactly like Huma's but Huma's sari had a better color combination. We were so amused to notice that Mrs Gandhi kept staring at us, as if wondering "How come someone else managed to get a better Jamdani than us?" I found that aspect of her character rather charming.

Talking of Jamdani saris, I must relate another interesting aspect of how important decisions at the highest government levels are sometimes taken on purely human grounds. Some years after my husband's posting in Dhaka, he was invite for an international conference there. Being a member of the conference's steering committee, he went to

Dhaka a couple of days before it had started. This time, I accompanied him and decided to shop—particularly for Jamdanis—before the conference started. Almost all the Indian delegates had orders from their wives to get Jamdanis. So I was tasked to guide them in choosing the saris. It was decided that the next morning, we would miss a session and quietly slip out. After breakfast, my friends changed their dollars to *takas*[14] and we were about to leave when suddenly, we heard gunshots and loud noises. A coup had taken place in Dhaka and President Irshad had been deposed. There was sheer chaos in the city and we were advised not to stir out of the hotel. Next day, the conference was called off and the curfew lifted for a couple of hours. The hotel we were lodged in was very expensive, so everyone tried to leave Dhaka and prepared to rush to the airport. But all foreign airlines—except Biman Bangla—to Delhi, had cancelled their flights. Luckily, we were booked in that so we took a taxi and headed toward the airport. Halfway to the airport, the taxi stopped as there was heavy stone-throwing on the streets, so the taxi driver refused to go further and dropped us on the road. There we were on the road, shivering in our boots, trying to shield ourselves from the stones being thrown around us by the angry mob. Just then, an auto-rickshaw approached us and offered to take us to the airport through the by-lanes, which he assured were safer. We decided to take his offer. Fortunately, we arrived safely at the airport and flew to Delhi in one piece. However, the long and short of it is that the Indian delegates who managed somehow to get out of Dhaka, returned without saris. They must have faced angry, disappointed wives, especially the one who had a Bengali wife. To add salt to the wounds, a friend of ours published an article on the Bangladesh coup and added that despite the coup, a delegate's wife had managed to buy Jamdani sarees!

It so happened that the following year, the delegate who had a Bengali wife was appointed the Economic Advisor to the Government of India, and in that capacity, he played a significant role in preparing that year's National Budget. To our amusement, we found that in the year's budget, the import duty on Jamdani saris had been lifted and those coveted saris became available in India also at a reasonable price.

The girls were growing up nicely. Idrak was the most loving and indulgent father while I was more of a disciplinarian. I was obsessed with the thought that I should prepare my daughters to face any

[14] The Bangladeshi currency.

problem in life and be strong women. We decided to give them a good education and a strong sense of human values, what Idrak termed as Christian values. We could not provide many luxuries as I was not working and he, being in an academic profession, was not highly paid. But even when he moved up in his profession, becoming the Director General of the National Council of Applied Economic Research (NCAER) and we could afford a higher standard of living, we did not spoil them and continued with a modest lifestyle. Huma, after passing Senior Cambridge (in those days English-medium schools had Senior Cambridge as the school-leaving certificate) joined JMC. The Senior Cambridge exam used to be held in December while college sessions began in July, so she had six months to wait before going to college. In order to keep her busy and to get used to the life in Delhi as she had until then lived outside Delhi—in a hostel in Nainital—I decided to enroll her in French classes and also in a stitching and cutting class. My mother had taught us some elementary stitching which I have found useful in mending clothes and thus reduced my dependence on tailors. So, Huma used those six months fruitfully and learnt to commute by buses. We discouraged our daughters from using a chauffeur-driven car, a privilege that my husband had as the Head of his organization at that time. In our way, we tried to make our daughters aware of the realities of life in India and not become upper-class snobs.

Kiran and Nikki went to a nursery school in Nizamuddin and later went to Mater Dei School which was the closest to our residence. Idrak was keen that the girls go to a Christian school and in those days, Christian schools provided a more wholesome education too. Later though, we shifted Kiran to Sardar Patel Vidyalaya after a strange, unhappy experience at Mater Dei. We often talked to our children about the importance of being helpful to others. We had also told them that there were two kinds of sins: sins of commission (when one deliberately does wrong) and sins of omission (if one turns away from someone who needs her help). One morning, as Nikki got out of her school bus at the school, she found that her best friend had not gone inside as she was feeling unwell. Both her parents were working and used to leave the house early in the morning. So, she could not go back home as her parents would not be there. Nikki decided to bring her over to our house where my husband could take her to a doctor. But she did not take the school principal's permission. This was a mistake. Some girl saw Nikki and her friend getting into an auto-rickshaw and going away from the school. The principal suspected that they had probably bunked to have fun. The next morning she called Nikki and punished her severely by suspending her. Nikki came home very upset, so my husband sent a note to the principal, explaining the circumstances under which Nikki had taken her friend to our house and apologized on her behalf. But the principal refused to accept my husband's apology and said that she did not trust her father as he was a bad man since he had married a divorced woman and she did not take back her suspension order. We were absolutely shocked at the nun's behavior and Idrak decided to complain to the bishop but found the bishop unwilling to intervene.

In those days, it was so difficult to get a child admitted in a good school. We then approached our friend who was the principal of St. Thomas's School. To our utter disappointment, she also showed reluctance to admit Nikki. We, in any case, did not want any of our daughters to continue in a school that was so backward in social attitudes. Finally, I talked to my principal at JMC—a senior nun of the same order who was broad-minded and liked me—to intervene. She was quite unhappy at the Mater Dei's principal's action and managed to persuade her to remove the suspension order and allow Nikki to continue. Such socially backward attitudes prevailed even in educational institutions in India, as late as the 1970s. However, we did withdraw Kiran from Mater Dei and got her admitted in Sardar Patel Vidyalaya. We would have removed Nikki from Mater Dei too, but she was refused admission in Sardar Patel, as unfortunately, she failed the Hindi test. When I mentioned this incidence to Ivy Khan—the General Secretary of the YWCA—she told me that until the late 1970s, the "Y" had a similar attitude toward divorced women and did not allow them to hold any official position. No one gave a thought to the fact that divorce takes place between two persons, a man and a woman. Divorced men did not have to suffer such stigma. No wonder, I turned into a feminist. Fortunately, such attitudes toward divorced women do not exist now, at least not to the same extent.

11

Awakening to Feminism

The seeds of feminism, when I think back, were sowed in my psyche when I read the book *The Second Sex* by French writer, Simone De Beauvoir, way back in my early 20s. I remember being hugely influenced by it, although at that time, I did not find avenues to articulate my feelings. It was then that I also realized that my poet uncle Majaz was a feminist too, although at that time the word "feminist" was not much known in India. Some of his poems like "Purdah Aur Ismat" (Seclusion and female virtue), "Naujawan Khatoon Se" (To a young woman), and "Kisse Mohabbat Hai" (Whom do I love) had influenced me a great deal. In these poems, written in the 1930s, uncle Majaz lauded a woman's contribution to society and urged them to walk and work alongside with men, a concept almost unknown at that time.

In India, women's emancipation started with the freedom movement. For the first time, they came out of their homes and participated, along with men, in the independence movement. Leaders like Mahatma Gandhi and Pandit Jawaharlal Nehru encouraged and appreciated their contribution to the movement. When the constitution was framed for the newly established Republic of India, women found their rightful place in it and were granted equality to men as full-fledged Indian citizens. Indian women were happy to have achieved constitutional equality and a kind of complacency prevailed in the post-independence years despite almost zero impact of the newly acquired rights on women's everyday lives.

In 1973, the United Nations decided to focus on the developmental issues in developing countries. In order to give a boost to development in these countries, it had decided to devote a whole year to understand, assess and promote balanced gender-equitable development. For this purpose, it was decided to dedicate a year each to different developmental aspects such as women, literacy, family planning, etc. UN declared 1975 as the Year for Women and an international conference on this subject took place in the summer of 1975 in Mexico City. Prior to the conference, the UN requested all member countries to submit to it a report on the status of women in their country. In India, until then, no comprehensive study had taken place about the situation of women. The general public and even the government assumed that women were fine as they had been guaranteed constitutional gender equality. However, to meet the UN requirement, a detailed report had to be prepared. The task of preparing the report was entrusted to the newly formed Indian Council of Social Science Research (ICSSR). Fortunately, the council was headed by Mr J.P. Naik, a well-known and highly respected freedom fighter and a reputed social scientist with secular credentials. A committee of seven women members was formed to investigate the status of women in India and to prepare a detailed report for submission to the UN. The committee members were selected from different disciplines and it was headed by Mrs Phul Renu Guha, a dedicated social worker from Bengal and a member of Parliament at that time. Dr Veena Mazumdar—a political scientist and the most dynamic and outspoken personality—was appointed as Secretary to the committee. The committee did an excellent job. The members travelled to all parts of India, interviewed women and men across caste, class, religion, and region. It compiled the most comprehensive, unbiased document on the status of women in free India which was made public in 1974. The report jolted and almost shocked the public, the government, and the policy-makers. It exposed the poor plight of women across the country who were living in an archaic, traditional, harshly patriarchal social structure. The political freedom of the country and a democratic, socially just constitution—which guaranteed gender equality—had not made any significant impact on women's condition in India. They lagged behind men in all important development indicators, such as, education, health, and employment. The first census after India's independence showed that the male–female ratio in India had dipped even lower than what it was in the pre-independence decade. This led to a serious rethinking of women's place in independent India.

After the publication of the report, seminars and workshops started taking place on women's issues. Newspapers and journals also highlighted women's concerns. The journal, *Seminar,* devoted an entire issue to the status of women in India and requested me to write the lead article. How the choice fell on me, I am still intrigued. However, it led me to think seriously about women's plight and their status in society. Until then, I had only been an angry young woman, unhappy at my own and other women's plight in my country. This offer led me to look deeply into this most prevailing social malaise. I remember I made a premise that the gender injustice basically expressed itself in the fact that on the one hand, society ascribed a fixed role to women and on the other, placed zero value on that role. So, women were viewed as a social liability rather than an asset to family and society. Both their roles, reproductive and productive, were not assigned any value. This point somehow clicked. The seminar had nationwide circulation, especially among the educated, and my name became familiar among the educated elites. There was a US diplomat's wife by the name of Mary Hainey, who was familiar with the feminist movement in her own country and used to attend various seminars, etc., on women which took place in Delhi. Mary and I vibed together and became friendly.

In 1975, I was still working as a lecturer at the JMC on an ad hoc basis. As I have mentioned, the then Head of the Department of Sociology—Professor Srinivas—who had the casting vote, would not let my appointment come through.

It was June 1975. I was sweating away in the college library as a temporary lecturer, assisting in the library stock-taking, when the college peon handed me a large envelope addressed to me from the State Department of the United States of America's government, Washington D.C. I looked at it twice before opening. I could not think why the government of the USA would communicate with me. I had neither visited the US nor knew any American except my new acquaintance. The contents of the envelope further surprised me as it contained an invitation to participate in a travel seminar in the USA to familiarize myself, along with 21 other women chosen, one each from 21 countries. Wow, what an opportunity! I was dazed. It took some time for the mind to register. So, I immediately called my American friend Mary Hainey, the only American I knew in Delhi. I told her about the invitation and she blurted out, "Oh my God, it is a mistake. You should not have received it." "Why not, it is addressed to me and sent at the right address," I replied. She said,

"Come to me at once and I shall explain everything to you." So I went over to her place; she lived close to my college. She told me that according to the bilateral agreement between the Government of India and the Government of USA, neither of the two governments could invite nor identify an individual to officially represent the other without the prior permission of the individual's government. By sending an official invitation naming a person—in this case me—the United States government had gone against the official protocol. Naming an official delegate was the prerogative of the home government. The lapse probably offended the Government of India and it could withheld the permission for me to attend. She accepted that she had suggested my name and had insisted that just any Indian woman should not be invited because most were not as well versed in women's issues as I was. Therefore, I could benefit more from that experience than a nominee who would probably have just been a relative or a friend of an Indian politician or a bureaucrat. The seminar was scheduled to start in another week's time and the Government of United States, assuming the Government of India's nod, had sent the invitation directly to me. Mary also explained to me that the bureaucratic process required approval from four ministries namely, Home, External Affairs, Finance, and Education, as well as an approval from the Vice Chancellor of University of Delhi who was required to seek an approval from the Head of the Department of Sociology. Thus, it would take a long time. The first seminar was on the topic of education and so my presence in it was essential. Therefore, it was too late and even if the request was reopened and the permission granted, there was not enough time for the lengthy bureaucratic process to be completed. She or the US Embassy, in any case, could not intervene as their intervention could further antagonize the Government of India. Therefore, the only possibility was that I, on my own, could use my resources to get the government's permission. But I did not have any heavyweight in the government to help me. How could I let go of such a golden opportunity without giving it at least a try? So, I asked if she could tell me which department the invitation had been sent to. She did tell me, although reluctantly, that it was lying with the Joint Secretary in the Ministry of External Affairs. Maybe I could meet him, without mentioning her name, and enquire about the reason for not approving my candidature. I came home and called the Joint Secretary's office and as always, his secretary asked me the purpose for my request. When I told him about the invitation, he refused to give me an appointment. My enthusiasm was crushed but I refused to give up hope. My husband thought it was crazy to even try. I felt unhappy, frustrated, and mad at the government's callousness. There did not seem to be any way that I could move the government and that too in such a short time.

A day later, I received a call from the secretary of the editor of *Femina*—a women's magazine—who wanted to meet me. I went over at the appointed time, 11 a.m., to her office in Delhi. It was a one-room office; the secretary was sitting at one end of the office and a middle-aged gentleman was on the other, browsing through a newspaper. As I arrived, the secretary apologized on behalf of the editor and informed me that the editor had unexpectedly been called to the PM's office at 11.a.m., although the meeting was scheduled for the afternoon. It so happened that Dr Radhakrishnan, the then President of India, had passed away that day and it was declared a public holiday, so Mrs Gandhi had changed her appointment with the editor. But if I could wait a while, the editor would very much like to meet me and discuss the possibility of me writing an article for *Femina* on women's issues. I decided to wait. It was all quiet in the room—a kind of an awkward silence—so I started a conversation with the secretary. During the conversation, I told her about this wonderful invitation that I had received and how the government was not responding. I can only describe this as divine intervention. The gentleman sitting at the other corner of the room was apparently listening to our conversation because he suddenly intervened and said, "Why is the government not giving you permission? You are highly qualified and would be a suitable woman to represent it. I shall help you." I did not know who he was. However, it turned out that he was the proprietor of a newspaper and a very influential person. How he knew and how much he knew about me, to this day, I have no clue. But he turned out to be a Godsend. In my presence, he called the Principal Secretary of the Ministry of External Affairs, Mr Dongre, and told him that he was sending one Zarina Bhatty and that he should do his best to help her. I could hear a very respectful "Yes, sir, yes sir" from the other end. He then told me to go straight to Mr Dongre, take my biodata along and not wait for the editor. He would tell the editor that he had interviewed me and that I should now concentrate on my visit to the USA.

I did precisely that. As I reached home, my daughter Huma told me that there was a call from Mr Teja's office, asking me to meet him at 10 the next morning. I could not believe that it was the same Mr Teja who had refused to see me a day earlier. Next morning, on the dot, I was in Mr Teja's office. I was ushered into the room and Mr Teja stood up to welcome me, shook hands with me warmly and requested me to take a seat. He then explained the entire situation and the reason for not responding to the invitation and said that once I got the required clearances from the concerned ministries on my own, he would be happy to hand over the invitation to me. The task was no less arduous than climbing Mt Everest. I did not even know where to start from but I was determined to give it a try and I did it singlehandedly. Luckily, the process had already begun at the Ministry of External Affairs which had sent its approval to the Ministry of Home Affairs the same day. The final approval had to come from them. But the Home Ministry required clearance from the Ministry of Education before finally clearing my application. The Ministry of Finance's approval was required to get the foreign exchange. That was to be the last and my husband knew the high-ups there, so that was not my headache. The real problem was the Education Ministry, which had to get approvals from the Head of the Sociology Department and the Vice Chancellor, as my employers. I knew Mr Shah would never clear my application. Even then, I did not give up and sought to meet the Education Minister, who at that time was Mr Nurul Hasan. I knew Nurul Hasan's family as he was from Lucknow and one of his cousins had taught me at the Karamat Husain Muslim Girls' College. As usual, I could not get an appointment with the minister but met his secretary, pleaded my case, and requested him to at least give my biodata to the minister before rejecting me. The secretary did give my biodata to the minister whose curiosity was aroused by my Muslim name and by Lucknow being my hometown. He made enquiries about me and my family. My family was well known in Lucknow and my reference to his cousin impressed him. He decided to forward my application to the University for the required clearances before taking the final decision himself. So, my fortune hinged on the approval from the University's authorities, namely Professor Shah and the VC. I again almost gave hope.

But call it destiny, God's will, or the confluence of stars which were determining my course of life, it so happened that I had a younger colleague, Kiran Nanda, at JMC who admired me a great deal and apparently had been praising me to her father and told him how the government was not allowing me to go to the USA. Her father worked in the Ministry of Education and dealt with the affairs of University of Delhi. As luck would have it, he was entrusted with the task of taking my application to the VC for approval. He also knew how Professor Shah was antagonistic to me and how I had feared that I may not get the clearance from him. So, when he took my application to the VC and the VC asked for it to be sent to Professor Shah as it was only after his approval that the VC would clear it, Mr Nanda butted in and advised the VC not to send it forward as there was very little time and the Department's Head was out of town. The VC, who fortunately knew me, agreed to clear my application on his own. Mr Nanda took VC's approval the same day to the Ministry of Education and made sure that their approval was sent to the Ministry of Home Affairs at once. The Home Ministry had no reason to raise any objections after having the clearances from the Ministry of External Affairs and the Ministry of Education. They promptly informed the United States Embassy in India that their invitation to Zarina Bhatty had been approved by the Government of India. All these procedures took four days, that is, Monday to Thursday. It was on Thursday afternoon that I got a call from the Chief of United States Information Agency (USIA) about having received the approval for me to travel to the US and that I must see him the next morning at 9:30 a.m. I was overjoyed but unless I did not leave India on the weekend, I would not be in Boston on time for the seminar on education. However, I went to see the Director of USIS, Mr Roche, the next morning. He received me cordially but said that I was asking for the impossible as I had only one working day to get a US visa and then the clearance for foreign exchange from the Ministry of Finance. Only then, he would sanction my travel to the USA. The US Embassy issued visa forms only until 11 a.m. and the visas were collected at 4 p.m. It was already 10 a.m. on Friday. How could I possibly manage to go to the Embassy, collect the form, fill it, bring it here for his sanction, and submit it to the Embassy by 11? I could see that the situation was hopeless. I also had to get a seat on the plane the next morning. The biggest optimists would have laughed at the situation and would have given up. But for me, the game was not over. The Private Secretary to the Director, USIS, was in the room listening to our conversation. He interjected and said that he always kept a few visa forms with him, so he could give me one which I could fill then and there and the Director could clear it and sign it and he—the Private Secretary—could immediately take the application with my valid passport and submit it to the Embassy. It was amazing since I did not know him at all and he on his own offered so much help. He also said that he would immediately book me a seat on the next morning's Pan Am flight on a priority basis, which he did then and there. I decided to forego the foreign exchange as I had friends in the US from whom I could borrow dollars. Mr Roche was the most cooperative but I still remember his remark, "Mrs Bhatty, it will be a miracle if you board the Pan Am flight tomorrow morning." The miracle did happen. I boarded the Pan Am flight on that fateful Saturday in July 1975 which changed my life.

My Maiden Visit to USA

This was going to be my maiden visit to the US. My enthusiasm knew no bounds. My family could not believe that it was happening. I quickly packed my bags, deciding above all, to show off my Kanjivaram saris as I had only a few left at that time. I pushed my suitcase under our bed before sleeping the previous night; I was still not fully convinced that I was really going to the USA and feared that my suitcase may be stolen or some other unforeseen hitch may occur. However, nothing unfortunate happened and I boarded the plane as scheduled but without any American money which did make me a little nervous. I again had a bit of good luck and met Mr and Mrs John Bissell of FabIndia on the plane. I had known them in Delhi and told them why and how I was going to the States. I also told them that I was travelling without any dollars, as I was hoping to get some from our friends in New York on arrival. I was also very nervous about arriving at the New York airport alone. I had been informed that someone from the US Department of External Affairs would meet me and settle me in the hotel and also give me a ticket to travel to Boston the next morning. The Bissells thought I ought to have some dollars for any eventuality and very kindly gave me US$100 which I could repay on my return to Delhi. I felt somewhat reassured. I managed to meet my escort at the airport who took me to a hotel. Once lodged in the hotel, I called Saeed, a close friend of my brother, in New York. Saeed came over and brought some food and some more dollars. So I was all set to fly to Boston the next morning to attend the most exciting and eagerly awaited seminar. Thus, began my journey into feminism.

The rest of the group had their briefing in Washington and had already arrived in Boston. It was truly an international group composed of women from Asia, Europe, and Africa, as well as a young woman from Kuwait. Generous hospitality was provided to us in terms of free food, lodging, and transport. On top of it, we were also given some dollars as pocket money and were told to choose a city of our choice to visit a friend or a relative as a break from the work schedule. I chose to go to East Lansing to visit an American family who were close friends namely, the Days. Bud and Gene had lived in India for some years and had become very friendly with us. It was a wonderful opportunity to enjoy their hospitality. In each city, we held seminars and met eminent feminists from different fields. This acquainted us with the position of women in the US as well as in countries which were represented in our group.

Among all the cities that we visited, I liked San Francisco the most. I still put it on the top after having visited many other cities in the USA, subsequently. Another city that I liked at that time was Denver. It was in Denver that destiny patted me on my back and again opened another wonderful opportunity for me. One morning, we were having breakfast outside. It was a warm morning and I was enjoying my breakfast, looking at the mountains in the background, when one of our American escorts said "Listen Zarina, it just occurred to me that you should go to the Women's Conference to be held in Mexico next week. There are going to be very few women from the developing countries. You are already here and it will cost much less to the sponsors if you were sent there." But who would sponsor me? I had no clue. She advised me to send a request to the UN's NGO forum to sponsor me, as they feared that the NGO forum would be flooded by only Americans. She also told me whom to send the request to and the address of that person. I remember vividly that just then, I wrote a letter requesting myself to be sponsored and funded by the NGO forum and posted it from Denver itself. We moved on to our other destinations and I had almost forgotten about it.

My Participation in the Mexico Conference

After the completion of our travels, we went to Washington for reporting back before leaving the US. There, another surprise was sprung on me. I was given a huge envelope—addressed to me—from the UN NGO forum. It contained an invitation for me to attend the NGO forum at the Mexico Conference, all sponsored by the UN. It also contained my air ticket and vouchers for my hotel, etc. What a luck! I was, to say the least, overjoyed. So, instead of returning home, I proceeded to Mexico the next morning. I informed my family in Delhi, who were equally happy for me. I was concerned for my two little daughters, Kiran and Nikki, who had to be without me for another two weeks. But Huma was already a big girl and would look after her young sisters. My husband assured me not to worry; he would take care of them.

As it turned out, the NGO forum had only three other Indian women. One named Sudha, who lived in New York, was representing the All India Women's Conference in New Delhi; Jasleen Dhamija had come from Tehran where she was on a UN assignment; and Devaki Jain was heading a research institute on women in New Delhi. The official Indian delegation, strangely, was headed by a gentleman and had two women; Rami Chhabra—a journalist—being one of them.

There I was among thousands of women from all over the globe. The amazing opportunity to visit the US and then to participate in the International Conference on Women in Mexico gave a totally different direction to my life and opportunities started falling in my lap. As we—Devaki Jain and I—were the only two women who had gone directly from India and had participated in the NGO forum at the Mexico Conference, on our return we found ourselves in great demand to address meetings and seminars and talk about the conference. Devaki mostly stayed in Bangalore, so in Delhi the pleasant burden fell on me. These opportunities turned me into a "feminist."

12
Joining USAID

At about the same time, motivated and enthused by the Mexico Conference, international agencies decided to focus on women's development, particularly in developing countries. In 1974, the US Government enacted a law called Percy Amendment according to which, all United States Agency for International Development (USAID) missions overseas were required to appoint a gender specialist in their missions. The USAID mission in Delhi started looking out for a suitable person to fill this post. At that time, the post was referred to as "Women in Development cum Social Analyst." I—having studied Sociology in no less an institute than the LSE and having attended the Mexico Conference, plus because of my exposure to the feminist movement through the US traveling seminar—was eminently qualified for the newly created post, so I was appointed to it. However, it did not come to me directly but only after a little drama.

Around the mid-1970s, awareness about the fast-depleting forests in India was created and the concept of social forestry emerged. International agencies had decided to get on the bandwagon, so USAID decided to launch a project on social forestry in India and allocated a large amount of money for this purpose. According to the Percy Amendment, each project had to have a "Woman in Development (WID)" specialist. Mr Peter Bloom, the officer-in-charge of the Social Forestry Project, began to search for a suitable woman to work in this capacity on the project team which was to work in the state of Madhya Pradesh (MP). It so happened that Mr Bloom's wife, Gretchen, was studying for her Master's at Jawaharlal Nehru University (JNU), and had become acquainted with my daughter Huma, who was also studying in JNU at that time. Gretchen mentioned to my daughter about her husband's anxiety to find a suitable woman for the social forestry project. My daughter suggested me as a possibility. Gretchen had heard me speak on women's issues in a couple of seminars and at the Mexico Conference. She jumped at the suggestion and informed her husband about me. One fine morning, I got a call from Mr Bloom of USAID who wished to see me. Huma had forgotten to tell me about Gretchen's conversation, so it came as a pleasant surprise. I went to meet Mr Bloom, who informed me about the forthcoming project and after seeing my biodata, offered that I join his team on social forestry as a WID Specialist. The team was to start traveling in MP from the following week, but I was to join from the next day, if possible. I happily accepted his offer but told him hesitatingly that I did not know much about social forestry (in fact, I did not know anything). He laughed and said that not many people knew about it as it was a new concept whereby, forestry was promoted through people's participation and I, being a sociologist, should be able to handle it. He was kind enough to give me some literature on the concept of social forestry to read before we went into the field. So here I was, employed for six weeks by the Government of United States, working with American experts on social forestry. Like the earlier opportunity to visit the USA and then Mexico, this offer too had fallen in my lap without my even trying for it. I could not help but compare my luck with the time when, in the earlier days of my return to India, I used to wander from one place to the other looking for a job without any success. Indians believe in astrology and in the influence of certain stars on a person's life. I cannot claim to be a firm believer in this philosophy but it did appear that my stars were beneficial. I was also struck by how, since the time I became disassociated with my first husband, my luck had started to change. All those 12 years that I was married to Hayat, I had to struggle hard without achieving much, except getting two degrees from the University of London which did prove to be my greatest asset. Imagine how, earlier, with two degrees from the University of London, I could not even get a lectureship at the University of Delhi.

My First Foray into Social Forestry

The offer to work on the social forestry project led to other professional opportunities for me and I found that "lady luck" was smiling at me again. However, my immediate task was to learn about social forestry. I was totally ignorant about forestry itself, had no knowledge about trees, about their varieties, or the usefulness of different trees. I thank God for endowing me with quick learning power and I learned as much as I could and as fast as possible in the one week before going for the fieldwork. My job was to see that women participated fully in the process of reforestation and also benefited from it. Those six weeks in the field, working with highly qualified experts in their respective areas, taught me a great deal. The leader of the delegation, a Harvard professor, was very kind, understanding, and helpful to me as were the other members of the team. They were, if anything, not only appreciative but intrigued to be working with a middle-aged Muslim woman (I was 43 years old then). In fact, the mission had until then not employed any Indian at the officer's level. All officers and experts in the mission were Americans. A few Indians were later elevated to an officer's position who started out as typists and loyal PAs and kept a low profile on account of not having high educational qualifications. They were also unduly impressed by the "white" bosses and bent backwards to please them. I had to perform in that environment and maintain my dignity. I must admit that most of my colleagues, especially the Americans, were cooperative and behaved decently. The fact that my husband, at that time, was heading a prestigious economic research institute in Delhi, National Council of Applied Economic Research (NCAER) and was a well-known economist, also helped me in establishing myself as a respectable, qualified, and competent officer.

I found my first experience of working on the project highly informative, interesting, and exhilarating. It provided me an opportunity to interact with the officers dealing with forestry from the highest bureaucratic levels, that is, the Secretary of Forestry and Environment, to the panchayat level. I began to learn about my country's development issues, specifically about the importance of forests in the lives of people and their significance as an important national development resource. It was all new learning for me. We visited all the forests of MP, stayed at forest guest houses, talked to local people, and discussed the issues with the officers. Social forestry officers of the Government of India always traveled with us and provided lavish hospitality. While hospitality is no doubt a positive cultural factor in Indian society and I am all for preserving it, the kind of lavish hospitality that I experienced during our field trips was totally unnecessary and a callous waste of public money.

Our first stop was in Gwalior. When we went to have breakfast in the morning, I was highly surprised to see what was served. There were half-fried eggs for twice the number of persons and as many boiled eggs and omelets. There was porridge and cornflakes, a mound of toast, dozens of parathas, sabzi, tea and coffee, and a variety of fruits. The same style of hospitality continued throughout our trip. Lunches and dinners were served in lavish style, with beer during lunch and imported Scotch during dinner. The Americans were not fond of hard drinks and abstained from having beer at lunch as they said that it made them sleepy. Our Indian counterparts though fully enjoyed the food and alcohol. Almost all the Indian foresters had huge paunches. I found that they nurtured an exaggerated feudal lifestyle. I noticed that even the jeep parked in the compound had to be brought right to the door for them. They would not walk even the few steps needed to get on to the vehicle. The foresters wore uniforms and carried a staff; they functioned like the army, behaving like generals and hardly had any contact with ordinary people while the concept of social forestry was based on their involvement and required close contact between the officers and the people. The creed of the profession was, "Forestry was about people, not about trees." This behavior was totally against the training and the ethos of the foresters. As a result, regular forest officers resented being a part of the social forestry division. It was looked down upon by the forestry service in the beginning, despite being the most important tool for reforestation and afforestation. So, to embark on reforestation was a Herculean task. It involved not only stopping deforestation but also changing the entire culture of forestry and the mindset of foresters. Corruption was so rampant that the villagers would tell me that the forest officers did collect their "salaries" on time; they had so much *balai aamdani*[1]. In social forestry, such *balai* income was not possible and they were required to shun the uniform and the stick, befriend the villagers, and stop being authoritative.

Gender Discrimination in the Forestry Service

I discovered to my dismay that women were not allowed in the forestry service (unofficially) although it was a national-level service and operated in the same fashion as the IAS, IFS and IPS. While women

[1] Bribery.

were not barred constitutionally from joining the service, it was a gender-discriminatory practice imposed by the forestry service itself. Strangely enough, it was not questioned by the government or the people. I suspect this was not even known to the public at large. The USAID project in MP was the second such in India. The first one had been launched by the World Bank in the same state as ours. But that project functioned more or less on the traditional pattern. I was the first Gender Specialist on a social forestry project. I remember meeting the World Bank team in Bhopal who looked at me blankly and asked me what was I doing in a social forestry project. When they got to know that I was a part of the team as a gender specialist, it led to raised eyebrows all around. Our project insisted that women should be encouraged to join social forestry and invited to compete along with men for the service. Fortunately, this request was within the ambit of the USAID, it being the funding agency. Besides, the Indian government could not defend its position as it was legally and constitutionally wrong to officially bar women. The foresters tried to defend women's absence from the service on the ground that women, being physically weaker, could not cope with the strenuous duties of a forester. One of the requirements for recruitment was that a candidate had to walk 15 kilometers on foot and it was assumed that women did not have the strength to do so. It was also pointed out that it was not safe for young women to visit lonely forests for fear of being molested. So they were to be "protected." It was assumed that for those reasons, women themselves would not want to join the service. However, their arguments did not hold water and when, on our insistence, women's entry into the service was opened, five women made it in that year through the usual competitive process. The administration was then faced with another problem—where to accommodate them during the training period as there were no hostels for women in the Forestry Research Institute (FRI) in Dehradun. The institute is situated on many acres of land which also has bungalows for the staff besides a men's hostel. It is such a beautiful place that I fell in love with it and wished I was a forester. At the same time, I felt angry at the thought that women were denied access to this luxurious place. However, finally the administration decided to allocate a bungalow for the five newly selected women foresters. But, they chose one which was located at the farthest end of the Institute in the loneliest spot. In doing so, did the women's assumed inability to walk long distances and the security concerns not occur to the administration? Such have been the prejudiced mindsets of educated Indian men. However, a big hurdle was overcome when women started entering the forestry service.

USAID's Social Forestry Project made another contribution toward women's entry at lower levels of the service. Until then, there was no separate forestry extension service as the forest extension was covered under the rural extension. With the introduction of social forestry, it was decided to establish a separate forestry extension service so as not to overburden the already heavily loaded rural extension service. This proposal was accepted by the government. But our project placed a rider that this newly created service should have female extension officers too. I insisted on this inclusion because I believed that women were better communicators and that village women and particularly tribal women might like to take up this job. Being more familiar with ground realities may even do a better job of it. This suggestion was also initially contested but I, with the support of the team, insisted on the inclusion of women at this level. Finally, with some reservations on the part of the foresters, the proposal was accepted and an undertaking was given that at least 25 percent women would be recruited as extension workers. I was happy that another battle was won. However, after six months, we were to take an account of the progress and an evaluation was carried on. To my surprise, I found that not a single female extension worker had been appointed. I naturally enquired about this and got the reply that no woman had applied for this post. I asked where the post was advertised. "In the National Gazetteer, where all forestry posts are advertised," came the quick reply. But how would the women have known that these new posts had been created, especially when they were kept away from the forestry service at all levels? However, I was not convinced that women would not be interested in these jobs which required a rural background and no high educational qualifications. So, I told them that unless the appointment of female extension workers as an essential requirement of the project was fulfilled, the project may be in trouble. Fortunately, I was senior in age, so I took advantage of my grey hair and even scolded the officer dealing with this issue. I suggested that they advertise the post in local and regional newspapers and write to girls' schools and colleges informing them of these newly created positions. Luckily, they followed my suggestions and within a short period, no less than 1200 applications were received, some from graduate and postgraduate women too. Thus, a minimum number of appointments were made. Again the problem of accommodation for these newly appointed female extension workers during the training period arose. I requested for some additional funding to build a hostel for them and it was granted. A hostel for women workers was constructed in Shivpuri, the training venue. Finally, when the female extension workers were appointed and sent into the field, their lives were made difficult by the chauvinist forest officers. Women were assigned the most difficult jobs, given areas which would not be accessible by road, and assigned areas which men would not like to cover. The forest officers would complain to me if female workers talked about their unusually difficult postings. The officers would taunt them rather than being sympathetic and helpful. I kept monitoring the situation closely and through conversations and arguments, kept trying to gender sensitize those officers to some extent.

During my 10 years' tenure with the USAID, I also had the opportunity to work with minor irrigation projects in Maharashtra and UP as well as mother and child nutrition projects in a number of North Indian states. I found that an important inhibiting factor in the development process was the patriarchal mindset of the bureaucrats. The bureaucracy in India mostly consists of the upper middle class, with a sprinkling of Scheduled Castes (SCs) and Scheduled Tribes (STs) under the reserved category. I observed that even the SCs and STs aspired to behave like their upper caste colleagues. I would notice, even among them, a near-complete lack of sensitivity toward people and their needs. The officers had very good technical knowledge but were insensitive about how the application of technology at the ground level affected people's aspirations and relationships. One of the things which used to irk me the most was the concerned officers' obsession with sewing machines as a panacea for reducing poverty and stitching clothes as an income-generating activity for poor women, without any understanding of the ground realities. In every village, there is a caste of tailors who do the tailoring work for the villagers. It may be noted that these tailors teach their craft to their sons, not their daughter like most other occupational castes. So, at a lower strata in the village, there were no expectations from women to learn stitching—a role which the bureaucrats were trying to impose—because upper class women liked to while away their time with such activities as stitching and embroidery. It did not occur to these development officers that training these poor women in tailoring would add another burden to their already heavily burdened lives and secondly, it was unlikely that they would acquire sufficient skills to compete with professional tailors. In their defense, the officers would say that in any event, women would save the money that they spent on paying the tailors, having no idea that the annual budget of a poor rural family would be almost negligible. The poor hardly have more than two sets of clothing. The sari—the usual women's dress—does not require any stitching; the poor women wear saris without petticoats as they cannot afford an extra garment. Children wear only one small garment and men's dhotis or lungis also do not require stitching. Even if these poor women were given training in tailoring, how much would they be able to save and how many would be able to buy a sewing machine? Such factors were not given any thought. So, sewing machine as a panacea for generating income for the poor families was a ridiculous idea because besides being uneconomical, it also strengthened a woman's traditional image and another traditionally gender role was being imposed on poor women. The development officers could not even think of training women for other professions where women could be taught to use natural resources which were locally available and make things for their use as well as add to their income, such as making soaps or extracting oil from locally available plants and fruits. The possibility of training women for the skills that modern technology had opened up were not considered. The notion was that technology too was only for men.

On completion of our social forestry fieldwork, we returned to Delhi to write the report. My inputs were on the participation of women in stopping deforestation and how they could embark on planting trees and give suggestions for future course of action. My two drafts were highly criticized by the project director but he was encouraging and helpful. The third time, I sat at a typewriter (there were no computers then) and started writing. I wrote as if I was guided by an invisible hand, kept typing till 2 a.m. and submitted the report in the morning. The project director was very happy with it and it boosted my self-confidence.

My appointment with the USAID was only for six weeks' duration of the project. On the last day, I was feeling a bit sad that my assignment, which had been enriching, was ending. It was then that I received a call from the mission director's office. The Mission Director, Mrs Prescilla Boughton, wanted to have lunch with me. I cordially accepted and thought that it was a polite gesture on her part to say goodbye. I went over to the staff canteen and chatted about my experiences on the project. She asked me about the feminist movement in India and I freely discussed women's issues. At the end of the day, just as I was leaving the office, Mrs Boughton came to my room and informed me that I had been offered the position of a gender specialist in the mission and that my lunch was actually an interview. Would I accept the offer? Most certainly, I did.

My Appointment as a Gender Specialist with the USAID

Destiny again played a role. The job as a gender specialist was not only to my liking but also highly paid. From a salary of ₹700, which I was earning as a lecturer, I was elevated to a salary of ₹5,000 a month, besides the enormous opportunities to travel and learn about my country and its development. It was a god-sent opportunity. I saw only one problem. With the USAID, I had to work from 8:30 a.m. to 5:30 p.m. for five days a week with only 15 days a year of earned leave while as a lecturer, I had the luxury of working only a few hours a day and even had the freedom to choose my hours of work, besides long summer holidays. I used to schedule my lectures in the morning hours so that I could be home by the time the girls returned from school. That kind of job suited me when my children were small as I could combine my domestic duties with my job. I used to walk with the children to the bus stop in the mornings and would be home to receive them after school. They were used to my presence at home all the time. My two younger daughters were in their early teens when I was offered the USAID job. Huma was in college. They did not need me as much as before. My in-laws had already passed away. I still had to consult my husband and the children, though. Fortunately, even before my husband opened his mouth, my daughters declared that they could manage without my presence all the time and that I must accept the offer. My husband too advised me to go ahead. I was entitled to three years' leave without pay from the University. I availed that privilege and took leave of absence without resigning from my University job. I wanted to keep my options open. There I was within a week, the first woman officer in the Indian mission of the USAID. At the age of 42, I had embarked upon a totally different career.

I found the long working hours at the USAID cumbersome but my work was interesting. At that time, the mission was funding in three areas namely, social forestry, medium and minor irrigation, and mother and child health that included family planning. The Government of India had assigned five northern states to the mission.

These were Haryana, Punjab, MP, Gujarat, and Maharashtra. I, as a gender specialist, highlighted the significance of women's participation in all development projects and tried to integrate women into the projects, both as active participants and as beneficiaries. I worked at all levels of the project, from project formulation to monitoring and evaluation. This provided me an enormous opportunity to acquaint myself with the socio-economic profiles of the five states, to suggest ways and means to improve women's condition through these projects, and to enhance their participation in the project activities. My ability to speak Hindi and to converse in North Indian dialects helped me establish a good rapport with the villagers which greatly facilitated my task. Initially, my fair complexion, fluent English, and working with white men created suspicion in the minds of the villagers. Some thought that I was a white memsahib but the moment I would open my mouth, speak in the local dialect, and behave like them—sitting comfortably on the stringed cot and addressing them in their familiar style—a rapport would be created. My earlier fieldwork experiences helped me in dealing with situations and I was soon accepted. I enjoyed my interactions with villagers, women and men, and gathered useful information about their problems and their views on how to solve them. Everywhere I went, I was struck by the villagers' sharp understanding and perception of their problems and their keenness to discuss them. But on a practical level, they showed great resistance in discarding old techniques and beliefs in agriculture, in accepting family planning, or in allowing women to come forward to handle village affairs. Their traditional mindsets, especially toward women, led to further resistance to change, which made my task a little more difficult. I also found that resistance to change was far stronger among the high castes than among the lower castes. I concluded that it was so probably because the lower castes had less to lose through socio-economic changes but the upper castes felt threatened that the changes may affect their higher position and power in the village structure. On that count, I found it easier to convince the lower caste women to experiment with changes such as, using smokeless *chulhas*,[2] accepting family planning, and using modern agricultural techniques. When the upper castes noticed the benefits of the new knowledge and techniques, they too adopted the changes, probably because they did not want to be left behind.

To my surprise, I found that the American men working on the projects were no less chauvinistic than their Indian counterparts.

[2] A small earthen or brick stove.

They did their job according to the objectives of the projects and left me, more or less, alone to handle the gender issues, often with a certain amount of cynicism, without being fully convinced of the important role of women in socio-economic development. I must admit that there were a few exceptions too. For example, sometimes I had a very understanding and supporting boss who almost gave me a free hand in using the funds available for women's development programs. When I joined the USAID, Indian development NGOs were not allowed to be funded by overseas donors. Some NGOs had misappropriated funds and some were suspected to be American agents. But later, this ban was lifted and the Government of India allowed bilateral funding of NGOs under certain conditions. This helped me in funding the NGOs working for women's development and empowerment. I had personal knowledge of some genuine women's NGOs and knew how they were struggling to carry on their work under severe financial constraints. I was also able to get a sanction for a women's training project with the support of my boss. In the early 1980s, women's NGOs were—though few—sincere and highly motivated to further the cause of women. But they needed training to efficiently carry on their work. Some small NGOs did not even know how to formulate a project and prepare a budget for submission for funding to foreign agencies. They also did not know about evaluation and monitoring techniques. Under the women's training project, I was able to upgrade their skills in these areas.

I also worked on minor and medium agricultural projects during my USAID days. While working with irrigation engineers, I realized how myopic their vision of development was. This was partly due to their education and training which only focused—at that time—on purely technical aspects. Both the irrigation engineers and the bureaucrats associated with irrigation-related issues felt that their task was only to create so many cusecs of water for irrigation. They did not consider it important to focus on what happened to people and their relationships with different castes and communities in the village, or when irrigation, an important development input, was introduced in the village. The engineers were competent in their limited expertise but ignorant of women's role in handling irrigated farming and its impact on their lives. When irrigation water is brought to an area, one most important factor to be tackled is its distribution among various sections of the population. I noticed that decisions about distribution of water were highly influenced by the insensitivity of decision makers toward social and cultural factors. These decision makers were also constrained by their own caste- and class-ridden mindsets. As a result, the high caste and richer farmers managed to get more advantages at the cost of smaller farmer and the landless. After working with irrigation projects, I understood better the reasons behind the uneven development of our country. The churning out of theories by the economists and the technology-based training of technical experts, I felt, has been responsible to a large extent for the continuing economic disparities in India's development.

During my work with the USAID, I also realized that unlike the general impression, the Government of India kept a strict vigil on the foreign donor agencies, more so on bilateral donors. For example, the USAID personnel were never allowed to go into the fields without being accompanied by a government officer from the relevant ministry. All foreign agencies had to work with the government closely at every stage of the project. The government had the authority to decide in which area(s) it would accept foreign aid and to allot the states for them to work in. The projects submitted by the foreign aid agencies were thoroughly scrutinized by the government before it was accepted. Bilateral agencies like the USAID faced stricter scrutiny than the UN development agencies. It was a happy learning for me that our government never buckled before the foreign donors and kept its sovereignty intact. During my tenure, a very large project with huge funding was rejected by the Government of India because it did not agree with the implementation mechanisms suggested in the project.

Some of my left-wing friends in the women's movement disapproved of my working with the USAID. They did not realize that I got more out of them, in terms of learning about my country and its development problems, than the USAID got out of my expertise. I never succumbed to their pressures; in fact, I do not remember ever being pressurized to do what I believed was not in the interest of our women. In any case, women's development funding was too small for the US Government to bother with. However, after working with the USAID for almost a decade, I resigned when I found that USA's policy was changing and that USAID, India, had decided to pull out of rural development and invest more in promoting high-tech programs, which I felt would not have a very beneficial impact on the poor rural women, at least at that point of time. It was not an easy decision to give up a highly lucrative job. Besides the salary, I also had the opportunity of meeting and interacting with the Indian bureaucracy from the highest to the lowest levels, an opportunity I would never have had as a university lecturer. But I had to be true to my convictions and I felt that by working with an Indian NGO, I could contribute better toward women's development and empowerment through the huge experience and learning that I had acquired during my work with the USAID. My quitting the job also reestablished my credibility in the women's movement.

Keynote Speaker in Washington

It was during my USAID days that I had an opportunity—which I regard as the highest point of my professional career—to deliver a keynote address at an international conference in Washington, D.C., USA. I felt particularly happy about that opportunity because the following year, no less a celebrity than Amartya Sen, the Nobel Laureate, delivered a keynote address at the same conference, though I can not even remotely compare myself to him. The American Association of Women in Development (AAWID) used to have an annual conference and would invite someone who had made significant contribution to women's issues in the developing countries to deliver the keynote address. I felt very honored to have been chosen for such a prestigious event. The session where I was going to give my keynote address was to be chaired by the Head of the USAID in Washington. My boss and the director of the Indian office of USAID were surprised that such an honor had been bestowed on me. One of my bosses even joked and said, "Hey Zarina, you are going to speak at a session which is being chaired by our ultimate boss. I have not even had the opportunity to shake hands with him and you will share the stage with him!" However, the director asked me to show him the address, which I did, and received his approval. It so happened that at that time, my husband, who used to edit whatever I wrote, was away in Bangkok on a UN assignment. So, I wrote my speech entirely on my own which further boosted my self-confidence. But I must say that my departure to Washington was not hassle-free.

As the US Government was paying for my air ticket, I was obliged to travel by the American flagship carrier, Pan Am. But at that time, Pan Am was on strike and had cancelled its flights from India to the USA. As a result, other international airlines going through New Delhi were overbooked and I could not get a seat. In the absence of availability of Pan Am flights, I was allowed to fly out of India on any other airline only up to the point from where I could avail a Pan Am and this was London. My daughter Huma was in India on a visit and was booked on Air India to travel back to the USA on the same date that I was to leave for Washington. I was running from pillar to post to get a seat on any airline but without success. The only possibility was that I go to some other country and try to get a seat from there but there was not enough time to procure a visa. Finally, I decided to meet the manager of Air India and told him about my plight. I could not possibly miss that opportunity. I showed him my invitation to the conference and requested him to treat me as a VIP and give me a seat on the Air India flight to London. I knew that national airlines reserve a couple of seats for VIPs and an invitation to give a keynote address at an international conference surely meant VIP status. The manager was sympathetic and allotted me a seat on the Air India flight, the same one on which Huma was also booked, to New York. It was a huge relief. We boarded the plane at 4 a.m. and soon after boarding, we fell asleep as we had not slept the previous night. After some hours, we woke up and felt that the plane was not moving and outside it looked like Delhi airport. When I looked at my watch, it was 10 a.m. Just then, we heard an announcement that we must deboard as due to a technical hitch, the airplane could not take off and another plane was coming from Bombay to take us to London and then on to New York. Huma was to fly onwards to New York on the Air India flight but I was to shift to the connecting Pan Am flight at London for Washington. Due to the delay in our departure, I missed the connecting flight which also meant that I would not make it to Washington in time to give my lecture and if I did not do so, then the US Government would not pay for my travel expenses. Being a Saturday, I could not even consult anyone in the USAID office. I was in a dilemma whether to proceed or not. I could see the wonderful opportunity slipping out of my hands. Huma insisted that I should try to get on the Air India flight that she was on and go to New York. From New York, there were flights to Washington every hour, so I could still make it. Fortunately, there was a vacant seat on that Air India flight. I availed that and finally made it to Washington on a Sunday evening and fulfilled my commitment to lecture on Monday morning. The AAWID had very generously booked me in a VIP room in an expensive hotel. Huma came with me to Washington and was thrilled to bits to share my hotel room. I woke up in the morning with butterflies in my stomach at the thought of speaking to an international audience. However, I tried to compose myself and took out what I considered my less flashy Kanjivaram silk sari in order to appear soberly dressed. Huma approved of my appearance assuring me that I looked dignified enough for the occasion.

My mind went back to the day almost a decade ago when I was sitting in the Royal Victoria Albert Hall to receive my BA (Hons.) degree and further back in time, when almost every year I had to face the threat of being stopped from going back to school. I certainly had traveled a long distance to be standing in front of an international audience in Washington. I noticed my American friend Mary Hainey in the audience, smiling away. She had reason to as she was instrumental in starting my journey toward feminism. I remain indebted to her forever.

While working with the USAID, I had no less than a dozen occasions to visit various American universities, both on the East and the West Coast, to talk about the growth of Indian feminism and gender and the development issues that we were dealing with. I had opportunities to go to such far-off places as Moscow and Pullman in the state of Idaho, not frequently visited by Indian scholars. I also visited San Diego where Huma lived, no matter which part of the States I was visiting. Huma used to say, "Mummy will en route herself through San Diego even if she was going to Timbuctoo." I was pretty well paid so I was able to travel to San Diego both the times to help out Huma when she had her babies. I cannot believe that those babies, Arman and Ayesha, are in their twenties now.

After resigning from the USAID, I joined an Indian NGO as Women's Development Officer on a salary that was one quarter of what I was getting at the USAID. This new job gave me more flexibility to take up short-term consultancies as a gender specialist. Opportunities came my way and I received a number of UN offers for short-term consultancies. Among them, the one I enjoyed the most were three consultancies with International Fund for Agricultural Development (IFAD). IFAD has its headquarters in Rome and this provided me an opportunity to work in the city I liked the most, even more than Paris. Luckily, I had an American friend who loved Rome as well and was very knowledgeable about the city. I stayed with her and she showed me around with such relish that my admiration for Rome, its architecture, its statues, and its people grew. I worked as a Gender Specialist on three IFAD Projects. We used to collect data in India, then go to Rome to analyze, and write the report.

13

Women's Movement in India

In 1981, when I was still with the USAID, I attended the first women's conference held in the SNDT Women's University, Bombay. The conference was an eye-opener as women from all corners of India had participated. The enthusiastic participation came as a delightful surprise to all of us. We had had no idea that so many women, even from smaller universities and colleges, were working on women's issues. In view of such wide interest, a decision was taken initiated by Dr Madhuriben Shah that an association of women's studies be formed and a year later, Indian Association for Women's Studies (IAWS) came into existence. Soon after the Bombay Conference, I resigned from the USAID and was elected to the IAWS executive. I later occupied the positions of its treasurer and, finally, its president. The IAWS had been mandated to integrate women and women's issues at all levels of higher education. This was to be done by generating gender-based data and encouraging research on education and gender issues in India, formulating curriculum for gender studies, and sensitizing academic disciplines and the academia toward the importance of gendering disciplines. Fortunately, it was decided since its inception that a separate department of women's studies would not be demanded as this would marginalize women. Instead, we wanted women's issues to be integrated into the higher education system and also into various academic disciplines. Along with this academic exercise, it was considered important to participate in advocacy programs and work closely with the grassroot organizations; we did not want to create armchair academics divorced from the ground realities of our country.

As mentioned earlier, Madhuriben Shah led the University Grants Commission (UGC) to establish women's study centers in universities and colleges. These centers, along with independent research institutes like the Centre for Women's Studies and Institute of Social Studies Trust (ISST, led by Devaki Jain) in Delhi, the SNDT Women's University, Bombay (under the leadership of Dr Neera Desai), and others, received funding from their respective universities. The private centers raised their own funds except for the Centre for Women's Development Studies (CWDS), led by Veena Mazumdar, which was partially sponsored by the Indian Council of Social Science Research (ICSSR). The institutes developed gender-based techniques of analysis, evaluation, and monitoring of women's programs. They also fed their knowledge and findings to the government and policy makers, besides assisting women's organizations in their work and making women's contributions to family and society visible.

IAWS Instituted

One significant contribution that gender-oriented research has made to academic disciplines has been in redefining concepts like "work," "employment," "family," etc. and in reinterpreting history with feminist perspective. These researches have not only added to the pool of human knowledge but have also contributed to a better understanding of development processes and thereby assisted in gender-sensitive policies. The IAWS—in order to coordinate feminist research being conducted in different women's study centers, research institutes, and by individuals feminist researchers—decided to hold biennial national conferences which would provide a forum not only for researchers and other academics but also women-oriented NGOs, to interact, discuss and, share their work with each other. The conferences rotated their locations and were held in different states, hosted mostly by universities, which had the added advantage of sensitizing students and inviting their participation in the women's movement.

The IAWS also brings out a quarterly journal to keep its members abreast with women-related developments and research and advocacy work being conducted at the study centers and elsewhere. Dr Madhuriben Shah, Chairperson of the UGC, also reactivated the Standing Committee on Women in the UGC to monitor the work of womens' study centers in the universities and colleges. I had the privilege of being a member of the UGC Standing Committee on Women during the tenure of Dr Armaiti Desai as Chairperson. My inclusion in the committee provided an opportunity to me to better understand the functioning of the UGC and the bureaucratic procedures involved in dealing with the government. Unfortunately, the Standing Committee in the UGC became almost dysfunctional after Dr Armaiti Desai left, when men were appointed as chairpersons and did not take much interest in integrating women into the higher education system. But the centers continued to function without proactive leadership. In the meanwhile, a large number of gender research institutes and organizations have been established which are pooling their findings to the government and policy makers and have resulted in a number of women-friendly legislations.

One positive result of feminist leadership has been sensitizing the government and the planning bodies toward women's concerns. Fortunately, in the 1980s when the women's movement was gathering momentum, a number of bureaucrats in the government and policy making bodies were persuaded by persons like Veena di (Dr Veena Mazumdar) and other first-generation feminist women to take women's situation seriously. Broad-minded officers such as Dr Swaminathan—the Deputy Chairperson of the Planning Commission at that time—Ashok Mitra, and Anil Bordia of the Ministry of Education, who were given the responsibility of drafting the new Education Policy, came forward and accepted the challenges. They were themselves shocked and unhappy by the findings of the Status of Women report and agreed that concerted action needed to be taken to improve women's situation in the country. As a result, women found their rightful place in the new Education Policy which focused on women's education among three other foci namely, education of minorities, Dalits, and STs. The Sixth Five Year Plan under the Deputy Chairmanship of Dr Swaminathan included, for the first time, a chapter on women's situation. These were some of the major achievements for the movement.

The Coalition of "Seven Sisters"

It was around the same time that another positive development took place. It was the formation of a national coalition of major women's organizations. The coalition was christened the "Seven Sisters." The objective of this was to put collective pressure on the Government of India to take a serious look at women's situation as identified by the Status of Women Committee and implement the recommendations of the committee to improve women's conditions. Initially, the "Seven Sisters" was composed of YWCA of India, the All India Women's Conference, the National Federation of Indian Women—a wing of the Communist Party of India (CPI)—the All India Democratic Women's Association (a wing of the CPM) University Women's Federation of India, Mahila Dakshata Samiti (a sort of coalition of women with socialist and liberal ideologies), Centre of Indian Trade Unions [CITU (a trade union of women workers)], and Centre for Women's Development Studies (CWDS), which along with the YWCA under the leadership of Ivy Khan, took the initiative to bring together such a medley of women's organizations. This was the most notable achievement of the 1980s that strengthened women's struggle in India. Finally, the coalition of Seven Sisters fizzled out but it was a useful tool as long as it lasted and some of the organizations, if not all, kept lobbying together for common women's issues.

The women's movement in India, since its inception, adopted a multi-dimensional approach. It looked upon women as an integral part of Indian polity and economy. It also focused on women's economic condition, their health status, their educational backwardness, and their legal status in family and society. This approach led to a closer relationship between the academics and the activists and both benefited from this proximity. The focus on gender discriminatory practices led to a number of gender-friendly legislations as the law was no less gender discriminatory than the socio-cultural practices. Constitutional gender equality remained only on paper, as was highlighted by the Status of Women Committee. The passing of the Hindu Code Bill in 1956 gave some property rights to women as well as the right to divorce and remarry, but patriarchal mindsets did not change and many social evils continued to plague the women's status. The practice of dowry was one such evil which was ever increasing, leading to the extreme step of bride burning in some cases. The rape law was also quite archaic. The women's movement took up these issues. As a combined effort of the Seven Sisters' coalition, a joint Dahej Virodhi Manch[1] was organized. The manch held dharnas[2] soliciting public support and urged the government to legislate against the

[1] Anti-dowry platform.

[2] Protests.

practice of dowry. It succeeded in persuading the government to pass an anti-dowry law.

Another important event which almost rocked the Indian Muslim community took place in 1986, known as the Shah Bano case, which questioned the credibility of the Muslim Personal Law and highlighted its bias. Minorities such as Muslims and Christians have their own personal laws which bring under their jurisdiction matters such as, marriage, divorce, maintenance, custody of children, and inheritance. Hindus and Sikhs are now governed under the modified and relatively more gender-equitous Hindu Code Bill. Christian law is somewhat liberal toward women but the Muslim Personal Law continues to be extremely gender discriminatory and archaic. It allows a man to keep up to four wives at a time (not that it happens frequently due to demographic constraints) and divorce a wife unilaterally, just by repeating three times "I divorce you" referred to as Triple *Talaq*,[3] without giving a reason or having witnesses. It may sound ridiculous but the Triple *Talaq* is legally valid even if the husband utters it in a state of drunkenness. The wife, thus divorced, is not even entitled to maintenance except for four months and 10 days, known as the period of *iddat*, same as in the case of widows. Shah Bano, a 70-year-old Muslim woman, was unilaterally divorced by her husband by his uttering the Triple *Talaq* and was denied maintenance even for the period of *iddat* as she was beyond the reproductive age. It is interesting to note that contrary to the religion-based personal laws, there is in India a Uniform Criminal Code which governs all Indian citizens, irrespective of caste and community. According to the Uniform Criminal Code, if one person throws another person into destitution, it is legally incumbent on the offender to compensate the victim by providing maintenance of a pittance of ₹500 a month to the victim. Shah Bano evoked this legal provision and demanded her right to maintenance under this law. Her husband contested her demand by claiming that this provision could not apply to Muslims as it contradicts the Muslim Personal Law. This Law is wrongly claimed to be the Word of God, thus sacrosanct and cannot be interfered with. Although in reality, the provisions are based on the interpretation of the Koran by Muslim jurists. It was claimed that any change in the existing Muslim Personal Law, which has remained unchanged for hundreds of years, would amount to heresy and would be a serious infringement of minority rights. Shah Bano's husband found supporters among the fundamentalist sections of Muslims,

[3] Divorce.

who created quite an uproar defending the Muslim Personal Law. The liberal Muslims rightly explained that it was misleading to say that the Muslim Personal Law was the Word of God. It was in fact the interpretation of the Word of God. They supported their argument by pointing out that there existed four fully recognized versions of Muslim Personal Law in India, namely, the Hanafi, the Shafi'i, the Maliki, and the Hanbali. But there is only one Koran. The four versions are based on the interpretations of the four Islamic schools. The fundamentalist approach was therefore, attacked by both the liberal and the secular Muslims who supported Shah Bano. Unfortunately, the feminist movement kept itself aloof from the controversy but a cross-section of feminists, Muslims and non-Muslims, decided to organize protests against the fundamentalist position through the media and launched a signature campaign in favor of Shah Bano. They managed to collect a large number of signatures. I wrote an open letter to Prime Minister Rajiv Gandhi, explaining the fallacy created by the fundamentalist Muslims regarding the Muslim Personal Law being the Word of God and requesting him to intervene. I also organized a delegation to meet him. This delegation was composed of both Muslim and non-Muslim women. We promptly got an appointment with Prime Minister Rajiv Gandhi. It was a very positive meeting. He absolutely charmed us. In fact, he called me and Promila Dandavati—the two senior-most members of the delegation—"Auntie" and promised to look into the matter. The same day, he raised this issue in the Parliament and asked for a White Paper on what was happening in other Islamic countries regarding the Muslim Personal Law. But alas, as it always happens, the fundamentalists and the conservatives won. Rajiv was advised not to stir the hornet's nest as it would jeopardize his Muslim vote bank. So he retreated and the fundamentalists had their way. Shah Bano was accused of heresy and of dividing the Muslim community; she got frightened and finally withdrew her case. However, the criminal code was slightly modified without contradicting the basics of the Muslim Personal Law. What saddens me is that not only was a golden opportunity lost to establish liberal and secular credentials of the Muslim community but also the neutral attitude of my feminist colleagues. Now, their stand to oppose a uniform civil code on the excuse of protection of minority rights, which in effect endorses the most archaic highly gender discriminatory Muslim Personal Law, is also baffling. The end result is that Muslim women continue to live under this almost barbaric law and as always, bear the brunt of preserving the Muslim identity.

Tempers were so high at that time that I was personally attacked for going to press in support of Shah Bano. I had written an article where I had quoted from a study conducted at a prestigious institute in Bombay which reported that in certain areas, majority of prostitutes were found to be Muslim. This was misquoted and a rumor was started that I have called all Muslim women as prostitutes. I was issued dire threats, including raping me and my young daughters. However, once the government buckled under the fundamentalist Muslims' pressure, the storm died down.

As I mentioned earlier, after quitting the USAID, I worked on a part-time basis at ACCORD—an NGO—headed by Kiran Wadhera who was an efficient young woman and had known me since my USAID days when I had provided some funding for her projects. When she heard that I had resigned from the USAID, she requested me to join her and head the women's development division. She was supportive and kind to me but we perceived women's issues very differently and after working there for three years, I decided to resign and do short-term consultancies.

While at ACORD, I had an opportunity to go to the International Conference on Women in Beijing. I owe Kiran Wadhera for her generosity as she offered to sponsor me with a view to make ACORD visible at the international level. I was thrilled as China held a special fascination for me and travel to China was restricted in those days. I enjoyed the conference thoroughly and the authentic Chinese food also. Chinese cuisine has been my favorite and after eating in China, I could make out the difference between the authentic Chinese cuisine and the Indianized Chinese that we have in India. We were taken to a restaurant which specialized in Peking Duck. There we were handed a written description of how the Peking Duck is prepared. Apparently, the process starts right from the conception of the duck to rearing it, until the time it is ready for slaughtering and to be cooked. Each part of the duck was served differently to enjoy the difference in taste. It was an amazing meal, worth visiting Beijing again, if for nothing else.

Fellowship at York University

On my return from Beijing, I received an offer from the Canadian embassy to write a paper on the then current issues faced by the feminists in India. My paper was highly appreciated and was sent to Ottawa. A friend suggested that I should apply for a Senior Fellowship at the Shastri Indo-Canadian Institute in New Delhi. The Institute was established to promote better understanding between the two countries through combined research and mutual visit of scholars to both the countries. It had also instituted fellowships in different subjects, Women's Studies being one of the subjects. I applied for Senior Fellowship there and submitted my research proposal entitled "Identity Symbols of Indian Muslims in Canada" and requested them to affiliate me with a university in Toronto that had a large Indian population. I had a personal interest in going to Canada too, as my two sisters were living in Toronto and a brother in Ottawa. My request was accepted and I was awarded the Senior Fellowship affiliated with York University in Toronto. I was very happy as it was my first visit to Canada and it also provided me an opportunity to visit our daughter in the States a couple of times during the duration of my stay.

It was my first exposure to the non-resident Indian (NRI) community in Canada and to my surprise, I discovered that the Indians of all communities living there were almost frozen in time, in the sense that, they imagined that India had remained the same—particularly culturally—as it was when they had migrated to Canada. They also suffered from a displaced sense of cultural superiority over the Western culture. This sense was heightened as a reaction to the racial prejudices that prevailed in the early 1990s even in Canada, although the country claimed that its society was a "mosaic" of cultures and every citizen had equal rights. Racism, though discouraged officially, did appear in personal interactions and even at workplaces, though probably not as blatantly as in the USA. Asians and in particular Indians, who have—to some extent—misplaced pride in their own culture, clung together and lived an almost secluded life within themselves, avoiding close interactions with the whites. They also perpetuated the same socio-cultural cleavages that existed in India and expected their children to follow them. This created a very unfortunate situation for the children of first-generation Indians who were born and were growing up in Canada. They felt frustrated as their parents did not want to follow the lifestyle of their peer group. Indian parents tried to impose upon their children the "superior" standards of sexual morality. They disapproved of dating and Muslims in particular strongly disapproved partaking of alcohol. They also practiced gender inequality and were much stricter with their daughters than with their sons. As I was focusing on Indian Muslims, I found that Islam was used as a weapon to impose moral values. I was very surprised to notice that Indian Muslim families only taught their children to be Islamic Indians; they did not inform their children about the contribution of Muslims in Indian society in fields of music, architecture, cuisine and such. I refer to "Indian" Muslims because the Indian Muslims in Canada distinguished themselves from the Muslims of other countries. Obviously, the pan-Islamic sentiment had not erased regional and cultural differences. Muslims of different nationalities even had separate mosques.

What particularly distressed me was the plight of Indian women, especially those who were first-generation immigrants. As it happens everywhere, the burden of transmitting a culture to the younger generation falls on women. It was evident there too, as Indian women of all communities tried very hard to present to their children the "sexual morality" of Indians, the superior family (to a large extent exaggerated notions), and of course religious values. Mothers were required to be the role models for their children and play the role of traditional Indian wives. Indian women continued to live under their husbands' domination. Soon after I arrived in Toronto, I got a taste of the highly gender discriminatory lifestyle. My sister, Resham, and I were invited by an Indian friend of my sister's for dinner. There, I noticed to my surprise that men and women did not mingle. Women sat together and discussed domestic matters although among them, there were a couple of professional women like a doctor and my sister who was the supervisor of a group of schools. Men sat together discussing Canadian politics, promotional avenues for their jobs, and indulged in India-bashing. When dinner was served, a gentleman got up and moved toward the dining table. I followed him and sat down next to him but I noticed that none of the other women or men followed. I also noticed that the gentleman who had come to the table seemed a little uncomfortable. I looked at my sister and asked her to come over and she rather abashedly said, "Let the men eat first, women eat after the men have finished." I was shocked at the prevalence of this now archaic Indian custom which had been discarded in India a long time ago, particularly among the educated urban Indians.

During another evening, we women were sent to the basement which was pretty shabby while the men sat in the proper sitting room. During meal time, men were served at the dining table and we women were asked to fill our plates from the kitchen. I took my food and finding the sitting room sofas empty as they had been vacated by the men, sat down on one with my plate in my hands. After a little bit of whispering among the host and other women guests, my sister came up and embarrassedly told me that our host wanted me to go down to the basement and eat there along with the other women. Such was the "superior" Indian culture exhibited there for the benefit of NRI children or was it for the benefit of our chauvinistic males?

Indian women in Canada also lost out on another count. Most of them were at least graduates and a number even held postgraduate degrees from India. A fewer number were medical doctors; some had even practiced medicine for several years in India. But Indian degrees were not recognized in Canada. So, these qualified women could not get jobs without further qualifying from Canadian institutions. In an overwhelming majority of cases, the Indians had migrated to Canada for a better standard of living, which was possible only if both men and women took up jobs. In most cases, the men had superior qualifications and managed white-collar jobs but women with BA degrees had to take up manual or semi-manual jobs and ended up with low self-esteem. They were the real losers. During my investigations, I came across families where there was a great deal of domestic discord and the wives would suffer it out because divorce was looked down upon and would have damaged the "superior" image of Indian family life. There were exceptions, but those were few and far between. Most families practiced gender discrimination in bringing up their sons and daughters, often resulting in anger and frustration among the daughters. I looked into some police records in areas which were predominantly Indian and found that many late-night calls to police stations were made by neighbors who complained of noise caused by Indian parents shouting and even beating their grown-up daughters for staying out late in the night. This had led to a great deal of friction in families and created two kinds of youngsters. First was the one who rebelled, causing pain to their parents, and second were those who became rigid conformists, some ending up as religious fanatics and strongly disapproving of Western culture. However, they all enjoyed their prosperity which found expression in celebrating marriages and religious festivals with great pomp and show.

I enjoyed my time at York University. I always felt comfortable in university campuses and it was after more than a decade that I had had the opportunity to be on one again. Besides my research assignment which required a report at the end, I was also requested to give lectures at different departments and participate in faculty seminars. I did find that the campus life had undergone a great deal of changes as a result of computers. Both the faculty members and the students spend minimum time on the campus; they worked from home as much as was possible. This had reduced the frequency of personal interactions and there was less hustle and bustle of students as there used to be during my time in university.

The Gold Episode

After completing my assignment, my return to India was quite dramatic. India was then running out of gold reserves and the Government of India had decided to allow duty-free import of gold. As my Senior Fellowship was quite lucrative and I had stayed with my sister, I was able to save some money. Kiran's wedding was approaching. I decided to convert my dollar savings into gold to bring home. I considered it to be a patriotic gesture on my part, although it was only a small amount of gold, around two hundred grams or so. I checked with my economist husband whether it was the right thing to bring gold rather than dollars. He approved of my decision and further checked with an economist friend who was a member of the committee which had taken the decision to permit duty-free import of gold. After getting the green signal, I converted my dollars into gold. As soon as I arrived at the Delhi airport, I proudly declared my gold and presented the customs' officer the little plastic packet containing some ounces of pure gold coins. The officer looked at me with utter surprise because I could have easily slipped that small packet under my clothes and taken it out. However, there I was, disclosing the precious metal quite shamelessly. He said, "But madam, this is illegal, you cannot import gold coins." I reminded him of the ordinance allowing duty-free import of gold. He told me that he was aware of it but it had a rider which was that the person importing gold should have been away from India for a minimum of six months. I had been away for five and a half months, falling short of the requirement by 15 days. He had no option but to confiscate the gold coins. However, he was impressed by my honesty and suggested a way out to save the gold. He suggested that he would confiscate the gold but keep it in safe custody and if I went out of India again within the next 15 days, I could reclaim it. He suggested that I should go to a neighboring country like Sri Lanka, Bhutan, or Pakistan. I had no option but to leave the gold at the Custom's desk. I was surprised that my husband had given me incomplete information and was obviously very disturbed at losing my precious savings. The customs officer again examined my little packet and said that he could not keep it in a plastic bag. I should put it in some small container but he could not provide me one. So, I went to the duty-free shop and bought a small tin of chocolates, emptied it, and put the gold in it which was then tightly packed and sealed and taken away. I was given a receipt in case I came back to reclaim it. At that moment I had no hope of doing so.

My husband was surprised at the six months condition and called his friend, who was equally surprised, as the committee had not placed any such rider. Apparently, some bureaucrat dealing with the matter had placed the six months condition without consulting the committee. The committee looked into the matter and fortunately removed the rider with retrospective effect and I was given a green signal to recover my gold. I was happy and greatly relieved and my husband and I rushed to the airport customs. The customs officer did not question the validity of the official letter and signaled us to go to a room in the airport premises itself. Happily, we marched into that room which was dark and dingy. Two disgruntled gentlemen sitting at a table looked at us with suspicion. We showed the letter to one of them who looked at it disinterestedly and asked us to describe the article we were reclaiming. At our description that it was a small tin box, he gave us a dirty look and asked how he could identify a small tin box among the thousands of entries in the files. He pointed to a large number of files, some of them tattered and all dusty. Besides, he asked us how we could be sure that our little tin box was stored in that particular storage place as there were a number of such storage places in different parts of the city. He simply refused to even try to find the entry of my little tin box. We persisted in our request to try to do something as we were officially entitled to claim our gold. In utter disgust and to get rid of us, he pointed to a huge hall and told us to go there and request the caretaker to try and find it. We entered a huge hall full of suitcases of all descriptions piled one on top of the other, almost up to the ceiling. The caretaker, after listening to the description of our valued article, looked highly amused and said, "Tell me, where I should start looking for your little tin box in this jungle of boxes?" We could see the absurdity of the situation but how could I forego my precious possession, especially when I had the official orders that it should be restored to me? We insisted that he should at least try, so he finally picked up a long staff and poked it between two huge boxes. There came my little tin box, tumbling down! The three of us gazed at it with utter amazement. For a few seconds, we did not even bend down to pick it up as we were so dazed. The caretaker could not believe that it was indeed my "object of desire" that had fallen. He looked at us and said, "Sahib, you must have bought it with very legitimate earnings." It was no less than a miracle, but my problem was not over. When we took the gold to jewelers, they also at first looked at us with suspicion as if we were smugglers and would offer much less than the going price. Even then they could not give us cash; we would have to buy jewelry of the same amount. I was not interested in buying jewelry as I already had enough to give Kiran. We needed cash for the reception and other related expenses. I shared my problem with a colleague in the office. Luckily, she had an uncle who as a hobby used to design gold ornaments. So, he offered to buy my gold which he knew was of the utmost purity and gave me the correct price. Thus, my ordeal was finally over and the money came in handy for Kiran's wedding. I became the talk of the town as whispers went around, "Did you hear that Zarina imported gold from Canada?" All my patriotism melted away in suspicion and in public perception I was turned into a smuggler.

Formulation of a Course on Gender Sensitization

In the last 30 years or so, many schemes had been formulated and implemented to improve women's status in health, education, and in employment, but despite these multi-pronged efforts, no substantial change had taken place. Some adverse situations such as the rising incidents of female feticide and high occurrence of crime against women were further pushing them into being disadvantaged. One of the reasons for slow change was identified as the lack of gender awareness in those who were involved in women's development programs. It was found that the workers, particularly those in rural areas engaged in women's development schemes, were themselves the victims of discriminatory perceptions. They lacked the knowledge and the conviction to bring about any change in women's status. Most of them came from rural backgrounds and were tradition-bound. They had limited access and exposure to modern liberal ideas. While I was still with ACCORD, I had the opportunity to design and write a distant education course for the grassroot development workers. The course was sponsored by the National Open School. It was conceived as a small contribution to inform, train, and gender-sensitize the workers so that they could perform their duties more effectively. The course did very well while it lasted but unfortunately, thanks to the callous attitude of the National Open School bureaucracy, the course was discontinued after a few years of my leaving ACCORD.

Bidi Study

Another contribution that I made toward understanding women's issues, in particular their economic contribution to the household and to the national economy, was a study I conducted of women workers as bidi[4] makers. While highlighting women's role in households and society, we found that women's economic contribution was almost invisible and was the main factor which was mostly responsible for them being perceived as having a lower status. Women were regarded as liabilities rather than assets for the households and society since their economic contribution was viewed as nil. There was very little understanding of the unorganized sector of the Indian economy which comprised nearly 90 percent of women workers. These women workers were referred to as home-based workers. They comprised garment makers, lace makers, many kinds of handicraft producers, bidi makers, garland makers, and hundreds of other daily wage workers, paid on piece rate basis where payment is made on the basis of the number of articles. There were no unions, no regulation of working hours, wage rates, or compensation regulations in cases of injuries or health problems. Most of them worked through contractors who exploited them heavily. One large category of home-based workers was that of bidi makers. In the 1990s, it was estimated that nearly 90 percent of the workforce making bidis was constituted by women. More women took to this profession because it required no education and hardly any training. The only raw material required for making bidis is a kind of leaf called *tendu*, some dry tobacco, and thread to tie the tobacco inside the *tendu* leaves in a conical shape. The contractors provide the leaves and tobacco to the workers and demand a certain number of finished bidis in return. The dry leaves are usually given to the workers in sacks. These leaves are often very brittle and while twisting them into a conical

[4] Thin cigarette made by filling tobacco flakes in a *tendu* leaf.

shape of a bidi, they break and are wasted. The contractors do not take into account this problem and cut the wages if the required number of bidis are not given to them. Another very unfair practice has been that the contractors select only the perfectly made bidis and reject those that they consider to be not of the required standards. The worker is not paid for those not selected but the contractor keeps them and even sells those bidis, without paying the worker for them. Often the bidi workers have to borrow money to buy the raw materials in order to provide the required number of bidis to the contractor, thus losing on their wages. I conducted the bidi study in Allahabad district of UP. The study's findings exposed the exploitative nature of the bidi industry and led to the government enacting the Bidi and Cigar Manufacturers' Act to regulate the system. This Act aimed to abolish the contractors and define the manufacturers themselves as "entrepreneurs" who could market their produce directly. The Act also fixed a minimum wage. In the early 1980s, it was around ₹4 per 1,000 bidis. The rate must have gone up but the contractors continued to function in the garb of "buying" from the entrepreneurs and selling for them. The manufacturers, not having the requisite marketing skills or facilities, had very little choice but to depend on the contractors. However, the Act has made some difference and a few bidi makers have been able to take advantage of the legal provisions and market their products directly.

Along with the study of bidi workers, the ILO had also commissioned two more studies of home-based workers; one was the lace makers of Narsapur. I have forgotten the name of the third study. The researcher was Suma Chitnis. These three studies drew the attention of the government toward the plight of such workers and a commission called the Women Workers in the Organized Sector was set up under the chairpersonship of the well-known social worker, Dr Ela Bhatt.

"Shram Shakti"

An important contribution of our studies was the awareness created among the policy makers and the government about the neglected unorganized sector of the Indian economy. This awareness took shape in the establishment of a national commission on the unorganized sector of the economy under the chairpersonship of Ela Bhatt who had been working among the home-based workers and had formed a kind of a trade union called the Self Employed Women's Association (SEWA) to protect their rights. SEWA was a very successful model and almost became a household term. A comprehensive and revealing report of the commission on the unorganized sector titled "Shram Shakti" was the first report of its kind. It must be noted that an overwhelming majority of workers in the unorganized sector were and continue to be women. Shram Shakti had the desired effect in making the unorganized sector visible and its contribution to the national economy began to be recognized.

My Association with IAWS

While working at ACCORD, I was elected as the Treasurer of the IAWS. It was a responsibility that I was ill-equipped for; I always had a kind of aversion to accounts. But it so happened that the treasurer had to be from Delhi and only Sujaya and I were elected on the National Executive of IAWS that year. Sujaya—being a government servant and the Joint Secretary in the Ministry of Women and Children Welfare at that time—felt that it would not be appropriate for her to take up the treasurership, so the choice fell on me. I learnt about keeping accounts and all the related work on the job. It also fell upon me to apply and procure the Foreign Currency Regulation Act (FCRA) in order to accept foreign funding for the biennial National Conference. The cost of holding the Conference was going up and IAWS had very limited resources. Fortunately, Netherland's embassy offered to bear the cost of that Conference which was held in the University of Mysore that year. In the role of a treasurer, I also had an opportunity for the first time in my life to deal with the Indian bureaucracy. How the lower rank officers with whom I had to deal in the Ministry of Home Affairs to get the FCRA sanctioned, harassed me! They unnecessarily took a much longer time to complete the formalities, apparently fishing for a bribe. Finally, I received the FCRA certificate a day after the conference had started.

I had a long-lasting desire that an IAWS national conference should take place in the University of Lucknow as, despite Lucknow being my home town, the University had been out of bounds for me because I had to observe purdah in my youth. So even now, I get a thrill whenever I go to the University of Lucknow to give a lecture or to participate in seminars. My long cherished desire was fulfilled when the Silver Jubilee Conference of the IAWS was finally held in the University of Lucknow in 2008. It was also very gracious of the University to honor me for my contribution to knowledge and development by presenting me with a plaque which will always remain dear to me.

After I turned 70, I had decided not to take up any professional assignment. But it so happened that out of nowhere, I got an offer to work on an Asian Development Bank project called "Building Highways as a Gender Specialist." The job description looked attractive and the emoluments were pretty high. So, I accepted the offer and enjoyed working in an area where I was until then unfamiliar. My job was to look into the issues of land acquisition for building roads and highways and how it affected women. The assignment was for nine months and, although posted in Delhi, I once again had the opportunity of traveling to a number of states to hold training workshops, etc. I then realized that I still had a head on my shoulders and that in India, the retirement age of 60 or 65 is too early. However, that was my last professional assignment. My husband had been retired for almost 15 years by then, so I also finally decided to call it a day and took full retirement. I was still a member of the IAWS Executive Committee when its silver jubilee conference took place in Lucknow. After that conference, I decided to pull out of all voluntary positions. I was then 72 years old; it was already long overdue for me to vacate my position and provide opportunities for younger women to take over. The movement had reached a stage where the younger generation could take over and infuse new blood into it. Fortunately, there were plenty of young women, although hardly any young men, to take the movement forward.

The timing appeared to be ominous as soon after the conference, I discovered a lump in my left breast which turned out to be malignant. I believe it was once again divine intervention as the cancer was at its primary stage. I went for radical surgery without losing any time and fortunately have not suffered any emotional trauma on account of it. But the disease affected my physical stamina. So, even if I had not pulled out of official commitments, I would not have been able to continue working at the same pace. It has been seven years now since I had the surgery and I am fine and leading a normal life, or shall I say, as normal a life as it is possible for an octogenarian.

14

And Life Goes On

My family was moving on. Idrak and I had taken our roles as parents pretty seriously and had decided, in the wake of limited financial resources, to fix our priorities, which were to provide good education and good human values to our daughters. We took pains to explain to them that they should find good human beings as life partners and that good human beings are found in all religions and communities. We encouraged them to choose their own spouses. Huma chose a brilliant Bengali scientist—Shoumitro Ghosh—whom she met at Chicago while pursuing her PhD. Idrak was not very happy about her choosing a Hindu; he had hoped that she would choose either a Muslim, as her father was a Muslim, or a Christian, as she had grown up in a Christian home. But I accepted her choice and persuaded Idrak to do so too, because since we had trained them to make their own choices in their personal lives, we could not now go back and dictate our preferences. Fortunately, the young man was very eligible, highly educated, and liberal in his views. It so happened that his father, Dr R.C. Ghosh, a forester by profession, had after retiring as the Director of Research at the Forest Research Institute in Dehradun, joined NCAER—which Idrak was heading at that time—as a consultant. Idrak and Dr Ghosh had become quite fond of each other without any knowledge that their children were courting in the States. When Shoumitro wrote to Idrak, asking for his daughter's hand and we discovered his parentage, we felt assured that our daughter had made the right choice despite choosing a person of another religious community. Dr Ghosh's own sister was already married to a Muslim. So, the Ghoshs also welcomed their son's choice. Shoumitro's mother, Shahana, was a delightful woman and she and I got along very well with each other. Huma and Shoumitro have been married for over 27 years now and have two wonderful children, Arman and Ayesha. Huma is a professor and currently Chair at the Department of Women's Studies, University of San Diego, California.

Kiran and Nikki also chose their own partners. After completing school, both Kiran and Nikki joined St. Stephen's college. Fortunately, both had done well in the school-leaving certificate exams. Kiran opted for Economics (Hons.) and Nikki chose English Literature. Kiran went to the USA for a Master's in Economics from the University of Chicago at De Calb, and Nikki joined Mass Communication at Jamia Millia Islamia for her Master's. After completing her Master's, Kiran married Aslam, a UP Muslim, who belonged to a well-known family of Allahabad. Aslam had joined his family business. I had known that family well before Kiran and Aslam met. After her marriage and a daughter, Lyala, Kiran joined the LSE for a PhD. She balanced her family requirements and studies remarkably well, just as Huma had done earlier. She returned to India after spending a year at LSE as a residential student which was the minimum requirement for PhD, completed her fieldwork in her chosen area in Himachal Pradesh, had her second child Danyaal, then got back to writing her thesis. After a short stint with UNICEF India and a year at the National Commission for Child Rights as the National Coordinator, she is now working as a Senior Fellow at the Centre for Policy Research, New Delhi. She is interested in social issues and has been associated with a couple of landmark legislations like the Right to Information Act and the child rights' legislation. She, along with Huma and Nikki, has grown to be highly socially conscious, which delights my heart. We are fortunate to have two sets of delightful grandchildren. Both our granddaughters—Ayesha, who is now 24 and Lyala, who is 16—have grown into stunningly beautiful, bright, and talented girls. Ayesha is an all-rounder, good at studies, an excellent swimmer, and a Bharatnatyam dancer too. She completed her Bachelor's from the University of Berkeley and is now studying architecture in New York. Lyala too is doing very well at school. She likes to draw, takes part in various extra-curricular activities, and is turning out to be a good debater. She even tries her hand at poetry for which there is no dearth of genes in my family.

Both my grandsons, Arman and Danyaal, are growing into real gentlemen. Arman, after completing his education, is now working in Chicago. He loves his job and is doing well in his profession. He played soccer in school, to his *nana's* delight, who himself was a champion footballer in his younger days. Danyaal, 13, is too young to decide what he would like to do, except that he aspires to be an international football player and is almost obsessively fond of the game, which again delights his *nana's* heart. He loves cooking too and has declared that in case he does not succeed as a world-class footballer, he will become a chef, but is changing his mind about cooking now. Fortunately, he is doing pretty well in school too. Both Lyala and Danyaal are showing some talent in music, with the genes inherited from their father's side. Lyala is learning piano and Danyaal is learning guitar.

Nikki chose Manu Khurana—a Punjabi architect—for a husband. He is a fine fellow and very liberal in his views. His family is very open-minded and accepted Nikki wholeheartedly. She has no children as is more absorbed in her profession. After completing her Master's in Mass Communication, she worked as an assistant director in a couple of Bollywood films, directed a number of serials on television, and is currently working on a film script.

We have had a good relationship with our sons-in-law and their families. Manu's father, Gulshan, is a great admirer of Urdu poetry. In fact, he formed a group named Tarannum which periodically organizes ghazal-singing sessions. He has a tremendous memory and his conversation is always laced with appropriate Urdu verses. I belong to a literary family and Idrak was a poet too, so Gulshan's fondness for Urdu poetry has created a bond between us, crossing boundaries of religion and region. I must also mention an incidence which shows how with a will and understanding, religious and cultural barriers can be overcome. Soon after Nikki was married to Manu, the festival of Karva Chauth was to be observed. Married women have to fast on this day for their husband's longevity and it is the most difficult fast as not even a drop of water can be taken the whole day. The fast is broken only after one sees the moon. Santosh, Manu's mother, and her sister-in-law were planning how they were going to spend the day. The fasting women usually get together and play cards or some other indoor games to while away their time. While the two ladies were planning the day, Nikki was sitting with them and Santosh's sister-in-law remarked, "I suppose Nikki will not fast for our dear Manu." Nikki noticed an expression of expectation on her mother-in-law's face, although she had not asked her to fast knowing that Muslims and Christians do not fast. Nikki did not want to disappoint her and promptly said that she would fast along with them although she did not believe in such superstitious practices. Nikki told me later, "Mummy, I felt what was there in fasting for a day if it made Manu's mother happy, as she did believe that fasting increases a husband's longevity." Manu though was angry that Nikki had conceded to his mother's unexpressed desire. In the evening, Santosh's sister-in-law asked the servant boy to prepare three trays to be taken to the temple for prayers. But Santosh interjected and asked the servant boy to prepare only two trays as Nikki need not go to the temple and asked Nikki not to wait for them to return but break the fast as soon as she sighted the moon. I feel this is a perfect example of tolerance and understanding of each other's customs, leading to happy relationships.

But despite these factors, unfortunately both Kiran's and Nikki's marriages did not last. Nikki parted amicably after being married for 10 years and Kiran's marriage lasted for 12 years. This is a phenomenon common in urban areas among educated families. I feel that our young, educated, and economically independent women aspire for careers and personal freedom, whereas men, when they become husbands, find it difficult to accept that equality and continue to have traditionally defined expectations from their wives. This seems to be a major cause of the rising rate of divorce in urban India and indicates the drastic changes that are taking place in educated urban society.

My family shows how from a grandmother (my mother) who did not even have proper schooling, it has progressed to a granddaughter educated at the University of Berkeley, USA, and preparing to be an architect.

I have mentioned earlier that I had tuberculosis in my 1920s, a brush with heart condition called tachycardia, and then cancer to top it all and I have survived. I certainly have been a survivor and hope to have an easy exit from my rather eventful life. Looking back, I feel I have led a rich life, not in terms of money, but certainly in terms of experiences.

After having conquered three major diseases, having paid my dues to society through my professional and NGO engagements, and rearing three children, my husband and I decided to retire in Mussoorie in "Woodside," our house. We stayed here for nearly eight months a year. It was an ideal retired life and we are grateful to our daughter Kiran and her former husband Aslam for making it so comfortable for us. "Woodside" is not only a spacious house but also beautifully located in very quiet and serene surroundings. I kept myself busy writing my memoirs; my husband had been busy writing a book on peasant economy which, alas, he could not complete. He passed away in November 2013. We used to spend our spare time playing scrabble and bridge whenever we got four persons to play with, or with our children and grandchildren when they visited us. We enjoyed watching sports on the television too. I am crazy about tennis while my husband preferred to watch cricket, which I also learnt to enjoy.

Now, Idrak has gone after 49 years of companionship. We did have our ups and downs as in every marriage, but the secret of our sustained togetherness, despite both of us having strong personalities, probably lies in the fact that we did not lose sight of each other's positive qualities and tried to understand and accommodate the differences in our outlook and perceptions. The young readers of this account should give some thought to this aspect of married life. However, I have to somehow reorient my life and learn to live without him. It seems very difficult but I know I must accept the reality and move on.

My daughters, grandchildren, and siblings visit me as often as their own busy schedule allows. That brings a deal of cheer to my rather quiet life up here in Mussoorie.

I wish to conclude this account by thanking my friends, teachers, parents, and all those I came in contact with, for their love, affection, and encouragement; and most of all to my husband, who despite belonging to an earlier generation of men and having streaks of male chauvinism [he himself would often jokingly say that he was a male chauvinist pig (MCP)], provided encouragement and support to my professional endeavors.

I am grateful and touched that my daughters, Huma, Kiran, and Nikhat, suggested that I write my story. I owe thanks particularly to Huma for mooting the idea that I write about my life, although—as I have mentioned earlier—I have no illusions about my being an important person but I did want to record the social changes that I have observed and experienced during the long stretch of 80 years of my life. I hope this account reflects those changes that have occurred in my community, region, and indeed in India, although a great deal is still desired in achieving socio-economic and gender equality. I very much hope that the struggle for gender equality, in particular, that was initiated by my generation, will be carried on until we achieve a society where every individual—irrespective of gender, caste, and class—will be able to fully utilize his or her potential for the common good of society.

Afterword

There is a Persian proverb, "*Himmat-e-mardan, madad-e-khuda*" which when loosely translated means that a man's (or woman's) courage receives God's help. I often thought of this proverb while writing this book because I have achieved my dreams and aspirations, unmatched both by my personal circumstances and by the socio-cultural environment, and felt that some divine force kept pushing me into a certain direction, despite the fact that I am not very religious.

I have tried to give a glimpse of the Indian Muslim society of my growing-up years, its customs, and rituals in the Oudh region of the province of Uttar Pradesh, India, as well as my experiences of the British society in the second half of the twentieth century, when I lived for nearly 10 years in London.

The Indian Muslim society was highly feudal as well as caste and gender discriminative, yet it had a certain grace of its own. It took pride in its *tahzeeb*, refinement of etiquette, polite manners with subtle humor, sweetness of Urdu language, and high standards of hospitality. I am reminded of my father's saying that hospitality was his religion. The society had respect for age and openness toward other communities where Hindus and Muslims lived their kind of life peacefully.

I have tried to bring out the dilemma of Indian Muslims who chose to remain in India, the land of their ancestors and whose Indianness won over the religious pull toward Pakistan, the newly carved out Islamic state. They participated in the freedom movement, opposed the partition of their country, and had been an integral part of its polity and society. The partition of India on religious basis turned them into a minority in the country which they regarded as their own, notwithstanding the fact that these Muslims had the option of migrating to Pakistan and yet had chosen to stay in India. My family was one such family among many who had disapproved of the division of India and stayed behind holding on to their roots. Those Muslims who were allured by the newly found "Islamic state" and migrated to Pakistan, found themselves being unwelcomed by the Punjabis and Sindhis, the original inhabitants of that part of the subcontinent. The immigrant Muslims in Pakistan found it difficult to adjust to a different culture and language and missed what they had left behind. Some of them even decided to return, as long as it was possible.

I have also tried to show how Indian Muslims as well as Indian Christians adopted the predominant Hindu customs and rituals which depicted a highly patriarchal structure of Indian society. Many customs and rituals have been practiced by Indian Muslims and even by Indian Christians which are contrary to their religious teachings, like caste consciousness and treatment of women. Most glaring of these have been the social stratification practices analogous to the Hindu caste system, the socialization of girls' imposition of purdah (seclusion), and the treatment of widows, which I have dwelt on in some details. It is somewhat heartening to notice that due to wider exposure and education, even among Muslim girls, there has been a rise of feminism, and above all, the modern ideas of equality and social justice enshrined in the Indian Constitution. A process of change has begun, although it is rather slow.

Among Indian Muslims, the continuing practice of the Muslim Personal Law is a serious stumbling block for the improvement of Muslim women's progress, especially when the Law is now regarded as a symbol of Muslim identity. This is not to deny that desirable changes are taking place, such as the treatment of widows has improved a great deal and many personal restrictions on them have been removed, divorce does not have the social stigma attached to it as before, education among Muslim girls and women is on the rise although they are still lagging behind, and employment of women is also better tolerated socially than earlier. One hopes that such advancements will not only be sustained but accelerated, although the rise of communal fundamentalism does pose a threat and some regressive signs are also visible.

I would like to repeat the Persian proverb with which I began, "*Himmat-e-mardan, madad-e-khuda*". May we all, especially women, have the strength to move ahead despite the obstacles. I have done it, and so can you.

About the Author

Humanist by faith, sociologist by profession, feminist by conviction, **Zarina Bhatty** was brought up in burka (seclusion) in a traditional Muslim family in Lucknow in pre-Partition India. She is the former President of Indian Association for Women's Studies (IAWS) and of Young Women's Christian Association (YWCA), New Delhi. She has researched, published, and lectured extensively in India and abroad on Indian Muslim Women's issues and on women in the unorganized sector. Her pioneering study on women in the bidi industry, undertaken and published by the International Labour Organization (ILO), received considerable recognition. Zarina Bhatty studied sociology and political science at the London School of Economics and taught at the University of Delhi. She later worked as Gender Specialist with United States Agency for International Development (USAID), International Fund for Agricultural Development (IFAD), and Islamic Development Bank (IDB). She is also the recipient of the Devi Awards 2015. After retiring from work, she has been living a quiet life in Mussoorie, Uttarakhand, India.